The Art and Practice of Marquetry

The Art and Practice of Marquetry

WILLIAM ALEXANDER LINCOLN

with 180 illustrations
in half-tone and line

This Special Edition distributed in America by

CONSTANTINE—Largest Source for Marquetry Veneers

2050 Eastchester Road, Bronx, New York 10461

To 'Ernie'

Mr Ernest Walter Oppenheim, Past President of The Marquetry Society, and founder of the Marquetry School of Toronto, Ontario, Canada

Contents

Acknowledgments

This book is a condensation of twenty years' experience and eight years of preparation and research. The actual writing of the manuscript took place from 1 p.m. until midnight, seven days a week *without interruption* until completed and it is therefore my first duty to acknowledge the patient understanding and fortitude of my wife Kathleen who created the conditions which made this task possible and who carried on the business in my absence during this period.

Thanks are also due to my son Andrew, who gave me detailed and frank criticism which proved valuable, and who then undertook all the line drawings which illustrate the book.

Extensive use has been made of the copyright material of The Art Veneers Co. Ltd, including *The Veneer Craftsman's Manual, Wood Technology, Techniques of Intarsia, The Fascination of Marquetry* (by Clifford Penny) and photographic material from the International Open Marquetry Competition for the Lincoln Awards.

My special thanks are due to Mr Ernest W. Oppenheim, past President of the Marquetry Society, of Toronto, Ontario, Canada, for translating periodicals, articles, leaflets and books from French, German, Italian and Spanish sources and for introducing me to American and Canadian publications. He also introduced me to two German authors on marquetry, Hans Beblo (*Intarsie und ihre Techniken*), formerly of Munich, now residing in British Columbia, and Dr Gert Kossatz of Dresden (*Die Kunst der Intarsia*), both of whom have been most helpful in making further introductions to marquetry craftsmen.

Ernie – to whom this book is dedicated at the express wish of Kathleen – inspired me to write the book by his enthusiastic encouragement, and tireless correspondence, often running at a rate exceeding twelve letters a week. I salute his zeal and dedication to marquetry, without which my research would not have been so comprehensive.

Thanks are due:

To Mrs Gertrude Constantine of Albert Constantine & Son Inc., New York, for providing data and information regarding American methods and to Mr E. Paul Boege of The Dover Inlay Manfg. Co. Inc. for fullest details of modern workshop practice.

To Mr and Mrs Robert Dunn, who kindly gave me most valuable information regarding professional architectural marquetry and access to their collection of prints.

To the Hon. Julian Guest of the furniture department of Christie Manson and Woods, of St James's, London, who gave me permission to draw upon the photographic records of all post-war sales of marquetry furniture of both Christie's and Sotheby's.

To members of the British Antique Dealers' Association and curators or librarians of museums in most of the art capitals of the world for providing me with more than five hundred prints from which to make a final selection; my especial thanks to all those who do not appear in the list of picture sources.

I must also acknowledge the help received from Mr L. J. Benjamin, past President of the Society, who provided me with back numbers of *The Marquetarian* which were missing from my own files; from Mr Paul Jobling who made available his private collection of prints and transparencies of prizewinning pictures from Society exhibitions, and his hands for the photograph on the dust jacket; from Tony Guglielmo, a New York policeman and ardent marquetry artist, who carried out research in the Metropolitan Museum of Art in New York and supplied prints and background information free of charge.

I must thank the executive committee of the Marquetry Society for making available to me the portfolio of prints of members' work and for their permission to draw upon material first published in *The Marquetarian*, the official journal of the Society.

To all members of the Marquetry Society, many of whom have become close personal friends and customers – who will understand they are collectively too numerous for individual mention – I am indebted for their valuable help and encouragement through the years.

Lastly, I am delighted to acknowledge the keen interest and enthusiastic collaboration of Stephen England, the managing editor of the publishers, in editing the manuscript for publication.

Mildenhall, Suffolk, 1971

1 The history of the craft

Is there anything whereof it may be said, See, this is new?
It has been already of old time, which was before.

ECCLESIASTES I:IO

My own introduction to the craft of marquetry was quite accidental. In 1947, my business was producing expendable products made from veneer, such as ice-cream spoons, lollipop sticks, pipe-smokers' spills and the like.

One day, as I watched the veneer being peeled off a steaming log, the pattern on the surface of the veneer caught my eye. There was a light-blue scattered stain across the leaf, with pinkish-orange streaks on a golden background. This particular veneer was destined to be converted into pipe-smokers' spills for the Woolworth counters. I picked it up, held it at arm's length and half closed my eyes. In my imagination I saw a blue sea and a sunset sky. While this moment of whimsy lasted, I indulged it by picking up a darker piece of veneer from the factory floor and roughly hacking it with a penknife to form the outline of a pier or jetty. Then I pinned both pieces to the wall with a drawing-pin. The illusion completed, my mental picture had come to life. I had discovered marquetry.

At that time I did not know that the two veneers could be interchanged or inlaid, or that the veneer should be glued to a baseboard and the picture polished. It was sufficient in itself.

However, my imagination had been fired, and it was easy to see that if greater care was taken in the selection of veneers, in the correct flow of the grain direction and the arrangement of the natural markings of the wood, most attractive pictures could be created.

I founded a company to develop the idea further, and our first marquetry sets were produced. To me, this was a more constructive purpose in life than the production of wood products to be thrown away or burnt.

Then I made the sobering discovery that there was nothing new in the idea at all. Marquetry had existed for centuries, and its origins were lost in antiquity.

When primitive man first learned how to fashion a flint with which to cut the inner bark – or bast – from a tree, he used these strips in the same way as reeds and bulrushes, to weave mats and baskets. Later, when flints were made to fell trees and slice veneers, he used the veneers to repeat advanced basketweave patterns in his woodwork, using the earliest decorative form of mosaic, in this case mosaic parquetry.

The ancient Egyptians were skilled in all veneering techniques and decorated their caskets and tables with mosaic parquetry in herringbone and basketweave patterns.

The Byzantine mosaic arts were kept alive in northern Italy throughout the dark ages by the monastic orders, in particular 'certomosaic' or monastery mosaic executed in wood to decorate church furniture, examples of which are to be found in the vestry of St Anastasia in Verona.

In Gothic times, the monks broke away from mosaic art forms and developed a new technique known as the 'shoulder-knife'. By this method, skilled wood sculptors and carvers chiselled and gouged out the solid base, using a long wooden-handled knife, which was tucked into the shoulder and levered with the weight of their bodies. The few native woods at their disposal were cut into thin boards of about $\frac{1}{4}$ in. thickness. This permitted simple arabesque, flower and tendril motifs to be created, usually in woods of two or three contrasting tones.

The first order of artisan monks devoted entirely to working in intarsia was the order of Olivetans at Monte Oliveto, near Siena, which became the cradle of intarsia. It was from this order that the famous 'cloistered intarsiatori' or masters of intarsia went out to decorate churches throughout northern Italy.

Marquetry, as it then developed, cannot be studied in isolation from the whole history of furniture and the development of furniture styles.

This study reveals an ever changing pattern of the decorative treatment of furniture. The style periods were transitional, and always in a state of flux. They were affected by the dictates of Church and Crown, the cause and effect of civil war, revolution, religious conflict, persecution, pestilence, disease and fire. Unrelated influences, such as the voyages of discovery, new materials and techniques and in particular the imprint upon history of the talent and genius of individual craftsmen – all played their part in the story of the development of marquetry. It is only in recent times that marquetry has departed from its historic role as a form of level surface decoration for furniture, to become the greatest challenge to the craftsman, in the creation of beautiful marquetry pictures using the many rare and exotic natural woods as his artist's palette.

There are several lessons from history worth underlining. One is, that a craftsman can cut an inartistic line in veneer just as proficiently as an artistic line. The early intarsia craftsmen of Renaissance Italy were all artists in other fields, such as painting or sculpture, carving or architecture; their marquetry designs were artistic, and their work has been greatly admired and has been treasured for centuries.

Supreme among them was a Dominican friar, Fra Damiano da Bergamo, whose contemporaries considered him to be the finest artist of his time; 'with his woods', one of them wrote, 'coloured to a marvel, he raised the art to the rank of real painting.' Like his fellow Dominican Fra Giovanni da Verona (1456–1525), Fra Damiano achieved a more vigorous effect in his pictures by the use of dyes, boiled in penetrating oil, as well as stains of mercury sublimate, oil of sulphur, a solution of corrosive sublimate and arsenic, gallnuts and urine. Fra Leandro Alberti wrote: 'Damiano has become a man of as much genius as is to be found in the world at present, in putting together woods with so much colour that they appear pictures made with a brush.'

The work of Fra Damiano can be seen in panels depicting Biblical scenes, decorating the choir stalls in the churches of S. Domenico at Bologna and S. Pietro at Perugia.

The greatest periods in the history of furniture have been times when the designs for decorative treatment were created by artists. When marquetry craftsmen tried to imitate paintings the results were bad, with marquetry showing itself nothing but a crude parody of the original. Striving after even closer realism, craftsmen resorted to dyeing their woods and faking with the use of bleaching, branding, burning and painting. When used very sparingly as tints, the effect was to enrich the work, but this encouraged attempts at designs which were far too difficult for both their technique and the limited range of woods which were available to them. They attempted figure-crowded historical and religious scenes. Their virtuosity hampered their artistic expression and the resulting pictures went far beyond the limits proper to marquetry. They had not learned to respect the limitations of their materials.

This, in turn, led to 'faking' tricky parts of a picture with a brush, painting in difficult effects which nature could not provide in wood. This was taken to the extreme on the cupboards in the sacristy of S. Maria delle Grazie in Milan, which are actually painted in imitation of wood intarsia. In the Colleoni Chapel at Bergamo, the brothers Caniana were not content to do this, but then employed all the skills of the copperplate engraver to further enliven the surface with fine line detail. The resulting marquetry picture did not have the appearance of a wooden picture at all. These practices brought about the decline of marquetry as a form of decoration. This process has repeated itself throughout history.

The next major development in the story of marquetry came around 1562 when the first fretsaw was invented. Fine saws were cut from clock spring steel and used in wooden bow frames made in the workshops of the intarsia craftsmen. This new sawing technique freed the design outline from the limitations imposed upon it by the chisel and shoulder knife, and made possible far more intricate and elaborate pictures.

It enabled the design to be cut and assembled in jigsaw fashion, and this completed assembly could then be *overlaid* upon the groundwork instead of inlaid as hitherto.

It was then possible to cut simultaneously both the background veneer and the veneer motif to be inserted, in one single cutting operation. Two contrasting woods were used and the parts interchanged. This took the craft out of the hands of the artist-craftsman into the hands of the skilled sawyer, and brought about a general lowering of artistic standards.

Also at about the same time, using a water-mill to power a pitsaw, the first veneer mill was established at Augsburg in Germany to produce veneers of about $\frac{1}{8}$ in. in thickness from imported logs. This gave a fresh stimulus to the use of marquetry as a decorative treatment for furniture.

There are two forms of decorative treatment: decoration by shape and decoration of surface. The proportions, outline and shape have to be balanced carefully and tastefully with the decoration of the surface. Marquetry should always be subordinate to the surface it is intended to decorate; as a form of level surface decoration it must never be allowed to intrude or dominate.

For example, when the joiners grew so skilled in their craft that they lost their sense of pride in accomplishment, when they could proceed no further with the development of constructional techniques, they invented difficulties of decoration, and created furniture which was a mere prop for lavish display of marquetry and other types of ornament.

When the era of the cabinet maker arrived, new constructional problems were met which had to be solved. While the new techniques of veneering curved surfaces were being learnt, marquetry decoration was drastically modified. Shape itself became the main feature of decoration.

After the cabinet makers had mastered shaped panels, they invented difficulties by making the panels even more shaped, both concave and convex, until they had solved all the problems of construction. Having reached the limits of their ability to cope with constructional difficulties, they then returned to the problems of decoration and began to create difficulties of technique which led to over-ornamentation.

And history shows that when virtuosity and technique predominate, style decays and dies.

The Bourbon kings of France, of whom Henry IV was the first, established Paris as the world's centre of culture and the arts, and as such it was to flourish for two hundred years.

Louis XIV, the Sun King, provided free workshops in the Louvre, accommodation at the Arsenal and Temple, and a special factory at the Gobelins. He freed privileged craftsmen from guild supervision and allowed emigrant craftsmen, who had sought refuge at the Abbey of St Antoine des Champs, to practise their craft as 'free craftsmen'. The Paris guild of *Maîtres Menuisiers et Ebénistes* admitted marqueteurs in 1743 and laid down stringent regulations for admission to the guild. Six years' apprenticeship had to be followed by a further six years as journeyman before a man was allowed to submit his masterpiece for approval, or confiscation, by the jury.

From this guild of marquetry craftsmen came the next invention to affect the development of marquetry – the French Horse,

13

or English 'Donkey', which was invented in 1780 according to the archives of the Paris Guild.

This ingenious device enabled the marqueteur to sit astride the 'horse', using his feet to operate a simple clamping device to hold the veneers in a vertical position, while the fine saw blades, cut from watch spring steel, could be worked in a horizontal position. The saw arm can be slightly pivoted laterally to allow for the thickness of the saw blade and veneers, by angle or bevel cutting. It was also possible to cut twelve or more veneers at a time, which led to the earliest form of mass production and brought a revival in the popularity of marquetry.

From Paris emerged some of the greatest masters of marquetry that the world has ever seen, including such men as André Charles Boulle (1642–1732), Charles Cresscent (1685–1768), Jean François Oeben (1720–1763), and Jean Henri Riesener (1734–1806).

David Roentgen (1743–1807) is generally acknowledged to be the greatest marqueteur of all time. His original factory was at Neuweid near Coblenz in Germany, where in 1772 he produced luxury furniture of great beauty, employing over a hundred craftsmen to produce spectacular marquetry cabinets and wall panels for the courts of Berlin and St Petersburg. His favourite subjects were allegorical and pastoral scenes, *chinoiseries*, and crowded historical scenes. He perfected a technique of progressively dyeing a veneer to varying depths, in order to achieve greater perspective and contrast in his pictures. He created a wonderful tonal range, by arranging the tiniest pieces of dark and white woods in mosaic style, to give his pictures dramatic highlights or subtle shades and fine lines, equivalent to pen and ink etching, for the minutest detail. Favourite subjects for this treatment were stories from classical mythology.

Roentgen was summoned to Paris by the Dauphine Marie Antoinette in 1774 as she was most impressed by the extraordinary range and flexibility of his talent. He was then described as *le plus grand ébéniste de l'Europe entier*.

During the reign of Louis XVI he produced pictures by using dyed veneer of one colour but several tones, for his most expressive figure studies *en camaieu*. This technique was also used with dramatic effectiveness in his portrayal of vividly coloured floral subjects.

14

By 1789 he had turned away from dyeing veneers, and he showed a table described as 'a veneer mosaic, with shades not burned or engraved or darkened with smoke', and made entirely from natural freak veneers.

But fashions change, and David Roentgen died relatively poor in Wiesbaden in 1807. One of his beautiful cabinets can be seen in the Victoria and Albert Museum in London, in the Jones Collection. The marquetry pictures depict scenes from the Italian Comedy.

The interesting point about Roentgen's work in marquetry is that although the brilliant colours of his woods have now completely faded, his panels reproduce beautifully in black-and-white (see pl. 28). This is because they were originally conceived as line compositions, with carefully studied balance between line and mass, tonal harmony, and contrast in line and form rather than in colour. They were conceived as black-and-white pictures but created in colour; their beauty of design took precedence over beauty of colour.

The use of colour photographs as original designs for marquetry could therefore provide a temptation to seek colours in wood that nature cannot supply, to make demands on the material that wood cannot meet. Monotone photographs are to be preferred, and these will require adaptation and artistic licence in translation into marquetry. It is the shape and form in nature that should be used for marquetry, rather than its colour contrasts and subtleties.

Many highly skilled marquetry craftsmen today demonstrate their superb virtuosity and patience by cutting minute detail, such as blades of grass in the foregrounds of landscapes, every leaf on the tree, cement mortar in between the brickwork, in pictures no larger than a matchbox. This is a retrograde step, for the individual pieces comprising the picture are so splinter-like and fragmentary as to show contempt for the material. There no longer remains any point in using wood for these masterpieces of cutting skill; the material might as well be plastic, for the craftsman has placed the demonstration of his skill before his respect for his material. The whole idea of a marquetry picture is to demonstrate the beauty of natural woods, not the cleverness of the craftsman.

The marquetry pictures being produced in Sorrento, Italy,

today are often overprinted with fine black line detail, such as eyelashes in portraiture, to achieve greater realism. A similar practice in Victorian times led to the introduction of marquetry transfers, which were simply applied to piano fronts. This rapidly brought the craft into disrepute. What is needed now is a new approach to marquetry. We have arrived at a point when a return to the use of marquetry for the decoration of furniture is overdue. Space age furniture is uniform, boxlike and devoid of any form of marquetry. The time is ripe for a change.

Before the modern designer can interpret the mood of his contemporaries, by the introduction of a new style of decoration in a form suited to the age in which he lives, he must first familiarize himself with all the known techniques of the past. Technical manuals in this field are lacking, for the craft has always been shrouded in secrecy. Many of the methods used by the old masters died with them, and when the craft died out, their methods were forgotten and have had to be redeveloped by trial and error and practical experiment.

This book now sets out to describe the various techniques used in different parts of the world in producing marquetry assemblies, with proven methods and actual workshop experience. These should be taken not as definite rules to follow, but as a stimulus to fresh thought, an encouragement to inventiveness, and an appeal to the hidden desire that lurks in everyone, often side by side with the dormant talent, to create.

The latest development (an invention of my own, for which world patents are pending) is an entirely new method of producing marquetry pictures and furniture motifs in quantity; these will be available in kit form, with all the parts cut out and having the correct grain direction, figure and marking.

This is not an attempt to reduce an art form to an exact science, for the craft has now passed beyond the handicraft stage of development and marquetry pictures of great artistry are being created today, deserving to be treasured for posterity.

It is hoped that this book will make a significant contribution towards raising marquetry from a craft to an accepted art form.

Thus equipped with the technical knowledge necessary to enjoy the legacy endowed by the masters of this ancient craft, I hope that marquetry pictures created by modern artists will, in turn, be perpetuated as a heritage for craftsmen of the future.

A word on definitions

There are two popular misconceptions, both in Britain and America, about the meanings of the words *marquetry* and *intarsia*.

In the course of my work I am in continuous correspondence with craftsmen in Europe and most countries of the English-speaking world, and I have discovered that in practically every country in the non-English-speaking world, with the single exception of France, the word 'marquetry' is not used. The work is described everywhere as 'intarsia', with slight variations in spelling in different languages.

In the English-speaking countries the word 'intarsia' means inlay – a design or pattern of wood or other material inserted into groundwork which has been suitably incised, gouged or routed to receive it. But the use of the word 'intarsia' in this sense is actually wrong; there is no such word in the Oxford English Dictionary, neither is it in common usage among the people who practise the craft.

To describe any form of decoration which is actually sunk into a solid base, the correct English word is 'inlay'.

The word 'marquetry' is used to describe a pattern or design of wood veneers, assembled together and overlaid, with glue, to completely cover a surface. This definition can be read to permit various refinements of technique, which might allow only part of the marquetry assembly being laid first, with other parts laid subsequently – such as border veneers or inlay lines, bandings or motifs. It does not alter the basic difference that the veneers are not sunk into the groundwork, but are overlaid on a flat surface.

The English-speaking world also extends the word 'marquetry' to cover the use of other materials as level surface overlays. In some cases 'applied marquetry' is used to draw a distinction between furniture marquetry and pictorial marquetry. But *boulle work* of brass and tortoise-shell (p. 215) is marquetry; pictures inlaid into a solid base are not marquetry but inlay.

In France, the overlaying techniques are known as *marqueterie*, and so are all of the inlaying techniques; the French do not use 'intarsia' or 'inlay' to describe patterns which are inlaid.

2 *The artistic approach*

Since marquetry is both an art and a craft, the work is restricted by the limitations of the material and by the technique adopted by the craftsman; both aspects will be dealt with in subsequent chapters.

We are concerned here with the artistic approach to the craft. There is no recipe for producing an artistic marquetry design. The talent of the designer is the decisive factor. As in all creative work, technical skill alone is not enough, there must be artistic appreciation. In fact, some argue that the cutting skill of the marquetarian is of little value; it is the artistic content that counts – but the danger of this approach is that it makes an excuse for poor workmanship.

It is better for a man with no talent for original artistic creation to rely upon others more gifted with the talent for design, or upon other forms of art such as photographs, prints or paintings.

The disadvantage in copying paintings is that problems are met which wood cannot solve. Although natural wood tones are manifold, they cannot be mixed like oil colours to suit the desire and intentions of the artist. This leads to the temptation to use tinted or dyed woods, which debases the work. There are no true blue or green woods in nature. It is a challenge to the marquetry designer to submit to the limitations imposed by the tonal range of his woods, when designing his picture.

If the craftsman recognizes the fact that his talents do not embrace original design, there are numerous sources where suitable subjects can be found. The local stationer will have many excellent full-colour views in calendar form, or postcards of famous beauty spots; travel brochures are another excellent source. Art galleries sell small prints of famous paintings for a few shillings.

The use of colour photographs, including enlargements of colour films and transparencies, requires special care. The temptation is to try to reproduce faithfully the original colours. One of the biggest errors of the amateur designer is to try to achieve photographic realism and accurate colour matching. The wise marquetarian will use 'marquetry licence' and adapt his coloured print by altering the time of day, or even the season of the year, to make better use of his available veneers.

By changing a high noon scene to late evening, with its darkening tones and shadows and sunset skies, the use of blue for the sky and green for the grass is overcome, and reddish-toned woods can be used for the sky and golden-brown tones for the evening grass in shadow. A spring scene can be changed into an Indian Summer scene of gold and russet-brown autumnal tints; or a mass of foliage may with advantage be adapted to winter snow.

It is safer for the beginner to use a black and white photograph, as this gives a true tone guide.

The drawing

The next step is to produce a drawing of the right size for your picture. This can be done in various ways. The pantograph is the usual instrument; another simple method is to trace a grid of ½-in. squares over the original print. Or if you do not wish to deface it, make an indian ink grid on a sheet of transparent plastic film, through which you can see the original photograph. If you want the final drawing to be four times larger than the photograph, draw 1-in. squares on a sheet of cartridge paper and copy the outline in map fashion. This is a very simple process; you merely watch where the line enters and leaves each square and repeat this on the larger squared paper.

There are many other ways to produce a suitable drawing: for example, you can trace from a photograph or reproduction, or project a colour transparency of the subject on to a mirror rigged up at an angle of 45 degrees, and reflect it down on to a sheet of paper of the required size. Then trace the outline of the projected picture, carefully noting grain directions and colour hues required. Depending on the cutting technique to be followed, you may require a reverse design, which can be made simply by turning the transparency around in the projector.

The following two techniques are very useful. First, a suitable photograph is enlarged to the required final size. The negative is

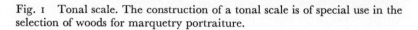

Fig. 1   Tonal scale. The construction of a tonal scale is of special use in the selection of woods for marquetry portraiture.

then projected through an enlarger on to a sheet of white cartridge paper to the required size. With soft charcoal sticks a sketch is made on the paper, filling in the white spaces on the cartridge paper a dense black, and gradually working through six to eight graduated tonal shades, leaving the black parts white. This is done in conjunction with the photographic enlargement, using it as an additional guide. This way of 'breaking down' the photograph into a set of six or eight tone changes is particularly useful for marquetry portraiture. From this sketch a picture with the correctly balanced tonal values can be created. For this purpose a tonal values scale can be constructed (see fig. 1). If veneers are examined through a pair of sunglasses, which will eliminate much of their colour hue, and compared with the tonal values scale, the ability to select the correctly toned veneer to suit the charcoal sketch will be developed, and this greatly enhances the artistry of the resulting picture.

Another method is to produce an enlargement of the required photograph on matt-surfaced paper, and to work over the design to make a waterproof indian ink drawing. As each pen stroke actually represents a line to be cut by the saw or knife at the cutting stage, this drawing requires the elimination of all fussy detail.

There are two basic methods of producing the drawing. First, by placing a sheet of tracing paper *over* the chosen design or photograph, large enough to include the border margins, both the design and tracing paper are pinned to a drawing board. The design is then traced with an HB pencil, including the border outline.

The alternative method is useful when the details of the picture to be traced are not too clear through the tracing paper, in which case the tracing paper is placed *under* the design, with a leaf of black carbon paper between. The outline is then traced over with a stylus point as used for stencil work, or a sharpened knitting needle.

Figs. 2, 3 Adapting a subject for marquetry. A good adaptation does not rely solely on simplification and the deletion of details as in the example of the castle and the cottage. By adding foliage to the tree the necessity of cutting additional branches was avoided; similarly, greater balance was given by the introduction of foliage to the top left-hand corner of the picture. The modern bridge, flats, street lighting, cranes, etc., were replaced by an ancient footbridge of a type in keeping with the subject. A beached rowboat completes the composition.

Streamline the outline as much as possible; omit any distracting detail which adds nothing to the charm or composition of the picture. Emphasize those features which lend themselves to expression in wood, such as half-timbered houses, old boats, tree trunks and branches, interior scenes. Nothing reproduces in wood quite so well as wood itself. It is a matter of trial and error and experience.

When the ink has dried thoroughly, prepare a solution of 1 oz. of fixing solution to the strength of 4 oz. of hypo or fixer to 1 pint of water. Then add 20 gr. potassium ferricyanide until the solution becomes straw-coloured. The chemical should only be added when you are ready to use it, as reaction occurs between ferricyanide and hypo and it quickly loses its power. Swill the enlargement around in this solution for three minutes. If the picture is now rinsed in fresh water, the photograph will have disappeared and the indian ink line drawing will remain. Care must be taken not to handle the ink drawing during the washing process or it will rub off. If allowed to dry thoroughly, the drawing can be handled and is indelible. In practice this process is quick, simple and trouble-free.

An alternative formula for this process is to make up a 5 per cent solution of potassium iodide, say 1 oz. in 19 oz. of water, to which is added as much iodine crystals as the solution will dissolve. Immerse the photograph, making sure it lies flat and is covered by the solution. This will leave a brown stain. Then the print is rinsed under running water before being laid in another solution, this time of hypo or fixer, 4 oz. to 1 pint of water, which will remove the brown stain. Further rinsing under a cold tap will render the print ready for drying and handling.

There are commercial designs for marquetry on sale, with arrows to show the desired grain direction, and showing the correct veneer to use.

For a modest outlay, the services of professional commercial artists are always available to assist in making line drawings.

Whether you intend to try to create your own original picture, trace a photograph, or copy a calendar or travel brochure, the final step is to prepare the working line drawing, featuring only the outline you intend to cut. Such details as shading, reflections, lighting and minor detailed pieces are kept for reference on the original sketch, photograph or print, to be added later. At this stage, only the major sections, comprising the background and the main parts of the picture, are made into a line drawing.

About 1 in. working margin is allowed around the drawing, and centre lines are drawn at the top, bottom and both edges in this margin, to ensure accurate register with the work in the later cutting processes to be described.

For some cutting techniques it will be necessary to have a reversed or mirror-image drawing; this can be done by putting a sheet of carbon paper under the design, sticky side up, so that the carbon copy is made on the back of the original.

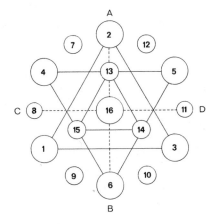

Fig. 4 The colour wheel. The construction of a veneer colour wheel with scraps of veneer will prove useful in the selection of woods for pictorial marquetry.

The colour wheel

The would-be creative artist will find an elementary colour wheel a useful aid, in conjunction with the tonal values scale.

This will give us three primary colours, three secondaries, and six intermediates. The centre circle of brown is surrounded by a triangle formed by the three tertiary colours (see illustration). All colours above the line (CD) are light colours and all those below are dark. Colours to the left of the line (AB) are warm colours and those to the right are cool colours.

Circles 1, 2 and 3 are the primary colours red, yellow and blue. Circles 4, 5 and 6 are the secondary colours orange, green, and violet. Intermediate circles are made of mixtures, e.g. circle No. 7 is yellow-orange. The tertiary colours 13, 14 and 15 are citron, olive green and russet. The construction of a veneer wheel with scraps of actual veneers will prove useful in the selection of woods for pictures.

23

The following types are suggested.

1 padauk	9 purpleheart
2 lime	10 dark mansonia
3 blue obeche	11 butternut or light mansonia
4 Honduras mahogany or opepe	12 myrtle
5 magnolia	13 afrormosia
6 Indian rosewood	14 green tulip burr
7 ayan	15 African mahogany
8 rosa peroba	16 Rio rosewood or Macassar ebony

The colours of veneers are in a far lower key than the colours used by the artist in oils but they have certain similarities. Every colour has five qualities. The first quality is hue (often incorrectly referred to as the colour), e.g. red, blue, etc. The second quality is tonal value. Thirdly, the degree of *brilliance*, which is governed, in the case of veneers, by their surface interest of grain and figure and the properties of light reflection that they present to the eye when polished.

Transparency – the fourth quality – is obviously difficult to define. It helps when the parallel in oil and water colours is considered. Vermilion is an opaque colour and rose madder is transparent. In marquetry it is said that gaboon has the quality of transparency, while sapele has that of opaqueness. The fifth quality is temperature, which is decided by the coolness or warmth of the colour.

It can now be seen that a comparison with both the colour wheel and the tonal scale will enable the craftsman to select the correct veneer for his picture – and these useful adjuncts to the craft can only be dispensed with when the artist advances to the point where he can decide on these hues, tones and harmonies from his own intuition and experience.

Let the wood tell the story
Every line that you draw on paper will eventually be used as a cutting line and therefore the aim is to draw as few lines as possible. In an original drawing, the first few lines will determine the size and position of the drawing; the next few strokes will aid the composition, and as the work proceeds, each successive line will have progressively less value until you reach the stage

where you are simply cluttering up your work with unnecessary detail. Try for simplicity: do not plan a project requiring a high degree of cutting skill, but a simple outline drawing in which you will allow the wood to tell its own story.

Never search for a veneer to suit a fancied picture. This puts the artist in a straitjacket. The first step is to acquire as large and varied a stock as possible of unusual, well marked, peculiarly figured, and freak veneers; interesting grains and exotic toned woods; and burrs, swirls, clusters and other odd types. These woods are your artist's palette. These are the woods that must inspire you to decide on the type of picture that can be made from them.

The first thing that you will discover is that your palette has no bright greens or blues. Therefore pictures at high noon which will require a preponderance of those colours must be avoided. Bring your colour requirements down to the level of your veneers, by making the same picture at evening sunset; you will find that veneers will provide you with russet browns and salmon pinks. Certain freak veneers can 'make' a picture by creating the most realistic sunset sky effects or stormy skies.

The artist must try to demonstrate the virtuosity and effectiveness of his woods; the result must look like a wooden picture without being 'wooden' in impact.

Perspective

When creating a marquetry picture, we are going to try to achieve the illusion of the third dimension of depth by the technique of linear perspective.

Three changes take place in the appearance of objects when seen in perspective at a distance: they appear smaller; they gradually lose their colour; and they become more indistinct and blurred.

As Master Brunelleschi discovered, buildings, courtyards, street scenes, interiors of rooms, cupboards, make the best subjects for experiment. Do not be deterred by criticism from making experiments with your own original drawings.

The following basic principles will give a working knowledge to guide your first steps.

First, determine the eye-level of your picture and fix a vanishing point to which all lines in your picture converge. When you

25

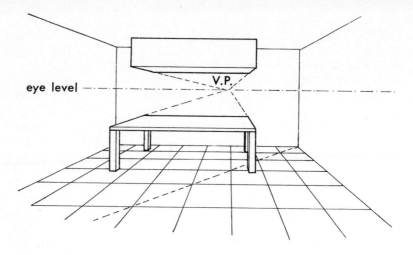

Fig. 5   All lines converge on the vanishing point at
eye level when it occurs within the frame of the picture.

have objects both above and below eye level, they may converge
on the same vanishing point or you may have two separate
vanishing points, which need not come within the frame of your
picture. Remember that vertical lines are always vertical. Never
use a ruler or straight edge to draw a straight line as this ruins
the appearance of a picture. At this stage, do not attempt to
draw a house, boat or tree, but simply try to draw a 'box' in
perspective or a series of boxes. When you have the perspective
and the overall balanced composition correct, begin to fit your
house, boats or tree, etc., into the pencilled 'boxes' which are
then erased.

You will soon be able to dispense with the preliminary 'box'
guide to perspective line drawing.

Still life

All forms of inanimate life are the best subjects for the beginner
to start with and will rapidly help him to assess his talent and
ability. The attic or cellar will reveal some fond relic that would
make an ideal subject if arranged in a suitable position. Excellent
composition is often available in nature if you have the ability
to visualize objects separately from their surroundings.

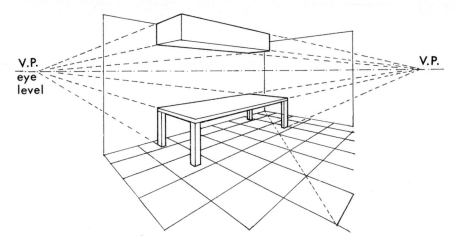

Fig. 6 The same objects drawn with two vanishing points at eye level occurring outside the frame of the picture.

The four basic problems to overcome are volume, proportion, light and shade, and composition.

The black-and-white soft charcoal sketch previously referred to, filled in with various tonal values, with particular attention to shadows, reflected light and highlights, is the first step.

If the project is tackled with bold strokes, aiming at a total overall composition and getting the masses right, and the correct tones, the attendant problems of shadows and lighting will resolve themselves. Flowers and plant life make excellent subjects and have always been favoured by marquetarians. Once you have mastered the fundamentals of creating your own designs, your sense of pleasure and achievement will be vastly increased.

Landscapes

A simple but effective aid for the designer of landscapes is a small pocket viewfinder, which need be only a small cardboard cut-out about 3in. × 2in. or in proportion to the picture size you intend to create. By closing one eye and moving the viewfinder about you will be able to see which part of the scene before you will best adapt into a picture for marquetry. Try to arrange for a

few branches or foliage to enter the top corner of the 'frame', for example, to aid the balance or composition of the picture; or contrive for a tree stump or fence or old wall to appear in the immediate foreground, which will appear in silhouette and provide the illusion of perspective. A scene pictured through an archway is another good idea.

There are two main types of landscapes: low-horizon and high-horizon. In a low-horizon picture the large expanse of sky is the main interest and will require a freak veneer, with plenty of natural mottle or other markings, to create the right effect. A good sky veneer is one in which the darkest part of the veneer appears at the top of the picture with the tone growing progressively lighter towards the horizon. Autumn skies taken just after sunset make excellent low-horizon pictures.

Clouds do not translate easily in veneers. By cutting in cloud scenes, there is the risk of making them appear like large balloons. Make sure that any clouds you do sketch in, are in aerial perspective, that is, with their lines converging towards a vanishing point on the horizon. Clouds should be lighter on top than at their base.

In high-horizon pictures, the foreground becomes the main interest, giving you the opportunity to display rock formations, shrubs, pathways, shadows falling across cobbled streets. This type of picture is very popular in marquetry because it is easier to find excellent foreground veneers than freak sky veneers.

Since perspective applies equally to colour and to shape, the foreground detail should be kept bold and clear, using the veneer colour wheel to provide you with warm colours which

28

Figs. 7, 8 *Left:* Low horizon scene requiring freak veneer for sky effects. *Right:* The same scene drawn with high horizon in which the foreground provides greater opportunities for marquetry.

appear to advance, and cool colours which retreat, to aid perspective.

Use the tonal values scale to provide brilliant-toned woods for the foreground and veneers lacking in tone for the distance, with medium-toned woods for the middle distance, lacking clear detail.

Try to capture an atmosphere by selecting woods for the distant hills, for example, which are very close to the chosen sky veneer in hue and tone.

Seascapes

It is always best to visualize your seascape picture looking towards the land rather than out to sea, as this would involve you in searching for freak veneers to represent both sea and sky. It is important that the sea should reflect the sky, but a tone darker. Reflections in water make good marquetry subjects, and should be a few tones darker than the main object they reflect. If possible, avoid cutting in an horizon, by trying to find a wide veneer with freak markings that will represent both sea and sky in one leaf, with the darkest part of the leaf at the bottom of the picture.

When selecting veneers for sea or sky, try to avoid using any veneer with a pronounced fiddleback ripple marking, if that mottled figure runs at right angles to the grain direction. When the veneer is cut into the picture, with its grain direction in a predominantly horizontal direction, the mottle will then run in a vertical direction and this will destroy the illusion of perspective, as the mottle should also be in perspective and converge to a vanishing point. It is perfectly all right to select a veneer with a cross mottle which runs in a diagonal direction, as this can represent passing clouds.

The same care should be taken with silver harewood or other veneer used to depict water effects. Also, when choosing veneers for roadways or fields, such as lacewood or elm, try to increase the perspective by using part of the leaf where the lace figure graduates from large to small, or where the grain markings vary from wide to narrow.

For these reasons, the best pictures rarely use one piece of burr veneer to represent tree foliage. It is better to cut several toned burrs into a tree foliage, with the lighter burrs to one side and top, to suggest light reflection and shadows.

Figs. 9, 10   Where the light source is outside the frame of the picture, all the shadows will fall in the same direction but in varying lengths. When the source of light is within the picture frame the shadows will run in different directions.

Light and shade

If you study objects which receive light from one source, you will see that when the light source is outside the frame of your picture, all the shadows will fall in the same direction, but in varying lengths. If the source of light is within or above the picture, the shadows may run in two different directions. The strengths of shadows will vary, too, so that the shadow at the base of a tree is a tone darker than the shadow of the treetop. Objects can also receive reflected light and reflected colour from nearby light or colourful surfaces.

One cannot start sketching a picture like writing a letter, at the top left-hand corner, and expect to finish at the bottom right-hand corner. Aim to achieve an overall sound composition with correct interpretations of tonal values. Start sketching the picture by putting in the dark tonal masses first, adding the medium and then the lighter tones, and finally bring the picture to life with highlights and reflected lights.

Figure studies

Pictures in marquetry will always have a lifeless appearance unless some form of life can be featured in the picture. It may be a bird wheeling overhead, or perhaps a dog in the distance, or a human figure. Incidentally, avoid cutting in smoke from a chimney. This never appears realistic as the outline would be too clearly defined.

These little incidental touches to the overall composition of a picture are all-important. The exact cutting of human figures and so forth in minute detail is unnecessary; only the basic outline in correct proportion is needed, and the clever arrangement of veneers to suggest clothing. The attitude of the figure, of course, should be a natural one.

A study of the human anatomy in terms of proportion is rewarding for the marquetarian. The hand should be no bigger than the face for example. The clothed figure cannot be fully appreciated until the nude figure is understood. Of course, classical nude studies make excellent marquetry. Art schools favour a 'seven-and-a-half-heads' proportion for the human figure, but for marquetry purposes, it is easier to adopt an 'eight-heads' proportion as figures in wood tend to appear dumpier than in other media.

Costume and drapery

Veneers are an excellent medium for depicting drapery. Delightful effects are to be discovered in the variations of grain, figure, markings and texture. This type of drapery marquetry should not be designed with a view to clever cutting, but should only be introduced into a picture if the marquetarian already has in his possession a freak veneer which can provide the effect.

Beeswing figure, fiddleback figure, and the swirl figure around knots and at butt ends of veneer make ideal material for depicting draperies.

Attention should be paid to the way a coat hangs, the fold of a skirt, a crumpled sleeve or worn shoe, the creases in trousers. Notice the way that materials of a light texture, like satin or silk, exhibit folds of an angular type; heavy tweeds or brocades hang in oval folds.

If your picture features figures in period costume, no matter how skilfully you execute the selection of woods and the cutting, the period style must be authentic or the work will be useless. The would-be artist must pay quite a bit of attention to details such as these before starting to draw.

A good tip when practising to draw drapery, is to dip a handkerchief or table napkin in a mixture of plaster, and after arranging it suitably, allow it to set. This will enable you to sketch the folds repeatedly over a period until you have perfected the sketch. A table cloth or curtain background is ideal for a still-life sketch.

Portraiture

This is perhaps the most ambitious and difficult of all marquetry subjects. It is good practice to commence with a self-portrait, using a mirror.

One of the Marquetry Society's leading portrait specialists, Mr Alexander Ephrat of Israel, has perfected his own technique. He projects a Kodachrome transparency of his subject on to a sheet of transparent drafting paper which is taped to a sheet of white cardboard hanging on the wall (or through a mirror rigged up at 45 degrees so that work can proceed comfortably at the worktable). The distance between projector and image can be varied to suit the size of picture required, and the focus adjusted accordingly.

The first step is to trace, with an HB pencil, the lines dividing the various degrees of shading and the highlights. Then, with a soft pencil or charcoal stick, the degree of shading and tones is sketched in. To blur the dividing lines between shaded areas a zig-zag line is drawn, which increases the amount of cutting to be done but improves the uniformity of the finished portrait.

The next step is to assemble all veneers with a smooth fleshy texture and to select the darkest and the lightest from all available veneers. Even if the darkest flesh-toned veneer is not as dark as the tone in the picture, it doesn't matter. Thereafter all veneer selection is relative to these two extremes. The next veneer chosen will be lighter than the preceding darker tone and so on.

The picture is traced in reverse on the background veneer, and progress can be watched as work proceeds, by holding the portrait up to a mirror.

The cutting commences from the perimeter of the portrait, tarting with the hair, forehead, eyebrows, neck, chin. The eyes, ears and nose are left until later and are only cut and inserted if the completed background and surrounding veneers have achieved a solidity and lifelikeness. Since the eyes are the most important feature, Mr Ephrat believes these should be one of the last features to be inlaid into the assembly, as they bring the portrait to life.

Begin with the general composition set down with a few basic strokes, then add a few lines of detail to keep the sketch moving. Add shading in the next stage to give the vitally important 'solidity' so necessary with a portrait, and finally try for a 'likeness'. To achieve this, remember that the eyes are the most important feature; try to get the exact number of highlights in the right places. Make the most of any predominant features by very slightly exaggerating a large nose, prominent teeth or protruding ears – the resulting portrait will be that much the better for it.

The light should come from a single source, as the shadows on the various planes of the face are most important; turn the head slightly – do not try a full-faced portrait as it will look 'posed'.

The selection of a background veneer is important to a portrait. If the right-hand side of the head is in shadow, find a veneer with the right-hand side rather lighter in tone than the left, in order to show up the shading of the face. The shadows on a face indoors are always in 'warm' toned woods; while the highlights are 'cool' tones; the reverse is true of shadows on outdoor portraits.

Really successful portraits require a face or head of some marked features. It is surprising how the general outline silhouette of the person, plus the correct clothing, can suggest the person even when the face is left blank. For example, portraits of Sir Winston Churchill, with spotted bow-tie, cigar, Churchillian attitude of neck, black jacket – these hallmarks suggest the portrait even before the details of facial expression are filled.

It is always good practice for a beginner to choose as a subject someone who is either so much a household word that recognition is immediate, as in the example of Sir Winston Churchill, William Shakespeare, or Abraham Lincoln, or go to the other extreme and choose a face of character, but completely unknown. Excellent portraits in marquetry can be made, for example, from a photograph of a wizened old Malayan, the face scored with the deeply ingrained lines of toil and age; here you are exploiting both the tanned, almost mahogany tone of the weather-beaten face – ideal for translation in terms of veneers – and also the fact that faces with furrowed brows, and lines of care or laugh lines, make good marquetry (pl. 67).

Another useful tip is to search for prizewinning photographs of subjects where lighting plays a big part. The dramatic effect of candlelight upon an upturned face for example, is excellent material for the portrait artist.

One of the most difficult subjects – and possibly one to avoid – is the attempt to portray a young woman's face, which is usually too smooth for wood. If this is attempted, ensure that the pose makes full use of hair or clothes and shadows, to assist you in veneer selection.

The effects of time

The colour tone of the wood requires attention, too. The process of steaming the log destroys wood insects, worm, etc., draws out various substances and chemicals, and inevitably changes the basic colour hue of the wood. The resulting veneer no longer matches the solid wood from the same log – a fact which often causes great concern when architects specify veneer to match solid hardwoods of the same species.

34

Veneers will also change their colour tone under the influence of the ultra-violet rays in both natural and artificial light. On exposure to light, some woods will fade and others darken. In other cases, strong light will fade and moderate light will darken – as in the case of purpleheart. Bleached woods will become yellow in time; chemically treated woods, such as silver harewood, all tend to fade and lose their original brilliance on exposure to strong light. The white veneers, such as sycamore, horse chestnut and maple, will gradually 'weather' into yellowish tones, and may eventually turn biscuit or tan-coloured.

Especially disagreeable is the resulting damage to veneer caused by exposure to partial light; for example, when the shadow of a window frame falls across a piece of work, resulting in discolouring stripes which are impossible to eradicate.

The task of the marquetarian is, therefore, to decide from experience which woods to use, not for their short-term artistic value in capturing a colourful scene in wood, but for their long-term, enduring tonal quality. It is his prime consideration to ensure that his finished work tends to become more perfect from year to year, by choosing woods which will blend harmoniously together and enhance the work uniformly.

Any slight fading, uniformly affecting the complete marquetry, and not with odd pieces standing out in stark contrast from the rest of the work, gives the work a mature patina of age which increases its appeal.

Resist the temptation to use woods which rapidly lose their brilliance and vivid colouring, such as purpleheart, padauk, rosa peroba, Indian rosewood and movingui, except for small parts of the marquetry, which may gradually fade a tone or two without detriment to the composition as a whole.

The skill in veneer selection lies in your ability to exploit the natural tendency of the woods to fade. For instance, silver harewood will eventually turn to a greenish tinge. Excellent! When used to depict water effects, the longer the picture is kept, the more realistic the water effect becomes. Fortunately, modern finishes containing ultra-violet light absorbers are now available which assist in retaining the natural beauty of veneers.

There are four main types of marquetarian. First of all, there's the 'colour-contrast' artist, who assembles a wide range of the most colourful, rare and exotic veneers, full of bright hues and

35

interesting textures, and then sets about deliberately injecting as much colour contrast as he can into his picture – to try to get away from the 'reddish brown and yellow' look of an old marquetry picture.

Unfortunately, many of the brilliant veneers react differently to light, after a time. The extremely attractive and colourful marquetry picture of today may look an eyesore in ten years' time, unless these colourful veneers are selected with great care based upon experience. There is a lot to be said for a picture which will mellow and mature with age, its overall initial freshness gradually replaced by the beauty of its harmonious patina.

The second type of marquetarian tries to exploit this fact by skilfully blending the veneers into a harmonious tonal range to achieve an overall sepia or monotone mood, with an obviously wooden appearance. One portraitist of some brilliance, for example, uses only walnut to create his pictures. They never grow dull with age and always look as charming as the day they were made. A whole picture may be made with only two or three woods.

The third type is not concerned with colour contrasts or tonal effects either. He is interested in exploiting the freak effects obtained from natural markings and odd figuring or grain contortions. He then creates a picture around these peculiarities, with the minimum of cutting, in order to let the wood tell its own story. Some of the best prizewinning pictures come from this group.

The fourth category, which far outnumbers the other three, is composed of men who are more craftsmen than artists, who strive to achieve photographic realism, involving a fantastic degree of minute detail and cutting in, and calling for the patience of Job.

Looking at it from about six paces away, a person who had never seen a marquetry picture before would not be able to detect any difference between this type of picture and a print or painting. The fact that it is made of wood is really incidental – an added extra – for the pieces are so small that they might just as well be cut from plastic or some other material.

A marquetry picture should not attempt to rise above the limitations of nature, as all history demonstrates that once the craftsman attempts to imitate effects obtained by other art forms such as painting or photography, by adding to nature's range of colour hues, by using chemical dyes and tints, he hastens the decline of his craft.

This is because the painter can paint a better picture, and a photographer can print a better reproduction of nature in all her glory. Marquetry was never intended to compete with those other forms of artistic expression.

Occasionally one finds a marquetarian with the ability to create his own style. One close friend, who is a water-colour artist, always manages to achieve a pastel appearance with his subjects; another chooses subjects which can best be portrayed on a simple white background – rather like Chinese art – and his style is most effective. Yet another believes in cutting the focal point of interest into a one-piece background, rather like a symbol, in keeping with modern décor, so that the panel retains an obvious wooden appearance yet loses none of its charm.

Fortunately for the craft of marquetry, there are as many different sub-divisions of style as there are craftsmen, each with their own personal taste and talent to express it.

3 Veneers – from the log to you

The path to success in the production of marquetry lies in the approach to the study of wood, as ultimately it is the wood that you use that will determine the success or failure of your work.

No two trees, even of the same species, are ever identical. There are differences of grain, figure, texture, colour and markings which will vary even in the same log. Every angle of cut through a log produces a different pattern of figure and grain effect, and it is this physical appearance which largely governs the value of a decorative veneer, and which the marquetarian considers when making his final selection.

From the cross-section of the stem of a tree, we can see mirrored in its cell structure all the events and hazards the tree was subjected to during its life – whether it enjoyed years of plenty or suffered drought, hunger, or maltreatment; whether it was plagued by insects, disease or fire. These external influences serve to produce the freak figures so sought after by marquetarians. It is the veneer cutter's task to decide how to cut each log to extract the best figure. To begin with, let us therefore consider how veneers are cut from the log.

There are four generally accepted methods: sawing, slicing, rotary cutting and half-rounding.

The veneer log – that is, the straight, cylindrical section of the tree trunk from just above the root-butt end up to the first limb – is kept in the mill pond under water until required, to prevent it from splitting at the ends and to protect it from attack by insects.

It is then hoisted into the mill and clamped to the moving platform 'bed' of a giant bandmill saw. The blade may be up to 50 ft. in length and over a foot wide. A 'slab-cut' is made at one side, which will enable the log to be turned over and laid firmly on this flat base.

The next cut is usually to cut the log in two 'halves', through the heart of the log. As most veneer logs are grown in the tropics, and the heart is near the centre of the log, this cut virtually cuts the log into two approximately equal sections. In the case of hardwoods from Europe or from the southern hemisphere temperate zones, more growth will have occurred towards the sun, with the result that the heart will be to one side. The object of this 'opening cut' is to remove the heartwood, which is spongy, and useless for veneer.

If the log is required for striped veneers such as sapele, it is then cut into four or six roughly squared-up sections called 'flitches', with the heartwood removed. If the wider flat sliced or crown cut veneers are required, the half-logs are 'squared-up', which simply means removing some sap from the edges.

Once the log has been opened in this way, the specialist veneer cutter can determine how to proceed to extract the best figure and value from the log.

Saw-cut veneers

For many centuries, all veneers were saw-cut, and most authentic antiques will be found to be veneered with saw-cut woods from about $\frac{1}{24}$ in. to $\frac{1}{16}$ in. in thickness. The flitch was cut into veneer on a large segmented circular saw of the ground-off type, of an overall diameter of from 4 ft. 6 in. up to 6 ft. It was a very highly skilled task, and a very wasteful process, as the sawdust wasted almost as much of the log as it yielded into veneer.

Today, the saw is used only in exceptional cases, to cut woods which are either extremely hard to cut by any other means, such as Gaboon ebony; or of such small girth or length as to make it either impracticable or uneconomic to cut the veneer by the other methods to be described. Other logs which were saw-cut were those of such irregular texture – such as curls – that other methods would risk tearing out the fibres.

Some of these small-diameter trees, such as holly, tulipwood, ebony, laburnum, and lignum vitae, are only available as 'billets', or small sections which have not been put through the saw to reduce them.

Incidentally, if you wish to experiment by cutting small sections of hardwoods into veneers for your own use, there are certain precautions to take. If holly is cut into veneer and then placed back in leaf form stacked one on top of the other, it will turn from white to brown. If separated immediately and exposed to the air to dry it may also turn 'weathered' – to a yellow tone. It must be stacked carefully with thin strips of wood between each leaf, and kept in a darkened room or cellar, with a free circulation of warm, dry air.

The only veneer sawyers that I ever knew – and I have had the pleasure of 'pulling through' for three of the best – all suffered from an occupational hazard – neuralgia. The velocity of the wind caused by the saw is in direct line with the intently watchful head of the sawyer, and after spending a year or two at this most exacting job, the sawyer was forced to wrap his head in a scarf. It is an extremely skilful task to saw a four-foot billet of ebony, and bring the veneer out at the same gauge at both ends without the saw cut wandering off. In fact, after about a dozen or so cuts, the saw had to be completely re-sharpened. The practice of saw-cutting has now virtually ceased and I know of only three sawyers in practice today, one each in London, Paris and New York.

Sliced veneers (quarter-cut)

These veneers are cut with a knife. To make this possible, the flitch is first placed in large vats or tanks, and boiled or steamed for a controlled period, varying from hours to weeks, and depending on the hardness of the log, the thickness it is. to be cut, the size of the flitch, and the species.

After a precise period, the softened flitch is carried by overhead crane into the veneer mill for slicing into veneers.

The flitch is fastened to a movable bed, and travels backwards and forwards against a knife held in a rigid framework. There is no waste, and after each slicing cut through the flitch, the knife carrier is given a fractional movement to correspond with the thickness of the veneer being cut. The huge knife, sometimes measuring sixteen feet long by a foot wide, remains stationary, while the flitch is brought with a shearing action across the knife.

In the case of striped veneers, the direction of the cut is from the outside of the flitch, at its sap edge, towards the heart side, across the annual growth rings and parallel to the rays. This radial cut produces the fine 'quarter-cut' striped veneers such as sapele, afrormosia, striped teak, etc.

Veneers cut by this process vary in thickness from about 0·6 mm., which is used mostly for backing or under-veneering, to

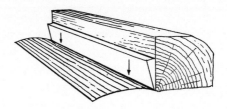

Fig. 11 Quarter-cut striped veneers are produced by radial slicing of a flitch.

0·7 mm, which is the thickness almost universally used for 'face' veneers throughout Europe. When a log is cut into 0·9 mm. it roughly approximates to the standard thickness used in Australia, Canada and the USA of $\frac{1}{28}$ in. thickness. It is important for the marquetarian to select veneers of about the same thickness for his work, to avoid trouble when laying the assembly, although this is not always possible.

Veneers are kept in precisely the same order as they are cut from the flitch, and each flitch is kept in the order it was cut from the log. This ensures perfect matching for decorative veneering, by arranging consecutive matching leaves in book fashion, to obtain 'mirror-matching' patterns. It is this continuity sequence which enables the marquetarian to produce four-, eight- and sixteen-piece turnovers, with only an imperceptible shift in the markings even in 32 leaves.

Some species, when radially cut, produce a striking medullary ray figure such as 'raindrop figured oak', 'lace figured sycamore', beech, etc.

Sliced veneers (flat-cut)

If an opened log is not cut into flitches, but is softened in a 'half-log' form, it may then be cut diametrically across its crown – a type of cut often called 'crown-cut' – to reveal a pattern of sap at each edge and a marbled figure heartwood at the centre. The full-width figured veneers, such as walnut, Brazilian rosewood,

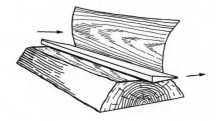

Fig. 12 A half log showing a diametrical crown cut across the full width.

teak, ash, elm and sycamore are cut in this way. They are highly prized by the traditional cabinet-maker, as they enable beautiful veneer matches to be created. These veneers are also cut into o·7 mm. thickness in Europe, and o·9 mm. for export.

Certain woods – such as sycamore, maple and horse chestnut, for example – cannot be given the heat softening treatment as they would immediately discolour. These have to be cut 'cold', and the log is worked over carefully with a metal detector, before cutting on the bandsaw, to ensure that it is free from small fragments of metal, nails, broken tips of penknives left in the tree by someone carving his initials, or pieces of horse-shoe. For these reasons 'hedgerow' timber is very rarely of any use for veneer logs.

After being cut into flitches the log is then cut without softening, and if the operator sees the smallest knot he must stop the machine and hack out the knot with an axe, otherwise it could result in the knife chipping. The expense in re-grinding the knife and loss of production while the knife is changed are reasons why few mills will attempt the cutting of sycamore, which is a native wood, and popular for marquetry work.

This is the reason why one often finds large man-made holes in sycamore. Another type of hole found in veneer – especially

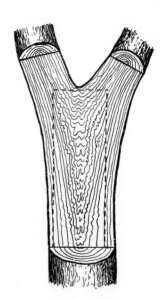

Fig. 13   Curl or crotch veneers are cut from the intersection of trunk and branches.

walnut – is the man-made bore-hole of a veneer auger bit. When buying a veneer log, it is permissible for the buyer to bore a hole into the log in one – rarely two – positions, in order to examine the pattern of sap and heartwood this reveals when the bit is extracted. This is not always an accurate guide, but explains why walnut veneers often bear a small hole through 'bundles' of 32 leaves.

By cutting through the intersection of a limb or branch with the trunk of the tree we obtain the figured curl veneers – known as crotches in America. The root base of the tree yields fancy figured butt veneers. To obtain this extremely beautiful figure, the veneer log has to be dug out of the ground with its rooted end intact, rather than felled by sawing through above the butt end.

Burr veneers (Burls)
Burr veneers are the end grain, wart-like growths which occur on some trees; they look like tightly clustered knot formations, and are the most highly prized of all veneers.

Rotary cut veneers
When veneers are required for constructional purposes, such as the laminations for plywood manufacture, the core stock for

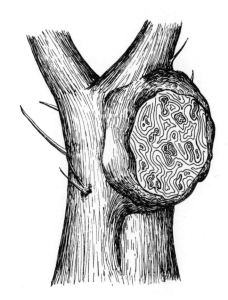

Fig. 14 Burr veneers (burl) are those end-grain, wart-like growths which occur on some trees, with the appearance of tightly clustered knot formations.

43

Fig. 15 Rotary cutting follows the annual growth ring of the log and is used mainly for constructional veneers.

shaped plywood, or the outer casing plies of blockboard and laminboard, they are rotary cut. They are cut with a knife, but from a complete log which has not been opened or cut in any way on the bandmill saw.

The complete log is steamed or boiled first, as for slicing, and is then placed in an automatic de-barking lathe to be 'rounded up', or made reasonably cylindrical and free from bark. The metal detector is used, as no risks can be taken with the expensive knives or production-time lost in changing the knife and re-setting the machine.

The log is then rotated against the knife and a continuous sheet of veneer is peeled from the log – rather like unrolling a giant swiss roll. The veneer is temporarily wound on large spools and removed to a clipper machine, where any defects are clipped out, and the continuous sheet is reduced automatically by the clipping guillotine into pre-determined widths.

Rotary-cut veneers can vary in thickness from $\frac{1}{100}$ in. up to a maximum of about $\frac{3}{8}$ in. thicknesses. The species most usually rotary-cut are Canadian birch, oneche, various mahoganies such as utile, sapele, tiama, 'coffin oak', gaboon, agba and cedar.

As an exception to the rule, this rotary-cutting process is used in exceptional cases to produce freak figured decorative woods such as bird's-eye maple, betula, masur birch, kevasingo and flame birch.

This is because the best figure of those particular logs is only obtained by cutting around the annual growth rings and not across its radius or crown.

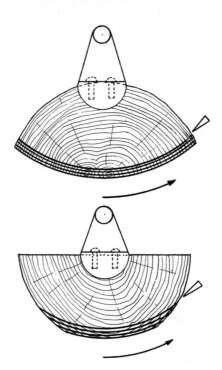

Fig. 16 An eccentrically mounted half log. Cutting that starts on the heart side is known as back cutting. True half-round cutting starts on the sapwood side.

Half-rounded veneers

In this type of cut, the quartered flitch is mounted eccentrically in the rotary lathe, so that the cutting starts at the heart side of the flitch – the technique known in the trade as 'back-cutting' – or, in true half-round cutting, at the sap-wood side. This technique gives a greater sweep across the growth rings at an angle which crosses them rather than follows them, as with normal rotary cutting, and is less likely to tear out the fibres.

Burry butt figured walnut, crotch or curl veneers, lacewood, and silky oak are cut in this way.

Drying the veneers

All veneers, by whichever knife process they were obtained, are then dried mechanically to an exact moisture content. The water found in wood is in two forms, as 'free water' in the cell cavities, and as 'absorbed water' in the cell walls. The weight of water in freshly felled 'green' timber can amount to more than 100 per cent of its dry weight. When wood is subjected to the veneer steaming or boiling process after being kept in mill ponds, it is usually saturated. It has to be dried to the point where it loses all its free water from the cell cavities, but leaving the cell walls still saturated. This is known as the fibre saturation point, beyond which, as the water in the cell walls begins to dry out, shrinkage will occur. The whole drying process is therefore aimed at reducing the moisture content to a point where the veneer will be in equilibrium with local atmospheric conditions.

By a carefully studied and scientifically regulated process, veneers are dried to about $12\frac{1}{2}$ per cent moisture content in Britain, but this will vary with humidity and climatic conditions in various parts of the world. Veneers to be used externally may be dried to 14–20 per cent, but as all wood is hygroscopic it will absorb or shed its moisture content with changing atmospheric conditions.

The dried veneers emerge from the hot mechanical drying kilns and are then given a cold air shower. If the veneers were stacked tightly together in the heated condition as they come from the drier, they would deteriorate and go spotty; the cold air douche enables them to adapt immediately to warehouse conditions, usually with humidity-controlled air conditioning, without waiting for a period of acclimatization.

The veneers are carefully replaced in a 'set' in exactly the same sequence as originally cut from the log or flitch. These irregularly shaped leaves, as cut from the log, are then clipped on power guillotines into veneers of uniform width. The wastage is collected by conveyor belt and returned by overhead cyclone extractors to the dutch oven which raises the steam for the softening tanks.

Veneer grading

It is at this stage that veneer grading begins. The grader, usually a man of great experience, marks on the veneers exactly where the trimming cuts are to be made to remove sap and other defects. Wide veneers with a wandering stripe may be guillotined at a slight angle to bring the stripe parallel with the edges, for instance.

The grading of veneers is a key job, since it is at this stage that their value is determined. They are graded according to figure, freedom from defects, knots, blips, soundness in texture and cutting, absence of mill defects such as a chipped cutting knife which will deeply scour the face of a veneer. There are very many other technical considerations as to length, even gauge at each end and both sides of the leaf, and so on. Or the drier may leave blue marks on the surface of certain woods such as afrormosia and oak, owing to the amount of tannin in those timbers.

This part of the operation is very detailed and specialized and there are therefore many grades for each species. 'Face' quality decorative veneers are usually worth many, many times the value of the 'backing' grades of the same species. It is therefore unwise, when purchasing veneers, simply to compare the name of the species with an apparent low price. The integrity of the supplier and grading experience are the vital factors in selecting veneers for any project.

The next phase of the operation of bringing veneers from the log to you, is the mechanical bundling of veneers. They are tied in 'bundles' of 24, 28 or 32 leaves – always in units of four for matching purposes – by automatic bundle tying machine. The tied bundle is now ready for measuring, which is not simply a matter of measurement and calculation. The veneer 'measurer' is another highly skilled man, who works with a marking crayon or chalk and a folding boxwood ruler, and he 'measures-out' and makes reasonable allowances for the bore holes, chopped out holes, patches, or other irregularities which might occur on some bundles in an otherwise perfect log.

The bundles are replaced in flitches, and eventually the complete log – now in veneer form – is taken by fork lift truck to the humidity-controlled warehouse, complete with detailed specification for any purchaser's inspection.

In my capacity as log buyer, I may visit six or more veneer mills to inspect more than one hundred logs of teak for example, before making a final selection of two or three logs. More than nine-tenths of all logs inspected fail to meet the exacting specification and grading requirements needed to supply artist-craftsmen with their veneers for decorative veneering and marquetry.

Grain, figure and texture
The *grain* of veneer, particularly the figured elements, is formed by its wood cells. There are six general grain types.

1. Straight grain – parallel to the vertical axis of the trunk.
2. Irregular grain, which occurs near knots or swollen butts.
3. Diagonal grain, which is usually a milling defect in otherwise straight-grained timber.
4. Spiral grain, where the fibres follow a spiral curve.
5. Interlocked grain, where successive growth layers have fibres in opposite directions – occurring mostly in tropical timbers.
6. Wavy grain, where the direction changes in waves.

The *figure* seen on the surface of veneer results from the interaction of several features – the scarcity or frequency of growth rings, colour tone variations, peculiarities of grain, contortion around knots, roots or limbs.

Irregular grain produces blistered or quilted figure; interlocked grain gives us pencil-striped or ribbon-striped figure; wavy grains yield fiddleback or beeswing cross-figure. Combinations of wavy grain and interlocked grain give rope-figure; other combinations provide such attractive figured effects as block mottle, pommelle, moiré figure, burry-butt, snail quilt, plum pudding, and other peculiar types of figure such as a burry-butt cluster, where a mass of eyes caused by dormant buds in burr formation are surrounded by an attractive finger-roll figure.

The surface of a decorative veneer may display, in addition to the distinctive grain effects and mottled figure, other peculiar markings which may be invaluable to a marquetry craftsman, even if of no account to a veneer craftsman. In fact it is often the case that the very piece discarded by the one will be eagerly sought after by the other.

Beautiful mineral stains – caused by the chemical action between the tannin in the wood and traces of iron in the soil, as found in obeche – can sometimes be found with a lovely scattered pale-blue stain or streaks, which makes a perfect sky effect. I have used this freak marking to portray both sea and sky effects in marquetry.

Often one can find a two-toned effect in a veneer caused by natural colour tone changes, which can be put to good use, for example in portraiture, where the darkest part of the background can be used to set off the profiled face of the portrait, and the lighter part of the background veneer can also set off the dark hair of the subject.

The markings in masur birch veneer are exceptionally important. This tree, which grows in Scandinavia, particularly in a part of Finland, is subjected to attack by insects which eat through the sapwood every year. When this species is rotary-cut into veneer, it is covered with tiny black specks and clustered brown markings, which makes the veneer an indispensable aid for marquetry.

Mansonia can be found with a light sapwood, sometimes streaked with golden brown markings, and the wood itself can give the appearance of twilight or the first light of dawn, for remarkable sky effects.

The physical *texture* of veneer is caused by variation in the size of its wood cells. Oak is coarse-textured; mahogany is medium-textured; sycamore is fine-textured. Diffuse, porous woods with narrow vessels and fine rays are even-textured; ring porous woods with wide vessels and broad rays are coarse-textured.

Lustre depends on the ability of the cell walls to reflect light. Some woods are dull, while others make excellent light reflectors. Generally, quarter-cut veneers of striped figure are more lustrous than flat-cut figured woods. The ability of wood to take a good polish does not necessarily coincide with its lustre potential.

The characteristic *odour* of some woods – such as camphor, pine or cedar – may be used for insect repellent purposes, to line blanket boxes or to retain the aroma of tobacco. Some veneers have a rather obnoxious odour until they have been laid and polished – for example Australian walnut.

Veneer defects

In selecting veneer for marquetry, the marquetarian should look first at the way the veneer has been cut. Make sure that it is of even gauge. Both sides of the veneer, at the edges, should be the same thickness, and also both ends of the leaf. Milling defects are quite frequent – sometimes not due to faulty machinery or workmanship but due to the log having a soft, or very hard, part which automatically affects the cutting.

Rub your fingers over the leaf to make sure the surface is smooth, and not with grain raised or torn by cutting. Some woods with a pronounced ray figure, such as oak, tend to become 'shelly' where the ray figure breaks out.

Bend the veneer slightly, and notice that it has a rough and a smooth side. The smooth side is the 'face' side, and although, when laying a veneer in matches, either side can be used, when cutting a veneer for a picture you should ensure that the smooth side is eventually seen.

For veneer matches, it is even more important that the reverse side is not really coarse, as smooth cutting is essential for all high-class veneer work.

The more slanted the grain of the veneer to the veneer surface, the greater the danger of dry checks; these are particularly noticeable on end grain veneers, such as burrs. Tiny hair checks cannot be avoided in rotary cut veneers, because the leaf has been torn from its natural position around the log and flattened out, thereby opening its underside.

Because of the conical shape of the eyes in bird's eye maple, the veneer should be laid face side – smooth side – down, that is, with the hair-checked side uppermost, to ensure that the eyes will not chip out.

Feel for a scratch mark across the leaf, which is a sign that the knife had a tiny chip out of it which has scoured the leaf. This may be impossible to paper out, and could ruin your work.

The veneer should also be free from shakes along the grain, and 'thunder shakes' across the grain, caused by tropical storms. Gum pockets, resinous patches – such as occur in zebrano and cedar respectively – are to be avoided. A natural dross or doat can form on some woods – it is a form of fungus – and can be found on canella, padauk, maidu burr.

Certain mineral stain defects are welcome, as explained in relation to obeche – stainy sycamore, maple, birch, mansonia, etc. But the majority of mineral stains, caused by the iron deposits in the soil reacting with the tannin in the wood, produce bad stains which are to be avoided, such as the heavy blue stain in oak, or afrormosia.

Injected veneer

An idea originating in Germany, and then developed at High Wycombe in Britain, is to inject the growing tree with vegetable dyes and other chemicals, which percolate through the tree from its roots to its topmost branches. The dye is carried through the sap until even the leaves change colour.

The dye diffuses through the heartwood too, with remarkable effects after the log has been cut into veneer. Experiments have been made by injecting the tree annually with a different dye; the result is rather garish. It produces a veneer which may have a novelty interest but is not of great value for marquetry.

However, some of the trees which have been injected with chemicals to produce pink variations, subdued reds, shades of green, and a spectrum of blues, have great possibilities.

The growing tree itself determines the pattern and nature of the veneer and no human control can be exerted over the final appearance – neither does the colour introduced in this way affect any of the original characteristics of the log such as grain, texture, figure and other markings. The idea itself is not new – for many years men have played at putting pieces of iron under their hydrangeas to change them from pink to blue.

Beech appears to be the most satisfactory timber for this process and is the one marketed in veneer form today. The lace-figured medullary rays do not appear to take the dye, and they show through the background colour.

The writer has a marquetry picture purchased in Moscow of a snow-scene, made of beech, in which the leaden sky, the swirling snowflakes, the snow-covered ground and the snowman being built by children have all been created from one leaf of beech, using these medullary rays to form the illusion of snow-flakes.

Weird effects of orange, brown and green have been obtained and its application seems best applied in architectural fields, although small articles of applied marquetry have been veneered successfully with injected veneer. The manufacturers of this type of veneer claim that the colours are fast to light, and they are available in green, blue, bronze and rainbow hues.

Dyed veneers

Only one firm in Europe specializes in the scientific production of chemically dyed veneers which are fast to light, and their methods remain undisclosed. The veneer chosen for dyeing is usually sycamore, but horse chestnut, pear, ash, birch, hornbeam, aspen, and all the maples, lacewood and abura are also used for special purposes. The colours are available in a wide range of delicate hues, from pastel yellows, through to black, and may be laid and sanded with other veneers without fear of sanding the colour out of the veneer as would be the case if the veneer was incorrectly dyed.

Attempts by amateurs to dye their own veneers, with the use of water dyes, spirit dyes and vegetable dyes, are successful only in the short term, since the chemical know-how of retaining light fastness, and preventing the colour from bleeding out of the veneer, or working towards one surface, or becoming incompatible with either adhesives or synthetic finishes, lies in the province of the specialist wood dyers.

The excellent book by F. Hamilton Jackson, *Intarsia and Marquetry* (1903), gives many recipes for traditional methods of dyeing veneer to obtain colour effects, but experience shows that the results are not permanent.

Marquetry craftsmen try to avoid the use of dyed woods but there are many traditional exceptions to this rule. The Marquetry Society in Britain admit the use of harewood – which is chemically treated sycamore (the monks used to immerse sycamore in artesian well water, to allow the iron to permeate the material and produce a greenish silver grey). Also, the restrained and limited use of dyed woods has recently been allowed by the Society in its competitions. The silver rose bowl which is the Society's highest award is often won by a picture in which dyed sycamore, in its harewood form, has been used. Professional craftsmen, however, have always used dyed black and dyed green, especially in mosaic bandings and inlay motifs.

The general principle is, never to use a dyed wood when there is available a natural one which will meet the need. Dyed woods are mostly used for applied marquetry decoration.

It is important to give all dyed woods, including inlay motifs and mosaic bandings, lines and strings, a brush coat of polish before cutting the veneers into the assembly, in order to seal in the colour. Otherwise, the sanding dust may rub into the open pores of surrounding veneers and this will discolour any light veneers such as sycamore, horse chestnut and obeche.

The different types of timber

It may surprise you to learn that there are estimated to be about 70,000 different types of trees known to man. There are thousands of people in all parts of the world with large private collections of woods, and more than 70 institutional collections possessing between 10,000 and 30,000 different types. The largest wood collection in the world is housed in the Samuel James Record Memorial Collection, at the School of Forestry, Yale University, which contains over 52,000 different specimens and maintains its own herbarium of voucher specimens.

For a sample of a newly discovered wood to be scientifically valuable, it must be correlated with a specimen of the leaves, twigs and fruit of the tree, but most important of all, with the flowers of the tree. All these together form a 'herbarium specimen'.

The wood scientist can positively identify every tree, with the same certainty that a detective can identify a man by his fingerprints, using a system of 'keys' for the swift identification of timbers; this enables even the layman without previous experience to make an accurate identification.

In his book *What Wood is That?*, Herbert L. Edlin describes 14 keys for easy identification:

1	general colour	8	weight
2	colour of heartwood	9	smell
3	growth rings	10	bark
4	pores	11	leaves
5	grain on longitudinal surfaces	12	country of origin
6	rays	13	sapwood
7	hardness	14	class of use

This book also contains a set of 40 veneer specimens of timbers popularly used for cabinet and marquetry work.

From the seventy thousand different species of timber known to man, exceedingly few are suitable for cutting into veneers by the large modern commercial mill. This is due to various reasons, some technical, some economic. Many of the trees are too small in girth to make their processing a viable proposition; others may not have a round cylindrical bole or stem. Yet others may be difficult to extract from their location and the effort unrewarding as more attractive similar timber may be obtained more easily elsewhere. Whatever the reasons, the timber specialists of the world have narrowed down their selection of the best veneer-producing trees to about two hundred, and this does simplify the task of the modern marquetarian. In fact, the leading stockists of rare and exotic wood veneers find it increasingly difficult to maintain a stock range of more than 100 types, permutated from this overall range of about 200.

There are excellent opportunities for home craftsmen, using power-tool saws, to produce their own veneers from small local or native trees, and vastly increase their 'palette' of woods.

Nomenclature

The accurate identification of woods is complicated by the fact that the same wood is known by different names in various parts of the world; some may be given trade names which sound glamorous or romantic but which actually refer to quite ordinary, common species. Many African timbers are known by their port of shipment, for example obeche is known as arere, ayous, samba, okpo, wawa, or African whitewood.

Pilot names are the names accepted in everyday trade usage in Britain, as listed in the British Standard Nomenclature of Commercial Timbers (BS881 and BS589). The same species may be known by an entirely different name in Australia, Africa or America. The pilot name is therefore only of value when used domestically in Britain, and this is the name used in the list of marquetry veneers given in this book.

The International Code of Botanical Nomenclature lays down a standardized code of *scientific names* in Latin, in order that scientists in every part of the world, whatever their native tongue, can understand to which species the name refers. This code uses the binomial latinized system. The first name indicates the genus and the second name, a specific epithet, indicates the particular species of that genus. The generic name is usually capitalized, whilst the specific name may or may not be. When a botanist has discovered and named a tree, it is the custom for his initials to be given after the binomial code names.

These scientific names refer to the geographic location or the appearance of the tree, or to the man who discovered it. Many of these names are of Greek derivation, but the scientific names are always latinized.

There are three advantages in using botanical names. Firstly, they are exact. Secondly, they indicate the true family relationship. For example all *Pinus* woods are true pines (*Pinus sylvestris*

54

is Scots Pine), whereas Parana Pine is *Araucaria angustifolia* and belongs to neither the genus nor even the pine family. Thirdly, the International Code is accepted in all countries and does not require translation into different tongues.

Common names are the ones in general usage and are often very misleading if they allude to some prominent characteristic of the tree. For example, if a tree is very heavy, it may be given the common name of 'ironwood'. In fact, there are more than 80 different trees of entirely different families known as 'ironwood'. Hornbeam is one example. Sometimes the common name refers to the colour of the bark of the tree as in the case of black Italian poplar, which is a very white wood grown in England and scientifically known as *Abele*.

Indian silver greywood – which sounds very exotic – is neither silver nor grey; Australian blackwood is not black but brown. Many of these common names derive from the scientific name. The larch comes from *Larix*, cedar from *Cedrus*, and pine from *Pinus*.

In the list of marquetry veneers to follow, I have listed the common names as a guide to other English-speaking readers who may know the timber by one of its other common names.

Vernacular names are the names by which the wood is known in its country of origin, usually in the native language. Here we get the reverse effect. Instead of different timbers being given the same common name, we have scores of different vernacular names for one specific timber. These names vary from region to region, and are often quite different at each port of shipment.

For example, afara (*Terminalia superba*) is known as *djombe* in the Cameroons, *eji* in Nigeria, *ka-ronko* in Sierra Leone, *fraké* on the Ivory Coast, *fram* in Ghana, *ofram* in former French territories, and *limba* by the British. In America it is given the name of korina.

As in the example of afara being sold in the USA as korina, the practice of giving timbers *trade names* is widespread in all countries. There are various reasons why firms invent trade names. In some cases it is to glamorize an otherwise ordinary species with excellent usage value. But more often it is due to a lack of knowledge of the true species by the unsophisticated trade merchant, who brushes aside the task of seeking true identification and provides a ready-made romantic or exotic name.

55

Inferior woods are given names to bask in the reflected glory of the original. Ayan (*Distemonanthus benthamianus*) is called Nigerian satinwood in imitation of genuine satinwood (*Chloroxylon swietenia*). The name 'African rosewood' is often applied to bubinga, and so on.

There are marked differences in nomenclature between nations in the English-speaking world. It is particularly noticeable in Australia, where oak, ash and elm are entirely different species from those we recognize in Europe or America.

The American gives different names to timbers from those accepted by both Britain and Australia. The following examples will illustrate how confused the situation has become:

Britain	USA
Silky oak (Australian) (*Cardwellia sublimis*)	Lacewood
Lacewood (*Platinus acerifolia*)	Sycamore
Sycamore (*Acer pseudoplatanus*)	Maple
Maple (*Acer saccharum*)	Sugar maple

But they know these timbers by the same scientific names, which underlines the importance of their use, as almost all other names can lead to confusion. This becomes patently clear when one considers the mahoganies. In the Meliaceae, the family of mahoganies, there are more than fifty different generic groups, producing over one thousand entirely different species growing in various parts of the tropical world. These include the West Indian and Central American *Swietenia* genus; the African *Khaya* and the *Entandophragma*; and every one of them may be known by a different common or vernacular name, or be given some exotic trade name.

The terms 'softwood' and 'hardwood' are universally accepted as conventional terms for the two main classes of commercial timber but the description can be misleading. Balsa wood is actually a hardwood, but pitch pine, although much harder and heavier than balsa, is a softwood. Most of the decorative marquetry veneers are cut from hardwoods, which provide the bulk of all commercial timbers, but there are many softwoods of sufficient hardness and beauty to convert into veneers. We get such attractive exceptions as pine, spruce, fir, larch, cedar and yew.

The flatting process

Veneers should be stored in a well ventilated, cool store, away from heat and if possible placed under a light weight to be kept flat until required for use. They should also be kept covered from the effects of both natural and artificial light. Sycamore kept for a few weeks without a cover will turn almost a light tan colour.

For various reasons, you may find your veneers are inclined to be overdry, resulting in a slight buckle, or waviness. Veneers kept in storage for a long time – especially in centrally heated homes, tend to shed their moisture content and start to curl up. Perhaps the local humidity is high, or there may have been a heat-wave. Whatever the reason, the veneer must be flattened before you can use it.

There are various ways of 'flatting' a veneer. The simple method is to sprinkle it with water from a sponge – not too wet – and place the veneer leaves between boards under a heavy weight overnight. This will allow the equilibrium of the veneer's moisture content to be restored.

A more certain way of flattening the veneers, is to heat two plywood panels, called cauls, and clamp them together with the veneers, lightly sprinkled with water, between them.

If you do use the heated caul method, the heat also serves to draw out any oiliness or resin from such veneers as teak or rosewood, which will make adhesion easier at a later stage. If the veneers are very resinous, brush them with a coat of carbon tetrachloride to remove the resin from the pores.

If there are a number of leaves to be 'stretched', sprinkle both sides of the veneer with weak glue size made of ten parts of water to one of scotch glue. Cover the veneers with a polythene sheet or clean paper to prevent sticking. Do not use newsprint as this may offset on the veneers. Place the veneers under the heavy weight as before or clamp them between the heated cauls.

If the veneers are very brittle, hard, or severely buckled – and certain burr veneers which contain many small holes and patches of ingrowing bark tend to buckle very easily – it is best to construct a simple home-made press formed by using four or six crossbearers and wing nuts, at the top and bottom of the two heated plywood cauls. It is a good tip to shape the top bearers slightly from the centre towards each end, to ensure that the pressure exerted by the nuts and bolts commences at the centre of the cauls when tightening the press down.

If it is not convenient to remove the wood cauls from the press in order to heat them before a fire, the alternative is to construct the press from blockboard panels, which may be made a fixture, and use thin metal cauls made from zinc or aluminium.

First, sprinkle the buckled veneers with thin glue size, and allow them to dry thoroughly. (I have successfully used cellulose paperhanger's paste for this purpose, such as Polycell, which dries invisibly.) Then place polythene sheets over the veneers to prevent them sticking together, or cover each veneer with a sheet of clean plain paper. Place them in the press, between heated cauls – which should be slightly larger than the veneers to be pressed.

The degree of heat is a matter for experiment and experience; generally I have found it only necessary to heat the cauls sufficiently to enable me to handle them without resorting to the use of gloves. If metal plates are being used, grease them with soap or candle grease to prevent them sticking if paper was used on the veneers, or remember to have a sheet of polythene between metal and veneer.

The press may be progressively tightened down, in stages; at each stage remove the metal cauls for re-heating.

Really brittle or buckled veneers are made sufficiently flexible and strong for safe handling by sizing with a mixture of adhesive for strength, glycerine for flexibility, and alcohol for quick drying. The following formula is recommended:

Cascamite 'One-Shot'	2 measures (1 part by weight)
Flour (not self-raising)	1 measure ($\frac{1}{2}$ part by weight)
Water	3 measures ($2\frac{1}{3}$ parts by weight)
Glycerine	$1\frac{1}{2}$ measures ($1\frac{1}{4}$ parts by weight)
Alcohol (meths)	$\frac{1}{2}$ to 1 measure ($\frac{1}{3}$ to $\frac{2}{3}$ part by weight)

This solution should be used cold.

Immerse the veneers for a few minutes, stand them on end to drain and as soon as the surface is dry to the touch, place between dry softwood caul boards which have been warmed. After 24 hours transfer them to another set of dry softwood heated boards for a further period. In this way the burrs or curls will be dried and shrunk slowly. At the end of the treatment they should be flat, strong and flexible and their further handling, cutting and laying will be easy.

If these burrs and curls are in a distressed condition after stretching, with opened cracks, splits, defects, holes or ingrowing bark – perhaps with plainer sappy parts, then use other leaves of the same burr to patch the leaf required for use. This is done by following the irregular contours of the burr's natural marking, using the veneer knife or one of the sawing techniques.

If the veneers are slightly split at the ends along the grain, pull the veneer tightly together with gummed veneering tape across the split and then along the split, and this defect will not show, as the split will lose itself in the grain. This special tape is placed underneath the split, and the veneer is vigorously rubbed along the split with a rounded hardwood 'rubber', which compresses the fibres of the veneer. The friction generated helps to dry out the tape, which contracts, pulling the join together more tightly. It is good practice to protect all veneers across the ends with veneering tape to prevent splits from starting.

Always keep veneers in numbered sequence, by chalking running numbers on each leaf, to enable you to use them for 4-piece or 8-piece matches if required.

For some of the fretsawing techniques, it is also advisable to glue a sheet of stout Kraft paper to the back of brittle veneers, so that any splinters or tiny fragments which may break off during the cutting sequences will remain fastened to the backing sheet, which can be easily removed at a later stage.

In practice, it will be found that ninety per cent of all veneers you purchase for marquetry work will be flat and ready for use, and will not require the foregoing stretching and flattening processes.

Many professional craftsmen, on the other hand, give *all* their veneers this heating and flatting treatment, certain that it assists the later glueing and polishing stages by filling the grain and pores of the veneer, rendering them softer, more flexible and, when given a strong paper backing, ideal for fretsawing and knife-cutting without fear of losing tiny fragments of brittle woods.

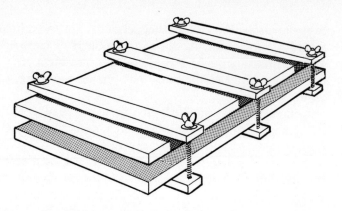

Making a simple press

The marquetry craftsman should construct a veneering press as the traditional veneering hammer cannot be applied to a multi-part marquetry assembly.

You may be able to find an old letterpress, of the type formerly used in solicitors' offices, with a centre screw. These presses can actually be the cause of blisters, as they provide simultaneous pressure all over the panel and trap the excess glue and air pockets. Another danger when using these presses is that if excessive pressure is applied with the use of a crowbar extension, pressures up to 300 lb. per sq. in. can be obtained, whereas the ideal pressure required for veneering marquetry work is only 30 lb. per sq. in. Excessive pressure results in damage to the cell structure of the veneer and also forces the glue into the groundwork, causing 'starved joints'.

Obtain two panels of 12 mm. plywood, or better still, blockboard, about 16 in. × 12 in. or sufficiently large to take the picture or marquetry assembly you wish to lay. Make sure these two panels are perfectly flat in each direction, as these are to become the pressing cauls.

Eight cross bearers are required, about 16 in. × 1½ in. × 1½ in., cut from hardwood, and eight 7-in. bolts, wing nuts and washers.

Drill a ½-in. hole about ¾ in. from the end of each bearer to take the bolts through the 1½-in. thickness. Through four of the bearers drill a hole about 3 in. from each end to take countersunk No. 8 screws.

Screw the four bottom bearers into position 2 in. from each end of the lower caul, with the other two bearers at 4-in. inter-

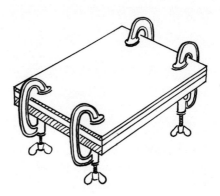

Fig. 17 *Left:* A simple veneering press. The top bearers must be slightly tapered from their centre towards the end. If the picture is only a small one, four 'G' cramps (*right*) are usually sufficient.

vals. The four top bearers must be shaped slightly, tapering all the way from their centre out towards the ends, which should be reduced about $\frac{3}{16}$ in. This gradual tapering will ensure that, when the bearers are tightened, the pressure will commence in the middle of the panels; this will force any surplus glue out towards the edges. Do not plane a few inches off each end, as this would have the effect, when tightened, of relieving the pressure on the centre of the caul. The tapering must be gradual along the whole length of the bearer from the centre towards the ends.

Tighten the bolts in sequence, beginning at the two centre bearers, then the outer ones, with the object of driving out any trapped air pockets. It is a good idea to have two sheets of aluminium or zinc the same size as the cauls, which may be heated on a hotplate to speed up the pressing time. Alternatively, two pieces of linoleum are useful, or thick rubber or plastic sheet, which will take up any unevenness in the assembly. Also have some polythene sheet at hand to place immediately on top of the veneer assembly to prevent any surplus glue from adhering to the press cauls.

4 Adhesives

The perfect marquetry adhesive has not yet been invented. All glues and adhesives possess certain advantages and disadvantages. The craftsman has to learn which to use for which purpose.

Animal glues, comprising bone, skin and hide glues, are water-soluble and therefore neither water- nor heat-proof. However they are widely used for interior decoration, and so are fish glues, which have the same limitations. The advantage of these glues lies in the fact that any defects in the laying operation can easily be put right; the bond is, to a certain extent, flexible, and will permit the panel to 'breathe' with changes in humidity. Repairs to the decoration can be made at a later date without difficulty.

These glues are of two types. The cold glues require pressure until cured, and the hot glues require heat or pressure. No amount of heat will cure a cold glue – in fact excessive heat will cause the glue to deteriorate. Only pressure is required. Hot glues have to be allowed to 'tack' before the pressure is applied, and these function best with heated cauls, to be described in the chapter on laying.

Casein glue, made from milk, is alkaline and therefore unsuitable for veneering owing to its staining effect on certain veneers with an acid content, such as oak, mahogany, obeche, afrormosia, etc.

Vegetable adhesives are mainly gums and only concern the marquetarian in his choice of gummed veneering tape, which should be of the type specially made not to stain delicate veneers.

Latex and rubber-based adhesives are emulsions with a high solvent content which has to evaporate, and the resulting bond is unsuitable for laying marquetry.

Each of the *synthetic adhesives* has its own special purpose. Balsa cement or marquetry cement is a special fast-setting synthetic used for butt-jointing assemblies, and for laying very small pieces of veneer into completed marquetry panels. Also, these transparent cements are useful for mixing with veneer dust to form a stopping paste for filling open joins.

PVA adhesives require special care as many contain a very low solid content in the emulsion. The resulting high moisture content has to escape through the veneer, causing it to swell and then split on shrinking. PVAs also have other disadvantages, such as being affected by water or excessive cold or forms of stress. These adhesives are used for butt-jointing and stopping paste in the same way as marquetry cement.

Impact adhesives are excellent for veneering generally, if the area to be veneered is reasonably small. In the application of the adhesive to both surfaces, as no moisture is involved, the marquetry assembly runs no danger of delamination or curling up as the volatile solvent evaporates immediately. To overcome the immediate bond upon impact, the use of the 'slip-sheet' technique developed, in which a paper separator is used.

An exceptionally strong mechanical bond results, which actually strengthens, as time passes, into a very durable bond. The big advantage of the impact adhesive is that veneers may be applied to any type of surface, such as hardboard, chipboard, plastic sheets, metal or ceramics. They are ideal for veneering around corners, and curves of small radii, and for curved and shaped work in general.

Ordinary household impact adhesives are not recommended, as they contain fillers of various kinds to enable the resin content to stick 'anything-to-anything'.

I have developed an impact adhesive specially formulated for veneering, known as Avco 539 and made by Evode Ltd., which is made to spread easily without stringing or other difficulties caused by the presence of these special fillers.

Glu-film

A recent advance in specially formulated veneering adhesive is the revolutionary hot-melt type of cast film adhesive which I introduced in 1966 under the brand name of Avco 'Glu-film'. It is a continuous sheet of thermoplastic adhesive film, with a siliconized paper backing sheet for protection. It is simply cut with scissors to the desired length to cover the groundwork, so that no waste results. The backing sheet is peeled off and the veneers placed in position. They may then be ironed on with an ordinary domestic electric iron set at 'rayon' heat – using the backing sheet to cover the veneer to prevent any scorching, although the iron is not really hot enough to cause scorching. The idea is to have the iron hot enough to melt the film, but not hot enough to scorch or dry out the moisture of the veneer. The film activates at 80°F. with a three-second time-pause. The veneers are then laid with the veneering hammer or seam roller.

One advantage is that joins may be made on the work, using traditional hand veneering methods. It may be re-heated and jointed, or re-laid in the event of repairs to blistered surfaces. The film is excellent for use in presses, where heated cauls are used. The film is of correct glue-line thickness of 0·005 in. and is waterproof, transparent, non-staining and gap-filling. The iron draws the glue up into the fibres of the veneer, giving a strong mechanical lock of great durability.

Glu-film has a storage life of several years and is most economical, since only sufficient for the exact requirements need be purchased. After laying, the bond will withstand 100°C.

There are other forms of adhesive, such as epoxy resins which require the use of a liquid hardener or catalyst. Some of these have such a fast cycle of operation that if they were mixed prior to application they would have an unworkable pot life. Therefore the hardener must be applied to the groundwork and the resin to the veneers. This type must on no account be used for marquetry veneering for two reasons. Firstly, moisture must never be applied to veneers, even for a few seconds before pressing, as this may cause damage to the marquetry assembly. Secondly, the acid catalyst has a staining effect on many veneers with a high acid content.

Some resin adhesives also accelerate the discoloration caused by the photo-chemical action of the ultra-violet light rays in both natural and artificial light. Others require special pore fillers in the subsequent polishing stage, otherwise the polish may be affected by the resin if the two are incompatible.

After very considerable experience in this field, I would recommend, as the best adhesives for marquetry, Cascamite 'One-Shot', a urea-formaldehyde type of synthetic resin, and Croid Universal clear liquid glue.

Cascamite 'One-Shot' is a mixture of urea resin, plus catalyst, filler, and flour extender, in powder form. This type offers the greatest scope for enduring bonds under all conditions and the greatest resistance to heat, moisture, and damage from other causes. Urea-formaldehyde resins do not stain even the most delicate veneers, and possess tremendous resistance to changes of humidity and all temperature extremes.

A common fault with any adhesive is that the amateur applies the film too thickly, believing that the more he puts on, the better the bond will be, but the reverse is true. The recommended glueline is only five thousandths of an inch thick, and when this is exceeded the bond tends to crack and craze after curing. To avoid this, modifications have been added to the urea powdered adhesive to make it gap-filling, when glue lines up to five hundredths of an inch are permissible without risk of crazing.

Once the bond has been made it cannot be undone: it cannot be reheated to deal with blisters. The laying must be perfect first time. Of course, this is the adhesive used in factory production, where all the necessary conditions are carefully controlled.

As the two main dangers to avoid with all marquetry assemblies are heat and moisture, an adhesive must not require very high curing or setting temperatures, which points to the necessity of using a cold glue; the marquetry must remain dry and the adhesive must be applied to the groundwork only, which eliminates all two-surface types.

Cascamite 'One-Shot', with water added according to the maker's instructions, has a pot life of one hour. The working temperature of the room must be 70°F., and after application to the groundwork, allow ten minutes' assembly time before applying pressure. The adhesive must be tacky to the touch before the press is tightened down, and the press must be kept at 70° for three hours for a perfect bond. Of course, by increasing the press temperature, the setting times are drastically shortened down to four minutes at 200°F. This must never be attempted with a marquetry assembly of any kind as this intense heat will cause severe damage to the veneers, especially in a marquetry picture.

Pressing at normal room temperature at 70°F. is ideal, but if a little gentle heat is used through the addition of heated metal cauls in the press, this will serve to draw the adhesive up into the pores of the veneer and shorten the pressing time to about four or five hours.

Once a panel is removed from the press it must be allowed to cure for a period of time – up to a week, for best results – during which time the adhesive will continue to harden and the bond to strengthen.

So much for the best adhesive for the serious marquetry craftsman or professional. The amateur marquetarian, uncertain of getting his marquetry assembly pressed correctly first time, wants a margin of error. The generally accepted adhesive used by members of the Marquetry Society is Croid Universal cold clear liquid glue, or Evo-stik Resin 'W'.

Croid Universal clear glue, or Evo-stik Resin 'W', is available in tubes, tins or plastic bottles. In cold weather it may require standing in warm water to restore its viscosity, but generally it may be used straight from the tube or tin.

It is applied thinly to the groundwork, and after a few moments it is tacky enough for the coated groundwork to be lowered on to the marquetry assembly, which is already in the press waiting to receive the groundwork.

It is best for this glue to be used at a room temperature of about 70°F. and a little gentle heat from heated cauls, although not necessary to the action of the glue, will help to speed the setting time and to draw the glue into the pores of the veneer. One should aim at absorption without penetration through to the veneer surface, which is why the correct thinness of glue line is essential.

The advantage of cold pressing with glue is that, if a blister should result, the glue may be re-heated and the offending veneer relaid; however, it has the disadvantage that the resulting glueline is not gap-filling, nor resistant to heat or moisture, nor likely to remain impervious to temperature and humidity extremes. It is ideal for amateur use, for laying pictures which will be kept at room temperatures.

A cautionary tale

The importance of adhesives, and the need for care in laying a picture, are underlined by a disaster that is still vivid in my mind after fifteen years.

At that time, a marquetry craftswoman came to see me with

her completed marquetry assembly taped together ready for pressing. This lady had spent nearly a year in creating her masterpiece, and had visited my veneer stockrooms on many occasions in her search for freak woods which would do justice to her picture of a galleon in full sail against a wild sky and storm-tossed sea. She had enlisted my aid in the selection of veneers and we had spent countless hours in discussing the craft.

The complete assembly was too big for her press, and she wanted me to supervise its laying. She knew of several cabinet-makers who would lay it for her, but would not entrust the task to anyone else. She insisted that it should be laid with compensating under-veneers, and should on no account be sanded after laying, as she wanted to allow the panel to cure well before introducing moisture to remove the tapes.

She returned with the picture a week later, this time with the border veneers affixed, and in a large, beautifully wrapped and tied parcel, complete with groundwork – or so I mistakenly thought.

I immediately took the parcel to the office of a personal friend who has a large veneer panel pressing business, with every type of press and equipment; I explained the requirement and he said he would give the matter his personal attention.

On my return to my own office, my friend was on the telephone, to tell me the panel was laid and I could come for it immediately. With great foreboding I drove back to the works and refused to allow myself to think what must surely have happened. He must have pressed the panel in the hot press at extremely high temperature, instead of using pressure only in a bag (vacuum) press. I had not presumed to advise him how to lay a picture.

He stood at the top of a flight of stairs, holding the picture up for me to see. I was horrified to see that it had been sanded, against my instructions. He explained afterwards that his men were so keen to see the picture that they took the panel from the press and sanded it before he could stop them. As I climbed the stairs, my initial shock turned to mortification when I realized, from ten feet away, that the picture was cracked and split all over, along the main grain directions. My hackles rose when I also noticed that they had sanded through the beautiful sky veneer which was 'freak celestial blue obeche'. My dismay turned to fury when I got to the top of the stairs and discovered that the picture was not even square and the border veneers were broken and splintered off.

With incredulity I took the panel out of his hands and, as I did so, discovered that it was not laid on blockboard as requested, but it was warped and twisted in both directions. I turned the panel over in my hands in speechless stupefaction, and found that they had actually laid the picture on a frayed old tea chest lid complete with tin bung at the back!

He shrugged it off as a great joke, explaining that he had simply given the package to his chief presser and told him to lay it. But my customer had brought the picture roughly taped to a tea chest lid for support!

There are two sequels to this story. Firstly, I immediately severed all trading associations with the firm who had been so indifferent to a marquetry masterpiece of this kind. Secondly, I learned a lot about restoring damaged marquetry panels: the tea-chest backing was coarse-sanded flat, then bonded to edge-lipped diagonal cross-veneered laminboard; after the panel had been soaked and steam treated to close up the cracks, new sky pieces were inserted and inlays made to other rubbed-through parts; the borders were removed and new borders applied; and finally a few tricks of the polisher were used to give it a perfect finish.

The resulting picture, under scrutiny of the most severe critic, would pass as not far short of a masterpiece. My customer, of course, disowned it, claiming that she would never make another marquetry picture as this one had broken her heart.

I always keep that incident before me whenever I think of laying a marquetry picture, and I hope it serves as a reminder to you too. Take great care that the groundwork is correctly and thoroughly prepared; that the picture is kept away from both moisture and excessive heat; and do not hurry the cleaning-up stages. Patience is a virtue!

5 The knife and the saw

Entirely different techniques have developed over the years for the production of marquetry, each governed by the thickness of the material to be worked.

In ancient times, when wood-carving tools and the shoulder knife were used, the veneers were actually thin boards from $\frac{1}{8}$ in. up to $\frac{1}{4}$ in. thick. Later, when the fine bow-saw was used, and the veneers were cut by pitsaw, the thickness was reduced to about $\frac{1}{8}$ in.

Then, when the large segmented teeth of the circular saw enabled veneers to be cut no thicker than $\frac{1}{28}$ in. to $\frac{1}{16}$ in., the 'donkey' (p. 14) was used to cut the marquetry.

Now, with knife slicing and rotary cutting of veneers, we have veneers of two main thicknesses in use. In Europe the universal thickness is 0·7 mm., which permits the use of the knife for cutting marquetry. In Australia, Canada and throughout the United States of America, they prefer to slice their veneers into $\frac{1}{28}$ in. or 0·9 mm. thickness, and these have to be cut for marquetry by fretsaw techniques and power saws.

The modern marquetarian must be able to employ any of the techniques of cutting if he is to be master of his craft and able to repair, restore or reproduce an authentic period piece of furniture, or picture; to use veneers of any particular thickness; or to use any of the many traditional materials such as tortoiseshell, mother of pearl, ivory, brass and other metals.

There are many advantages in using sawn veneer. It retains its original colour tone and vividness, as it has not been subjected to the steam treatment. Its thickness makes it more resistant and easier to work by fretsaw. You are not restricted to the hundred or so veneers which are commercially available in knife-cut thickness, but may use any of the local or native hardwoods from the thousands of different species known to man.

There is one important consideration when using sawn veneer.

The teeth of the saw cause tooth marks to appear across the surface of the veneer, obliterating the true grain, figure and markings of the leaf. It is necessary to plane one side to remove the tooth marks and reveal the true colour tone. If these marks are not removed, and the veneer is glued down with the saw marks in the glueline, eventually the tooth marks will be seen from the smooth polished side of the veneer, as the action of the glueline in pulling the veneer down will repeat this pattern on the face side.

If you consider this necessity to plane sawn veneers as a nuisance, it also has its compensations; the finished panel may be brought to a smooth surface, either with a traditional smoothing plane or a cabinet-maker's scraper, or by power sanding, with a great deal more confidence than with the thinner knife-cut species and with less risk of rubbing through.

Finally, it is as well to realize that many woods, such as gaboon, ebony and greenheart, lignum vitae and kingwood, are not available in any other form; also that holly and other small-dimensioned trees have to be saw-cut for economic reasons.

Therefore, the question of whether to use the knife or a fretsaw for marquetry does not arise. In fact, the proficient craftsman has to be skilled in using the chisel, the knife and the saw as tools of his craft. The choice of techniques is determined solely by the job in hand and the materials to be used.

The workshop

The amateur craftsman, using the knife-cutting technique to cut a marquetry picture for a hobby, can use the kitchen table, and slide the whole apparatus of veneers and knife into the table drawer in a few seconds. From that approach the craft of marquetry as a hobby does not involve the amateur with any more expense than a knife, a non-slip ruler and a tube of glue, with a few finishing materials.

However, amateur and professional alike should note that daylight is essential, in order to recognize the colour tones of the woods. The light should be strong enough to show up a crack even in dark veneer. Artificial light must not glare. Pure white neon light is completely unsuitable. The best arrangement is a well-lit room with a spotlight on your work. If you are painting or decorating the workroom, colour it green, which will prove quiet and restful to the eyes. The room should be dry, of even temperature and well ventilated. Try to avoid condensation even in winter, as wall humidity can affect the veneers. Central heating, too, is not advisable, for the same reason; air conditioning is to be preferred.

The tool kit

Knives. The craftsmen of old used to make their own shoulder knives to suit themselves, the length of the wooden handle being the exact length from their outstretched finger tip to the elbow. Knives still remain highly personal tools, and in the same way that no two people can get the same result with the same pen, a knife will give a different feel and cut from man to man. Some people have a tight grip, others can exert heavy pressure through their fingers without gripping the handle tightly; other craftsmen like the feel of a handle they can control, especially when making strong cuts.

This explains the shortcomings of commercial knives. A high-speed hacksaw blade, as used by engineers, can be broken in half and filed down to make an excellent knife. File off the teeth, and grind a 45° cutting angle to the blade, which can then be sharpened and honed on an oilstone. The blade can be fitted into a handle made of hardwood, into which a sawcut has been made to accommodate the blade. Bind the handle with adhesive tape. It is also a good idea to round the end of the knife to make a 'rubber'. The rubber is used for rubbing down gummed veneering tape or small fragments of veneer, and for coaxing small marquetry pieces into tight-fitting assemblies.

In addition to varying the length and shape of the handle, also make a few knives with different cutting angles on the blades. For trimming veneers along the grain, or for making two-piece matches, you may find a very long blade ideal. This is made by sharpening one long side of the blade; a 45° edge would be excellent for cross-cutting, and 60° for cutting fine, intricate shapes.

I once made a double knife, by making a double-width saw cut in the handle and grinding two identically shaped blades, with a packing piece between them to suit the width of veneer line to be inlaid. With one stroke I was able to cut a white line from sycamore, and with the next stroke to cut a groove into the background veneer of the precise width to receive the line. To prevent the blades from moving in the handle after a while, it is safest to drill two small countersunk holes right through the handle and blade, and retain the blades with small nuts and bolts.

Just as a wood carver has a multitude of chisels to suit every cutting need, the marquetry craftsman should build a range of knives to suit his handgrip and the types of cut he will meet in marquetry. There are many excellent commercial knives on the market. The Swann-Morton craft knife has a small plastic handle with a knurled knob to tighten one of three different blades, one curved, one hooked and one straight, the latter being the most popular for marquetry. This handle will also accommodate the specially fine surgical scalpel blades, as used by hospitals, of which the No. 11 is the best shape. Do not try to use the correct scalpel blade handle, which leaves far too much of the blade exposed; when pressure is exerted, the fine blade may snap off. In the ordinary craft tool handle, the scalpel blade fits almost completely inside, leaving just enough blade exposed to do its work.

The Multicraft tool kit has a range of handles and different blades to suit most needs. The Stanley Slim knife with five spare blades is another excellent knife for veneer work generally.

Straight edge. For small picture marquetry the Maun non-slip safety ruler, either in bright steel finish or painted black with white markings, is an essential piece of equipment. It has an M-shaped section, and when pressure is applied with the left hand along the shaped top section of the ruler the possibility of slipping with the knife, when using some pressure, is reduced.

For larger veneer jointing, such as small panels, table tops, etc., straight edges made from heavy-duty steel with accurately machined edges are available in 24 in. and 36 in. lengths.

Seam roller. The decorator's seam roller is a useful tool when laying veneers by the slip-sheet separator technique, and also for hand veneering as a complementary tool to the veneering hammer.

Toothing plane. This is a wooden plane with an almost vertical iron, which has minute teeth cut into the planing edge. It is used to work across the groundwork diagonally in both directions, to form a key before veneering. Any absence of tooth marks shows up slight hollows in the groundwork which might

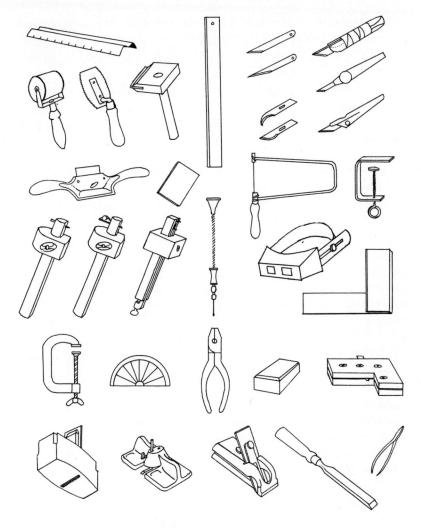

Fig. 18 The marquetry craftsman's tool kit.

otherwise not be detected. The teeth of a hacksaw blade, or an old tenon saw, dragged across the work answers the same purpose but the toothing plane is the correct tool.

Veneer hammer. This is not used like a hammer, but rather like a squeegee. It consists of a wooden holder about 5 in. wide and 3 in. deep and about $\frac{1}{2}$ in. thick, with a saw cut in the bottom end about $\frac{1}{16}$ in. wide. Into this is firmly fitted a rounded-edged metal blade – usually non-ferrous metal, to avoid any chemical reaction with the tannin in certain veneers. The squeegee is fitted with a dowel handle, mainly as a balance, for, in practice, professional users hold the hammer with the handle pointing away from them.

When laying veneers by hand, with the traditional hot scotch glue or Glu-film techniques, the veneering hammer is used to work along the grain in zigzag fashion, from the centre of the veneer leaf outwards towards the edges, to exclude all air bubbles and surplus glue and ensure a perfect bond.

Veneer saw. There are two basic types; one has a wooden hand grip with a curved steel blade fixed to one face and with teeth pointing inwards from each end; the other looks like a miniature backsaw except that it has a 3-in. blade with teeth on both edges, and the blade is attached to the handle with two screws, which enable the blade to be reversed so that either edge may be used, depending on the thickness of the veneers to be cut. It is used for cutting joints in veneer for matches, since a knife cut or chisel cut is actually a bevel cut, whereas the saw gives a square edge.

Although the veneer saw is still widely used in America for cross-cutting $\frac{1}{28}$ in. thick veneers, it is used in Europe mostly for cutting saw-cut veneers, or those of the 0·9 mm. or $\frac{1}{28}$ in. thickness.

Cabinet scraper. There are two principal types of scraper used in marquetry work. The Stanley type of metal scraper, fitted with a double handle and used rather like a spokeshave, is capable of fine setting but is unsuitable for use by inexperienced workmen. The type of scraper used by most professional craftsmen is a piece of mild steel about 4 in. × 2½ in. upon which one long edge is burred over slightly by rubbing it along a hard piece of iron such as the back of a chisel. The scraper is then grasped in both hands, slightly flexed, with both thumbs at the back, and the burred edge scythes its way over a marquetry assembly, removing a very fine shaving. With a little practice, to avoid digging the scraper into the veneers, it is an indispensable aid, as it may be used to remove traces of gummed paper tape, paper backing sheets, or parts of designs glued on to veneers, and to reduce varying thicknesses of veneer in a picture or marquetry assembly without glass-papering. All papering movements tend to cause a fuzziness of grain, whereas with the scraper the shavings are completely removed.

Marking gauge. After the picture has been laid, over-size, into the surrounding border margin, a marking gauge is used to mark a parallel line exactly true to the edge of the panel in order that the surplus veneer may be removed and the border or cross-banding veneer may be fitted accurately. The best types of marking gauge have brass strips let into the face of the gauge to prevent wear.

Cutting gauge. Instead of marking the work with a line from a fine point, the cutting gauge is fitted with a sharp knife blade, and will actually cut into the surplus veneer for easy removal. The best-quality cutting gauges are also fitted with brass strips in the face side, and they are adjustable to any desired width up to about 6 in.

Mortice gauge. The mortice gauge has two knives, which can be adjusted to make a double cut of any required width, and is ideal for both marking and cutting veneer to receive inlay lines, stringing or bandings. These also should have brass inlaid face strips to prevent wear.

Fretwork drill. The archimedean type of push drill with a very fine point is ideal for drilling a tiny hole in the working margin of veneer pads to accommodate the fretsaw blades.

Fretsaw frame. The F.S.70 Eclipse fretsaw frame has an 11-in. throat and is the best commercial fretsaw frame available.

Fretsaw blades are available in sizes ranging from W1/0 to W/0 (0·011 in. × 0·034 in.), which are suitable for the beginner to practise with. Marquetry fretsaw blades, size 2/0, are made with double teeth, each with a special set to allow for sawdust clearance, and with rounded backs to permit the blade to swivel around very tight curves without stress; the blades are only ten thousandths of an inch thick (0·010 in. × 0·021 in.). Metal-piercing jeweller's blades have single teeth and are extremely fine, varying from Grade 3 (coarsest) to Grade 1 (robust), 2/0 (medium), 4/0 (fine) and 6/0 very fine). It is possible to obtain 8/0 (extremely fine), but these are so delicate that great expertise is required in their use. These grades range from 0·016 in. × 0·034 in., 32 teeth per inch (No. 3) to 0·006 in. × 0·016 in., 76 teeth per inch (8/0).

Bench clamps are available in a range of sizes from 2 in. upwards for holding the cutting table to the workbench, and clamping straight edges to the work.

Pocket hone. Small pocket carborundum oilstone for keeping a keen edge on knives.

Squares. A carpenter's try square is a useful tool for testing the accuracy of border surrounds; T-squares for use in developing the design; and a combination try and mitre square for checking the accuracy of mitred corners.

A transparent *protractor* of 180° will be found most useful for parquetry cutting, as this involves cutting at 30°, 60° and 45° angles.

'G' cramps are useful for cramping heated wooden blocks over blistered veneer surfaces, holding battens in place for the application of edge lines, and for cramping heated cauls together in the flatting process.

Pliers are needed for tightening the knobs on knife handles, and the fretsaw frame winged nuts.

Magnifying glass. Headband binocular magnifying loupes may be worn, even over spectacles, for close work, leaving both hands free. This is useful when entering the fine piercing blades into the minute holes in the veneer pads for fretsawing.

Scratch stock. This is a simple home-made tool for cutting the grooves to accommodate inlay lines and bandings. Two pieces of hardwood or plywood $\frac{1}{4}$ in. thick by 6 in. long are screwed together, and a notch marked out and cut in both pieces. The two halves are screwed up tightly together to enclose a steel cutter, which is filed up square on all faces and edges. This may be made from an old saw blade and should be the exact width of the line or banding to be inlaid.

In use, the shoulder or fence of the scratch stock is pressed against the edge of the wood, and worked backwards and forwards with a scratching motion, which forms a groove to the required depth pre-set on the cutter. This should be slightly less than the thickness of the line or banding to be inlaid, so that pressure may be applied to the inlay when being laid.

For cross-grain inlaying, it is best to cut the two outer edges of the groove with a cutting gauge to sever the fibres cleanly, and then to use the scratch stock between the two cut grooves.

The scratch stock may be rounded to enable it to be used around curves or on hollow surfaces.

76

Small router plane. A router plane will be found very useful for removing parts of the groundwork for inlaying, especially where inlay motifs are to be inlaid into the solid, rather than assembled together with other veneers.

Small bullnose rabbet plane. When an inlay line of square section is to be inlaid on an edge, it is best to use a cutting gauge in both the width and depth dimensions and remove the waste with a rabbet plane.

Firmer chisel. Any good make of firmer chisel is useful, for instance in clearing out the corners of solid groundwork, before it is worked with the scratch stock, to prevent the cross-grain section from splintering out.

Tweezers. A pair of fine-point and a pair of flat-point tweezers will be found useful, both for handling tiny pieces of veneer when inlaying, or when sand shading, and for immersing the shaped veneer into hot sand.

They are also invaluable for the occupational hazard of removing splinters!

6 The double cut

This is the simplest of all fretsawing methods, by which two contrasting veneers are cut simultaneously and the parts interchanged to provide two identical marquetries; one in which a light motif is set against a dark background, and the reverse pattern in the other. The works of André Charles Boulle (p. 215) were made in this way – but using tortoiseshell and metal foil to achieve the effects known as the *première partie* and the *contre partie*.

A waste veneer is placed underneath the two contrasting veneers, to take the swarf of the teeth of the saw. The grain direction of the waste veneer should be opposite to that of the veneer above. The three veneers are slightly larger than needed for the chosen design. They are glued together at this working margin, or nailed together with veneer pins – the points of which should be nipped off to avoid splitting, and the heads nipped off just above the veneer. A commercial stapling machine is ideal for this purpose; for small marquetries, the three veneers may be bound together with adhesive tape.

Larger veneers may require special preparation to prevent the veneers from lifting on the upwards movement of the saw. The three veneers are lightly rubbed with soap to aid their later separation and then glued together, with a sheet of paper between each veneer. Alternatively, greaseproof paper may be used, or small sheets of polythene. A copy of the design to be sawn is pasted to the top veneer. Use a water-soluble glue, such as Scotch glue, to make this sandwich, which will melt with heat, when the parts are separated later. The sandwich is allowed to dry thoroughly.

A hole is pierced in the working margin, and the fretsaw blade, with teeth pointing downwards, is let in from the top. The saw is tightened to the correct tension – it should make a high-toned sound if flicked with a finger nail – using pliers if necessary.

The saw is held in the right hand, and led up and down without great pressure and in easy, smooth movements, avoiding jerkiness. The work should be held with the left hand, pressed firmly down upon the cutting table, using the finger tip of the left forefinger to exert light pressure downwards at the point of sawing (vice versa for left-handed craftsmen!). A thimble can be worn to protect the forefinger. Turn the work towards the saw, which is held perfectly vertical and is never turned at the corners of the design. To turn a sharp corner, it is best to back out of the corner along the cut just made, and approach the corner from the other direction.

Commence any small 'island' pieces first, to prevent the design falling apart at an early stage, working outwards towards the edges. It is a good tip to hook up your working apron under the saw table, to catch any small pieces that may fall out during the sawing process. Lay the sawn parts out in trays until all the sawing is completed.

Now to separate the parts. Take each sawn part, which still comprises three veneers, and slightly warm them by standing

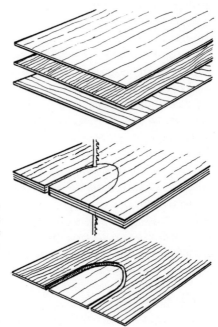

Fig. 19 Double cutting of two contrasting veneers. A third waste veneer is placed underneath to take the swarf of the saw teeth.

79

them on a hot-plate for a few seconds. Then, with a wide flat knife, work carefully between the layers of veneer – which peel apart easily – and assemble them on two further copies of the design. You now have two inlays, one light and one dark but both identical in design. Thoroughly cover the surface with gummed veneering tape or glue a sheet of Kraft paper over the assembly. When dry, completely turn the marquetry assemblies over to reveal the design with the open sawcut joins clearly visible. The open joins are now filled in, using a paste made from wood dust from the fretsaw, mixed with transparent adhesive to match the background wood colour tone. Alternatively, use a proprietary wood stopping such as Brummer. Sometimes the wood stopping is used in deliberate contrast to the background colour, as in the case of veins in a leaf pattern, the contours of which need to be emphasized. Then the veneers are wiped free from filler and glue traces and smoothed perfectly flat, ready for laying.

The obvious disadvantage of this 'double-cut' method is that the resulting inlay has the thickness of the sawcut visible around each section of the design. The advantage to the beginner is that even with his first steps at fretsawing, he will have no difficulty in making the parts fit – perhaps too easily!

If these inlays are to be laid on solid groundwork, then both the light and dark veneers must be in the same grain direction as the groundwork, in which case the grain on the waste veneer used to take the saw swarf would run in the opposite direction.

However, if the assemblies are to be laid on plywood, block-board or laminboard, the veneer used as the background must be opposite to the grain direction of the face veneer of the plywood, and the waste veneer in this case would be in the same grain direction as the plywood.

This is because you must always veneer *with* the grain on solid wood and *across* the grain on laminated boards. This allows for the natural shrinkage, in time, of the solid groundwork.

It is trade practice to use fretsaw blades with rounded backs. This permits you to rub the back of the saw against the cut you have just made, when changing direction, prior to making the forward movement in a new direction.

The bevel cut

The marquetarian will soon wish to progress beyond this stage,

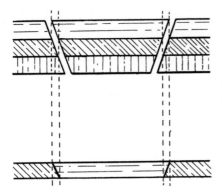

Fig. 20 Bevel cutting, in which the saw table is inclined 15° to eliminate the saw cut.

and will want to create an inlay where the joins are invisible. The same preparation is made, bonding the veneers into a 'sandwich' ready for cutting, taking careful note of the grain direction required in the finished panel as before.

This time, the saw table is inclined about 15° to 20° (this is a matter for experience and is governed by the thickness of the material being cut and the thickness of the saw blade you are using). A little more care is required this time in the actual cutting, because inaccurate cutting will result in the opposite effect, producing large gaps.

As the top veneer will now be fitted tightly into the lower veneer, the parts cannot be interchanged after separation. Therefore it is only possible to produce one inlay at a time by the bevel-cut.

In practice, a combination of both methods is used. First of all a multi-layered sandwich is made of various veneers, which is cut with a robust saw blade on the double-cut flat-bed saw table. The decorative motifs cut by this technique may be 'full', or slightly larger than required by the final drawing.

The motifs are separated and laid out in trays. Then each motif is glued directly in its position upon the base veneer, with its underlying waste veneer, and pressed until dry. Now the work is transferred to a bevel-cutting angled saw table, and, using a very fine saw blade, each motif is 'let-in' to the base veneer by sawing accurately to size on the required line. After separation, the motif will fit perfectly without visible joins.

Both of these sawing techniques were used by the intarsiatori

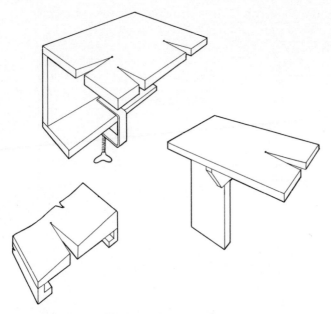

Figs. 21–3   Fretsaw cutting tables.

Fig. 24   The marquetry cutter's donkey or French horse.

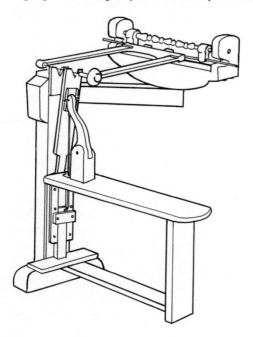

of old with their fine bow saws; they provide valuable practice exercises for beginners to the craft.

These methods quickly lead us to cut several layers at a time without the resulting saw cuts being visible, or the need to 'let-in' each motif individually by the bevel cut, and to produce inlays much more quickly and cheaply. This is exactly what led to the invention of the French horse or 'donkey'.

The 'donkey' enabled the work to be gripped by foot pressure and held in a vertical position so that the sawdust did not cover the design line, but fell away. It also left both hands free for holding the work and operating the shuttle movement of the saw arm, which gave not only forward and backward movement but a little lateral side play, permitting bevel cutting too.

However, the home made 'Swingsaw' and the modern power fretsaw machine are excellent for our purpose, and the sawdust can either be blown away or removed by the dust extractor which is fitted to most machines today.

The craftsmen of the past used to file their own saws from the finest clock spring steel; this is no longer necessary, as jeweller's piercing blades, and special marquetry double-toothed round-back blades (p. 75) are available for use in all saw frames or machines.

The commercial method

The design for a commercial marquetry picture or motif is known as the paramount. It is usually supplied by the client's designer, in the case of a picture or furniture 'lay-on' (as the marquetry assembly is known) or by the architect in the case of wall panelling or murals. The designer's original requirements are often in need of modification by the specialist marquetry designer, who brings to bear his knowledge of available veneers and the limitations of his technique.

The marquetry designer makes a water colour or pastel drawing of the design in order to develop a conception of the veneers required. For this purpose he mixes his colours to match his veneer tonal range. If the sky veneer for a picture is to be figured avodire, there is no point in the paramount design specifying a blue sky; the coloured paramount would have a sky painted in yellow to closely resemble avodire.

83

When the client and his designer or architect approve the coloured sketch, a final line drawing is prepared, usually on strong parchment, vellum, cartridge paper or white bond paper.

The master 'show' drawing is produced by working over every inch of this line drawing with a very fine needle, piercing holes through the paper as close together as possible. This is done by a special machine which works up and down exactly like a sewing machine. However, if a fine needle is run through an ordinary bottle cork, this will be easy to handle and makes an excellent needle pricker. This seemingly tedious task is amply repaid by the accuracy of the resulting work.

Having completed the master pricking, the next stage is to make several exact copies of the design. With a hard felt pad, made by tightly rolling a piece of felt and tying it securely with string, fine bitumen or asphaltum powder is tapped through the perforations, or 'pounces', of the original master design. The pounces are immediately held over diffused heat, such as a hot-plate, to 'set' the powdered siftings. This causes the paper to scorch slightly and fixes the powder, preventing smear.

In this way, exactly as practised for centuries, any number of identical pouncings may be made. Even if you are able to secure printed, duplicated or photostat copies by more modern printing techniques, the traditional method has the advantage of producing a needle-sharp line to follow when sawing, usually much finer than those made by other reproduction processes. The prickings may be used to produce either 'face' copies of the original master design, or 'reverse' copies, by pouncing from the other side of the sheet.

One control pouncing is made, 'face' side up – that is, exactly as in the original master design – and upon this is recorded the veneers to be used, their grain direction, and other information. For every part of the design that calls for a different veneer, a separate pouncing has to be made, to be cut up and fixed to that part. Note that it is not enough to have a pouncing for every veneer in the design; you will need one for every *part*, since the same veneer may be used but in a different grain direction.

The pounce drawings then go to the preparer. He roughly cuts them into the various segments of the design. The preparer also wants enough copies of the complete design to correspond with the total quantity of inlays to be produced.

The preparer then selects the veneers from the storage racks, guided by the veneer combination as specified on the master control sheet. He cuts a batch of each veneer to a convenient uniform size and makes a stack of up to 32 pieces to the pile. Two pieces of thin plywood are cut to similar size to sandwich the pile of veneers between, to hold the pad firm for cutting. The bottom piece of plywood will take the swarf of the saw, and the pounce drawing segment is glued to the top piece to guide the jigsaw operator.

The veneers will have been 'stretched' or flattened previously, by coating with glue size and drying under pressure between heated boards, with clean Kraft paper applied to one side. When arranging these veneers in the sandwich, care is taken to see they are kept in exact matching sequence, with papered sides uppermost. The other side of each veneer is rubbed lightly with soap to aid its later separation. The sandwich is technically known as a 'pad'.

The pad is compacted, and as a precaution against splitting the delicate veneers, tiny holes are drilled where each nail is to be inserted. It is then placed under pressure and nailed together with very fine steel wire nails. This cutting pad is usually $\frac{1}{2}$ in. larger in each direction, to provide a working margin for nailing. The points are nipped off before nailing through the drilled holes – the pad being supported on an iron plate – and the protruding heads are also nipped off.

Nailing is never carried out too near the edge, and often a nail or two is inserted within the design area. A pencilled ring is made around the position of the nails to warn the sawyer.

If only a few veneers are to be cut, instead of a complete bundle of 32 leaves, it may be possible to staple the pad together with a heavy commercial-type stapling machine. Large pads have their outside working edges coated with glue before nailing, and they are then allowed to set in a press until dry.

If only six or eight veneers are being cut at one time, no greasing of the saw blade is necessary, but for cutting more than this number it is usual to interlay a sheet of waxed paper, suet paper, or paper coated with Russian tallow to grease the saw. On no account should the fretsaw blade be oiled, as this would discolour the veneers.

A careful check is made to ensure that the grain direction

marked on the design section, glued to the top of the pad, is correct and corresponds with the master control sheet.

Holes are drilled, with a very fine spiral bit, around the working margin, close to any part of the design line which touches the edge near the working margin. The saw is let in from above, teeth pointing downwards; the saw table must be perfectly flat, and the saw itself must be vertical both in front and side elevations. Special round-back, double-tooth veneer-cutting saw blades, grade 2/0, are used for this work, which enables the sawdust to clear as the work proceeds.

For drilling 'island' parts of the design, a suitable drilling bit can be made by flattening the point of a needle, by heating in a flame and tapping with a hammer. It is preferable to use an awl or needle rather than remove wood by drilling, because it merely forces the fibres of the veneer apart; they will close again later if you put a bead of water over the split and then tap it with a light hammer.

The prepared pads are now skilfully sawn. This is carried out at 'half-mark'. As the line to be sawn is needle-thin, and the saw blade is only a few thousandths of an inch in thickness, great accuracy of cut is possible.

The sawyer aims to leave a hairline fraction of the needle-sharp cutting line visible on the top of the pad, in other words, to cut barely outside the line, very carefully following the curving contour of the design. This completely eliminates the saw cut when the design is assembled.

With practice, it is possible to cut at 'half-mark' to the inside of the line when cutting the background veneer and to the outside of the line when cutting the motif parts to be inserted, but for normal work, the trick is to leave the line just barely visible, to ensure a good fit, on the old principle that it is easy to take a bit off, but difficult to put a bit on! Obviously this accurate sawing is only achieved after a great deal of practice, and for commercial production allowance has to be made for human error and operator fatigue.

To compensate for human error in sawing, such as wandering from the intended design line – and who doesn't at some time? – expert marquetry 'donkey' cutters use the following technique. The pouncing is used for cutting out the components of the design or motif, but an identical pounce is not used for the background.

Instead, the actual sawn motif, or part of the design, is assembled over a piece of plain paper, with a leaf of carbon paper between. The veneers are held together with tape, and when they are rubbed over with a smooth tool such as the pene of a hammer, the slight saw swarf on the underside of the veneer prints a clear impression on the white paper. This can also be done by using heelball, as in making a brass rubbing. This actual outline is then used as the cutting guide for the background veneer, thus compensating for any sawing error in the first phase of the work. Alternatively, depending on the nature of the work, an assembled motif could be temporarily glued to a background pad, and the actual contour of the motif followed by the saw.

After each different part of the design is sawn into shape, it is placed in a sectional tray, divided to prevent mixing the parts, until all sawing is complete.

Many designs include portions which require sand shading, to create the effects of folds or shadows, or in ribbon and flowered designs, or segmented sunburnt designs, fans, etc. This process is fully described later (p. 153).

If it is an intricate design – there may be up to one hundred parts of different sizes and shapes making up the complete motif – the trays are then handed over to the inlayers. Using very thin-gauge headless steel wire pins, the 'field' or background veneers are first tacked down over a pouncing design laid out on 'inlay boards' – flat, smooth plywood boards large enough to accommodate the completed inlay. Then, carefully following the master control sheet, the assembly is begun, much as one would assemble a jigsaw puzzle.

A spot of rubber cement is placed under each veneer as it is assembled. It is wisest to assemble very small detail first, by butt joining them edge-to-edge or with paper tape, before fixing them into the main assembly. It is best to put down the outer background veneer and then work towards the centre detail, as it often happens that if you work from the centre outwards, the design comes out larger than intended.

Because of the moisture introduced by the rubber cement, it is necessary to place flat heavy weights over each area of 12 sq. in. as it is inlaid. The weights maintain an acceptable degree of flatness until the step is completed.

After careful inspection, and the removal of any minute

particles of foreign matter, the inlays are scrutinized against a strong light to check for flaws, small missing pieces which may have fallen out, bad cutting, etc., which must be rectified at this stage.

The marquetry assemblies, still tacked in place upon the flat inlay boards, are then placed in hand-screw sectional presses; meanwhile sheets of stout Kraft paper, of a size to cover each inlaid assembly, are coated with hot Scotch glue and allowed to become tacky before being placed over the inlay and the presses tightened down, using a heated caul to melt the glue, and the panels are left to dry overnight.

When the inlay boards are lifted from the presses, the assemblies are lifted from them with a broad flat knife, and the pounce design is dampened with a sponge and peeled off. (Rubber cement rubs off veneers easily and without trace.)

Next, a filler of finely pulverized sawdust mixed with glue size is thickly spread over the entire inlaid surface and then immediately scraped off. This fills the tiny voids, and fine saw cuts, some of them deliberately made in the form of vein lines in the leaves, and bringing the filler flush with the Kraft-papered side, which will ultimately be the face side of the veneer motif or picture.

This completed, the filled and inlaid faces are again returned to the presses between boards, with a layer of felt or linoleum between the upper caul and the filled surfaces to ensure uniform pressure. After at least four hours' drying time, the marquetry is removed from the presses, and made ready for laying.

This is done by gently working over the back with a medium grade of garnet paper, grade 6/o, wrapped around a cork rubbing block to ensure that the surface is perfectly smooth and flat and so to avoid any possibility of blisters in the laying process.

In America, where veneers are usually $\frac{1}{28}$ in. in thickness, it is customary to use a cabinet scraper to level the back of the inlay. Although it is possible to lay the inlay assemblies without first levelling the back, simply by placing plenty of packing – in the form of linoleum, plastic sheeting, etc. – over the inlay to take up any difference in the thickness of the veneers, faulty levelling is the principal cause of blistering, and the correct procedure adopted by all professionals is to prepare the back as described. Saw-cut veneers may be levelled with a finely set toothing plane.

The foregoing technique is exactly as practised to this day in many marquetry works, but there is a slightly different working method adopted on the continent of Europe.

In the above sequence, only 'face copies' – so-called 'sun' copies – of the pounced design were used. Consequently, the sawing and assembly sequences were carried out with the final 'face' side of the inlay visible throughout. The European practice differs slightly from this, in that reverse pouncings are made from the original pricking; some are to be cut up and glued to the top of the pads, and other complete designs are fastened with gummed paper tape to the inlay boards, upon which the completed inlays will be assembled.

It follows that the fretsawn parts are actually in reverse, that is, with the back of the inlay visible. The reverse design is brushed with hot Scotch glue and allowed to become tacky, and the parts are assembled direct to the design; the back is then filled, scraped off, and placed in the press to dry out before final cleaning up.

In another slight variation on this procedure which I have seen in both London and Paris, a metal hotplate is placed over a candle and warmed sufficiently to keep the Scotch glue in a condition between 'tack' and 'slide'. Instead of using a reverse design to assemble the parts upon, those who favour this method lay a sheet of ordinary newspaper or Kraft paper and brush this with Scotch glue; the glue remains wet, and the parts are slid into position by placing the background veneer on the paper first, and then fixing the parts into position with tweezers. The glued paper has an immediate grip; when the paper is removed from the hotplate for filling, it chills immediately and there is no danger of the parts lifting.

When placed in the press between heated cauls, the glue reheats and forms a strong bond. Left in the press overnight, the back is then cleaned, not only of the paste filler, but of the thin paper used in the stretching or flattening process, which would have been affixed to the back of the veneers at the earlier stage. The important point to remember is never to introduce hot Scotch glue direct to a veneer assembly, as the moisture will immediately cause the veneers to swell and the inlay motif will be ruined.

Whichever form of temporary adhesive is used during the

actual assembly, whether it be masking tape, rubber cement or ordinary gummed paper tape, this must be removed if the design is sawn and assembled from original pounced designs; if reverse designs are used, the parts may be assembled direct on to the Kraft paper layer, which will cover the face of the motif.

The techniques I have described are mainly used for the production of decorative motifs for furniture and are ideal for the beginner to practise with, to acquire skill in fretsaw cutting. The commercial method may be used for the production of pictorial marquetry, but all really successful and artistic pictures are made individually from carefully selected freak woods, where speed and economy of time or effort are less important than the creation of a first-class picture using the best features of grain, figure and colour tones of the veneers.

The American 'pad' method

By this method, mainly used for pictorial marquetry in the United States, it is possible to cut a complete marquetry picture from one single sawing operation, which ensures that the parts must fit perfectly together as they are all cut simultaneously.

Another advantage is that the method allows for very considerable error in sawing. It enables even beginners to cut brittle or hard woods, or veneers of $\frac{1}{28}$ in. or greater thickness, including sawn veneers, and this, in itself, is a factor which recommends this technique to amateur craftsmen using power fretsaws.

To begin with, a master control design is prepared upon which all relevant information as to choice of veneers, grain direction,

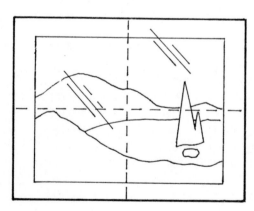

Fig. 25 The American pad method – the transparent viewfinder.

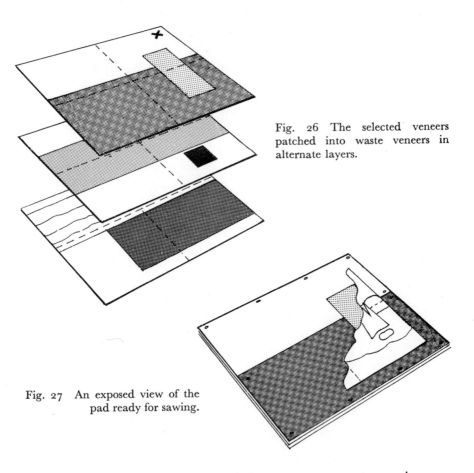

Fig. 26 The selected veneers patched into waste veneers in alternate layers.

Fig. 27 An exposed view of the pad ready for sawing.

etc., is recorded. From this control sheet, a transparent copy is prepared on celluloid, clear plastic sheet or perspex, using indian ink applied with a fine pen.

Leave a working margin of up to 1 in. around the picture area, which means that the transparent design sheet has to be 2 in. larger in length and width than the actual picture.

Now prepare several leaves of scrap or waste veneer, each exactly the same size as the transparent 'viewfinder'. Draw a centre line to ensure perfect register with the veneers, and repeat the centre line on each waste veneer; also mark each veneer with a X in the top right-hand corner. Sycamore, obeche, poplar, or any light soft wood is ideal for this purpose. These waste veneers are now laid aside until required.

Veneer selection. The veneer to be used for the sky is selected by reference to the control sheet. The viewfinder is placed over the sky veneer and is moved about in order to determine the exact flow of grain and peculiar markings required in the picture. Holding the viewfinder down with the left hand, mark the rectangular extremes of the skyline of the design, upon the sky veneer, allowing about $\frac{1}{2}$ in. all around the section to be cut, to allow for errors in sawing. Place the viewfinder back in position and check to see that the pencilled shape is about $\frac{1}{2}$ in. larger all around than required, then remove the viewfinder.

The rectangular pencilled shape is now cut from the sky veneer using a straight edge or non-slip ruler and a craft knife. This rectangle of veneer, which we will call the 'patch', will be let in, or patched into, one of the waste veneer leaves already prepared.

One of these waste veneers is placed under the viewfinder and checked to see that the register lines coincide. The sky patch is then slipped between waste and viewfinder and located in position, showing the patch to be overlapped $\frac{1}{2}$ in. into the working margin at the top and both sides. The viewfinder is removed, and the exact position of the patch is pencilled round on the waste veneer. The patch is now let into the waste veneer with the knife and straight edge, and fixed in place with gummed paper tape along each join.

Where several parts of a design call for sky veneer, for instance in a picture featuring a tree where the sky shows through the branches, make sure that all pieces for the sky are cut from one leaf, to preserve the continuity of grain and figure flow.

Similar veneer patches are prepared for every part of the picture; they are carefully patched into the waste veneers, endeavouring to get as many patches into one waster as possible. The fewer wasters used when making up the saw pad or sandwich, the easier and more accurate will be the result, with fewer possibilities of open joins. To hold the pad in register during this patching phase a simple jig can be made by driving a few nails into the workbench at the top and sides of the pad.

The patching may be in any convenient order, as it is impossible for any two adjacent parts of the design to be patched together because of the $\frac{1}{2}$ in. overall allowed around each section. However, it is important to patch adjacent parts of a picture in consecutive layers, to minimize the risk of open saw cuts.

The pictures are secured to the wasters by adhesive paper tape along the joins, tapes uppermost. The tapes may criss-cross without affecting the pad. In practice it is more convenient to allow the outside patches to run across the working margin to the outside of the pad, rather than cut them into the waste veneer and leave a working margin.

When this phase of the work is completed, all the wasters are located in the guide jig, and the register of centre lines checked to ensure that the X occurs at the top right-hand corner of every waster. Locate the viewfinder in position and then glue the design to be cut to the top veneer, under the finder which is removed. A waste veneer is placed underneath to take the saw swarf. The pad is then compacted in cramps, and nailed or stapled through the working margin, or touched with glue at the edges and pressed until dry. Tiny holes are drilled or pierced to accommodate the saw, where a design line meets the surrounding border margin, about ¼ in. from the beginning of each line.

Only two or three drillings are usually necessary. You will need to drill any 'island' pieces within the design, rather than saw across to them from the margin. Where possible, use an awl to pierce this hole, or better still, omit this detail completely from the original sawing, leaving it to be let in later by other techniques yet to be described.

Sawing. The saw blades used are the same as described for the commercial method (p. 83), grade 2/0 special thin, double-toothed, round-back blades, having 38 teeth to the inch, measuring only 0·008 in. × 0·028 in. The ideal rate of sawing is about 150 to 200 per minute of 2-in. strokes, speeding up to 250 strokes per minute when negotiating curves or bends, which puts added stress and side pressure on the sawblade.

Power fretsaws should be slowed down to 1,300 r.p.m. If you are making a picture too large for the fretsaw frame to encompass, saw along part of the design line and cut the pad in halves. Securely bind each half-pad with Sellotape along the cut edge, and continue with the work.

British piercing pad method

A variation of this method, for use with the thinner British veneers of 0·7 mm., enables very hard or brittle veneers (which may be too difficult for the normal knife cutting technique) to be used; this employs metal-piercing blades and a different preparation.

The patches are simply arranged together in one layer with sufficient overage around each part to form a complete layer, without using waster veneers at all. This layer is then glued to clean paper and arranged in a pad with up to six or more layers, and pressed until dry. The pad is then nailed or stapled together. The very fine metal-piercing sawblades, with single teeth and rounded backs, are obtainable from a robust grade 3, down through the grades 1, 0, 2/0, 4/0, 6/0 to 8/0 which is the finest. The finer blades will not stand the stresses of power machining, and this technique is best performed by hand. However, the extremely fine sawcut is invisible when the final picture is assembled.

The Canadian method

The Marquetry School of Toronto, which has pioneered the introduction of the craft of marquetry in Canada since 1936, under the presidency of its founder, Mr Ernest W. Oppenheim, uses a technique perfected and developed by its chief instructor, Mr Marion Magus.

A number of identical 'face' copies of the design are prepared by photostat or from pouncings. These are cut up by scissors, together with a selected veneer which should be about $\frac{1}{2}$ in. larger all around than the piece required for the picture. After checking to see that the grain direction and other features are exactly as required for the picture, the design and veneer are stapled to a $\frac{1}{16}$-in. piece of gaboon plywood, with an ordinary office stapler. A hole is drilled in the working margin to take the 2/0 fretsaw blade (with double teeth and rounded back) which is entered, teeth pointing downwards, exactly as for the commercial and pad methods.

With careful cutting at half-mark – in practice, this means leaving a little of the line visible on the part required – no joins are visible in the finished picture.

The cutting may be done on a power jigsaw or hand fretsaw, and if the resulting cut is a trifle oversize, the piece may be carefully trimmed down exactly to the required line by using a flexible shaft tool, fitted with a very small jeweller's burr, the smallest cylindrical shape obtainable. This enables the parts of

94

the picture to be tailored to fit, especially where the inexperienced sawyer may have wandered off the line fractionally. Until accuracy of cut is achieved through practice, you should err on the side of cutting slightly oversize.

One of the design copies is fastened to a flat surface with gummed paper tape and spread evenly all over with rubber cement, which is allowed to dry. As each part of the design is cut out, a fresh squeeze of rubber cement is spread over the section to receive the veneer, which is then pressed down on the paper design with finger pressure. When the picture has thus been assembled, jigsaw fashion, complete with fillet border and border mounts, the surface is levelled with a scraper and filled with a paste made from urea resin glue and sawdust; this is allowed to dry, and then levelled with sandpaper.

Reverse designs can be used in the same method, in which case the face of the picture will now be embedded in the rubber cement and the picture is ready for laying, with the paper design face side uppermost.

If a face design has been used (not in reverse) then the back of the picture will be embedded in the rubber cement. In this case, a sheet of strong clean paper should be glued to the face side, the picture turned over and the rubber cement removed from the back with the finger tips; it rubs off very easily without trace. The back can now be filled and levelled prior to laying.

This method has certain advantages. It is not necessary to make elaborate preparations; one does not have to handle a large pad of veneers when sawing; greater accuracy of work is possible in the elimination of open joins; the work is carried out on a flat sawtable with a saw held vertically; various thicknesses of veneers can be used; hard or brittle woods may be cut without extra effort; and in certain veneers a greater fluidity of line is possible than with a knife.

1 Part of a wooden box, inlaid on one side with triangles of coloured glaze and decorated with a border representing basket-weave; on the other side it is inscribed in the middle of the border with a falcon over a frame and the now illegible name of a king of the first Egyptian Dynasty (*c.* 3100-2890 BC). This was found in excavations at Abydos in Egypt.

2 From the tomb of Hemaka at Saqqara, first Dynasty (3020 BC), comes a box inlaid with native woods to resemble basket weave.

3 Marquetry casket from the tomb of Tutankhamen, inlaid in a herringbone basket-weave pattern in ivory and ebony and decorated with gold buttons.

4 Walnut and rosewood chest, inlaid with certosina or monastery mosaic. North Italian, c. 1500.

5 Italian sixteenth-century arabesque and flower and tendril marquetry, from Perugia—a transitional style between monastery mosaic and perspective marquetry.

6 Interior cupboard scene in perspective marquetry decorating the choir-stalls at Monte Oliveto, Siena, by Fra Giovanni da Verona.

7 Self-portrait by Antonio Barili (1502), one of the famous intarsiatori of Siena. This panel, formerly from the choir of the cathedral of Siena, was destroyed in the second world war. With the shoulder knife (see p.71) the artist is seen cutting the words: 'This work I, Antonio Barili, made with the knife, not the brush, in the year of our Lord 1502'.

8 'Flagellation of Christ', intarsia panel from the choir of San Domenico at Bologna by Fra Damiano da Bergamo.

9 Table desk of oak inlaid with bog oak and holly. On the front, back and sides are marquetry panels enclosing design of palace façades within borders of checker ornament and roundels; on each side is also an inlaid eight-pointed star. Late sixteenth century.

10 Tyrolean chest with elaborate marquetry decoration. The woods used are ash, cherry, pear, walnut, thuya and maple, veneered over deal. The mounts are partly of gilded and engraved copper, coated on the inside with tin. The entire chest is decorated with imaginary scenes in which strapwork combines with human beings, birds and animals in surrealist encounters with architectural ruins. Back, front, sides and top of the chest are decorated in this way and also the inner surfaces of the drop front and of the smaller doors and drawers within. About 1580-90.

11 Walnut vargueño with Moorish decoration in taracea. Sixteenth century.

12 James I marquetry buffet with cupboard above, the canopy supported by two bulbous balusters, fitted with two drawers and cupboard doors below. The panels are inlaid with various woods with a decoration of scrolled foliage on oak and walnut grounds, within carved borders of running scrolls. The cupboard door is inlaid with the initials CNA, dated 1615.

13 North German marquetry buffet saturated with pictorial and decorative marquetry.

14 Veneered cupboard decorated with three tones of walnut, oystered parquetry in floral sunburst patterns. North Netherlands, *c.* 1675-1700.

15 An oak cabinet veneered with walnut oyster parquetry with marquetry star and circle decoration. Netherlands, late seventeenth century.

16 Flemish cabinet veneered with engraved floral and grotesque marquetry incorporating birds, animals, etc. Flemish, c. 1675-1700.

17 Floral engraved marquetry of natural woods and ivory on an ebony background featuring birds, butterflies and jasmine flowers. Late seventeenth century, Flemish.

18 Walnut veneered cabinet with marquetry of ivory, mother of pearl, sycamore and ash, featuring engraved floral marquetry, birds and beribboned sprays of flowers with heraldic insignia of the arms of Lawson impaling Trotter. English, 1700.

19 Top of side table
decorated with engraved
floral marquetry.
Flemish, late
seventeenth century.

20 Seaweed drop-front
secretaire cabinet.
English, seventeenth
century.

21 *Opposite:* Veneered
ebony armoire with
tortoiseshell panels
inlaid with engraved
brass and mounted in
chased and gilded
bronze. André Charles
Boulle from designs by
Jean Berain for
Louis XIV, late
seventeenth century.

22 Bureau cabinet veneered on both the interior and exterior in architectural marquetry, including trophies of arms in the spandrels and cresting. Each of the upper doors has a throne room with a tessellated floor and Corinthian columns, the sides with scenes from the Italian Renaissance palaces. The flap also shows a simple throne room, the drawers of the lower part with architectural fantasies and the doors and sides with perspective studies of courtyards and galleries. German, mid-eighteenth century.

23 A parquetry library or centre table with a decorative mosaic of exotic veneers incorporating star motifs, bandings, parquetry etc. Portuguese, late eighteenth century.

24 Lady's small dressing-table top attributed to Jean François Oeben, with elaborate cube and water lily parquetry and a central marquetry panel of musical instruments. Louis XIV, eighteenth century.

25 Top of Louis XVI toilet table by Bernard Molitor (late eighteenth century), featuring a background of line-and-dot ebony parquetry with a border surround of trellis parquetry and a central motif of sand-shaded shell and decorative marquetry.

26 A superb Louis XV marquetry *table à dessus coulissant* (photograph of top only), the top finely inlaid with a marquetry of various woods featuring a bold basket of flowers in a shaped panel bordered with floral festoons and with panels of trellis work in ebonized and stained green ivory, on mahogany and dyed green grounds with geese, animals and a shell medallion with cross-banded rosewood border surrounds. Eighteenth century. This was sold for a record price of £35,700 at Christie's in November 1968.

27 Top of side table with a singerie or fantasy decoration with satyrs and monkeys playing with caged birds etc. By J. F. Leuleu, eighteenth century.

28 *Opposite, above:* Large pictorial wall panel by David Roentgen, 1779. 'The Abstemiousness of Scipio', 360 × 377 cm.

29 *Opposite, below:* Beautiful example of sand-shaded perspective pictorial marquetry by Luigi Ravelli of Vercelli. Italian, 1776-1858.

30 Bureau of Louis XV. The entire surface is richly veneered on oak with pictorial marquetry of holly, box, purplewood etc., featuring groups of flowers, cartouches, musical and military trophies. Each side of deep drawers is faced with floral marquetry and mounted with a handle in the form of a ribbon bow. The interior is mainly veneered in purplewood and holly on a ground of pear wood with a fret of marquetry enclosing leaves. Commenced by Jean François Oeben and completed by his pupil Jean Henri Riesener in 1769 for Louis XV of France. This bureau is in the Museum at Versailles and a copy may be seen in the Wallace Collection.

31 Boxes and a paper knife decorated with Tunbridge ware and pictorial marquetry. Nineteenth century.

32 Chippendale satinwood commode, with garlands, bowknots, and musical instrument motifs in marquetry, c. 1775.

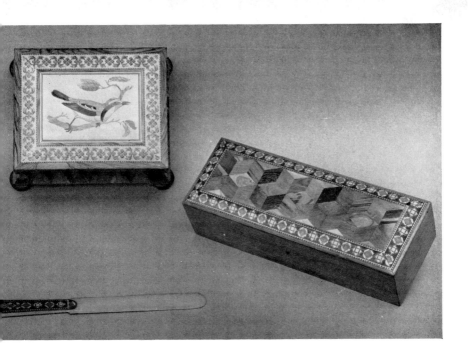

33 Sofa table veneered in amboyna burr with a kingwood crossbanding and brass inlays. Made in 1816 for Princess Charlotte, only daughter of George I, en suite of four. The other tables are in Buckingham Palace.

34 Mahogany Victorian sideboard with two-tone decorative marquetry of symbolic leaf formation, herringbone bandings etc. in William Morris style. Made by Morris & Company in 1891.

7 Knife cutting methods

The overlap technique

The European marquetarian enjoys many advantages over his transatlantic colleagues in being able to draw upon a much wider range of veneers, of a gauge (0·7 mm.) which permits cutting by knife. This has enabled cutting methods to be developed which make it possible for the beginner to create a successful picture the very first time he tries. Hundreds of thousands of amateur hobbyists have been introduced to the craft by way of the marquetry art set, which presents the craft in its simplest terms, with the veneers cut up into pieces and stuck to the printed baseboard in jigsaw fashion, piece by piece. Using a fast-setting glue, only finger pressure is required to lay the work, and there is no need for cauls or weights.

The marquetry set method

Let us assume that we are going to make a simple picture with only a sky, mountain and sea, with a foreground roadway.

The sky veneer is selected to match the design and the grain direction and markings are adjusted to suit. The design is then traced on to the veneer, using carbon paper and a fine point. Do not use a pencil as it tends to wear. A very fine point such as a stencil stylus or a worn dart is ideal. Allow a generous surplus of about half an inch at the bottom of the sky veneer, along the edge which forms the skyline of the picture.

With a very sharp knife, cut the veneer to the shape of the traced outline; make a light tracing cut at first and then work over the cut with a little more pressure to sever the veneer. Do not use heavy pressure; it is best to make a few light cuts, as too heavy a cut may split the veneer. Cut from the outer edges of the veneer towards the centre to avoid breaking out the veneer at the edges.

Do not wastefully cut your first pieces from the centre of the

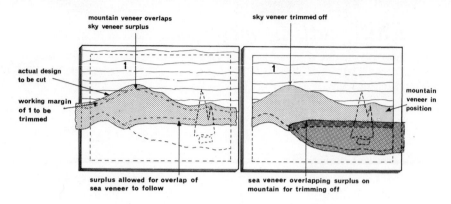

Figs. 28, 29   Knife cutting. The overlapping template
method used in marquetry sets.

veneer leaf, as other parts of the picture may require pieces of
the same veneer.

The method of proceeding with most marquetry art sets is to
apply some adhesive to the printed baseboard and place the sky
in position, overlapping part of the printed space where the
'mountain' veneer will eventually be positioned. Then the process
is repeated by tracing the required outline on the veneer selected
for the mountain, but this time, and from now on through the
picture, different tactics are adopted.

The mountain veneer is accurately cut along its top edge, and
again a generous surplus is left at the bottom where it meets the
sea. But instead of laying the mountain veneer in position on the
baseboard, it is positioned on top of the surplus which was left
at the bottom of the skyline veneer. Make a knife score into the
skyline veneer, using the edge of the mountain as the template
to guide the knife. Make one or two cuts along the groove until
the skyline veneer is severed. The surplus piece can easily be
removed from the baseboard with the edge of a knife. The
mountain veneer may then be laid by applying more adhesive
to the printed section of the baseboard and the mountain veneer
laid under a heavy weight.

Similarly, after tracing the sea veneer, and cutting its top edge
exactly to the design, it is temporarily laid overlapping the surplus at the bottom of the mountain, and used as a template to
guide the knife; the surplus is removed and discarded as before.

The procedure is repeated again, tracing and cutting the fore-ground veneer, always leaving a surplus at the bottom for trimming off, using the top edge of the new piece as a template for the final cutting of the preceding piece. The foreground is allowed to overlap into the surrounding border margin for trimming off when the borders are fitted.

Proceed in this way until all the large areas of the picture have been cut and laid, then the boat is cut out, overlaid on the background veneers, and used as a template as before, and finally the very tiny detail.

This method has the advantage that the beginner may see his picture growing piece by piece. Care should be taken to see that any excess glue which may ooze out at the edges of the veneers being laid is scraped away, to ensure a perfect fit when the next piece is laid.

To retain the advantages of this method, the groundwork must be sufficiently thick to resist the tendency to warp, if making the picture is a prolonged task. For this reason, the back of the panel should be veneered when the main parts of the background are laid, to keep the panel balanced.

To overcome the disadvantages of the 'stick-as-you-go' method, another method is to work from two copies of the design, one of which is used to trace the picture on to the veneers as already described, and the other copy is used as a base upon which to assemble the veneers instead of laying them to the printed baseboard.

Most methods require a reverse design because it is customary to work on the back of the picture, keeping the 'face' side of the veneer – the smooth side – free from pencil or knife marks. To reverse a design, either make a tracing, turn it over and work from the back or place a plain sheet of paper immediately beneath the design, and a sheet of carbon paper *beneath* the lower sheet of plain paper, but with the carboned side uppermost. When a tracing is made with a hard pencil or stylus, a reverse design will appear on the plain paper.

First of all, the reverse design is fastened to a flat surface with gummed tape. Then a little rubber cement is squeezed from a tube and spread out thinly and evenly over the complete printed area; this is allowed about five or ten minutes to dry. When the sky veneer has been cut out, with its surplus along the bottom

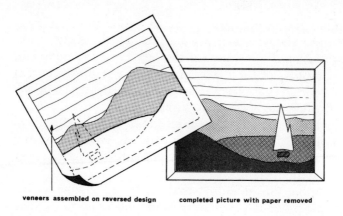

veneers assembled on reversed design   completed picture with paper removed

Figs. 30, 31 The American 'rubber cement' method using a reverse design.

edge, it is placed on the cutting board. The mountain veneer is cut out, overlapped as before, and the surplus removed from the sky veneer.

Now spread a second fresh coat of rubber cement on the sky portion of the printed assembly pattern and while the cement is still wet, lay the sky veneer accurately in place and press down with the fingers. Never apply cement to the veneer. Use the point of a knife to slide the veneer into correct alignment.

When the mountain has been cut to fit from the top edge of the sea veneer, more rubber cement is spread on the pattern and the mountain is positioned. The process is repeated until the complete picture has been assembled, including fillet strips and the four border mount veneers, which are mitred at each corner and the surplus discarded; the whole assembly is then pressed flat to the paper design.

The back of the picture is the side visible at this stage, and to avoid blisters when it is being laid, it may be levelled with a cork rubbing block and sandpaper, any minor defects remedied, where they will not show, and tiny cracks filled with plastic wood or stopping. The completed picture should then be laid under pressure, or with cauls and clamps, to the plywood groundwork, with the design-paper side uppermost. Also lay a backing veneer, which will keep the panel from warping. When the picture has cured outside the press, the design is simply peeled off, because rubber cement is only a temporary adhesive. The cement easily rubs off the face side of the picture without trace.

If the veneers are rubbed with the finger tips, the rubber cement comes off in a series of small 'balls', leaving a clean dry surface.

This method has many advantages over the previous method, in that parts of the picture may be discarded or replaced easily before being laid to the plywood.

A third method is to trace the design on stout Kraft paper or self-adhesive plastic shelf covering, and then cut up the design with scissors, fixing each section to the appropriate veneer with rubber cement. The veneer is cut out completely to size, either by knife or saw, and touched-up with a file to fit perfectly. It is then assembled to the printed design, using rubber cement as before. To prevent long narrow sections from twisting out of shape when positioned on the veneer, a separate tracing is made, including surrounding parts of the design, to ensure correct orientation. Some excellent results have been achieved by this method.

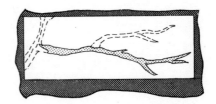

Fig. 32 The third method: separate tracing includes the surrounding area so as to ensure correct alignment of detail.

The window method

This is the traditional professional knife cutting technique, which has been used for the hand cutting of marquetry pictures for many years, and was adopted by the Marquetry Society. By this technique, the craft has been raised to great heights of artistry and skill. The name derives from the simple process of cutting a hole, or window, in a 'waste' veneer, which then acts as the template for cutting the veneer required to fill it.

Having chosen a suitable design (p. 18), the next step is to prepare a line drawing on a sheet of good-quality tracing paper, which should be about 1 in. larger in each direction than the design. Pin the original print and the tracing paper together with drawing pins, at each corner, on a drawing board or any flat surface, and carefully trace the outline, including the position of the border lines.

If you have any difficulty in seeing the print through the tracing paper, put the tracing paper under the print, with a sheet of black carbon paper between. Then make the outline tracing with a stencil stylus or sharpened knitting needle, or an HB pencil.

With the 'window' method, it is possible to work on either the back of the picture or the face side; that is, all the cutting and tracing may be done either on the side you will eventually see, or on the side which will be laid in the glueline.

It is necessary to understand the reasons why this is so, at the stage of preparing the design. If you will refer to the design printed on page 124 you will notice that the yacht is on the right-hand side of the design. If you traced the picture on the waste veneer exactly as printed, all the cutting and tracing would be carried out on the side of the picture which you will eventually see when completed, the face side, and the tapes would be fixed underneath, on the back of the picture.

This poses two problems: all the tapes you fix to the underneath or back will have to be removed at a later stage in order to glue the picture to a baseboard; and the face side is not necessarily the better side of the picture, because the knife cuts a 'V' shape into the veneers, forcing the fibres apart. In fact, the back of the picture has the better joins, because they are made by the tip of the knife.

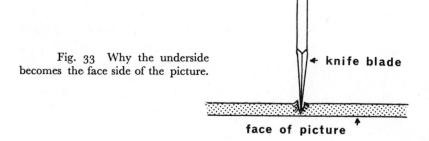

Fig. 33 Why the underside becomes the face side of the picture.

← knife blade

face of picture ↑

Therefore, if the design is reversed to start with, so that the yacht appears on the left-hand side of the design to be cut, the underside with the best joins will become the face side, and the tapes need not be removed.

Conversely, if you use the design exactly as printed, and tape the underside, which you can nominate as the face side, then the resulting picture will be in reverse when made. This does not matter in many scenes, but it may be important if you make a portrait, or an actual scene of a known beauty spot, in which case you always want the finished picture to be the correct way around. There are two simple choices:

1 Make a reverse design and tape the back of the assembly, which, when laid, will be the face side of the picture when it is the correct way around.

2 Use an original design; tape the back of the assembly until the picture is complete, and then lay a sheet of paper completely covering the face side, and remove the tapes from the back. This is the method advocated by the Marquetry Society, and it has the advantage that you will eventually see the picture in exactly the form in which it was made.

For the purpose of these instructions, we will use the design exactly as printed; the finished picture will appear in the same form, that is, with the yacht on the right-hand side.

The tools required. Have a cutting board about 16 in. × 12 in., with a soft, smooth face – plywood veneered with obeche or sycamore is ideal, or the actual groundwork upon which you propose to lay the picture. The knife cuts and general scoring of the surface will make a key for laying the picture. A knife which you have decided is best suited to your own grip and style, with a very sharp pointed blade, is needed, also a fine oilstone or pocket hone with which you can repeatedly sharpen the blade as work proceeds, as continual cutting rapidly blunts the edge. You will also require a small tube of either balsa cement or PVA adhesive for butt-jointing small details edge to edge, and a small reel of special veneering tape, extra-thin, double-gummed, about 1 in. wide, which you may cut into small pieces about $\frac{1}{2}$ in. × 1 in. as work proceeds. A try square, and a non-slip metal ruler complete the tools required to commence making a picture by the window method.

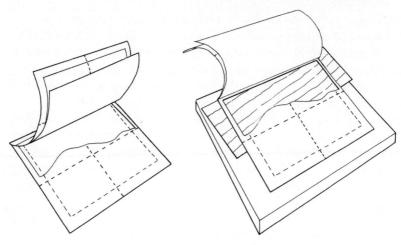

Figs. 34, 35 *Left:* The window method: an aperture cut in veneer waster to receive sky veneer. *Right:* Testing the sky veneer for effect.

Preparing the waste veneer. Select a leaf of veneer, the same size as the tracing paper – that is, about an inch larger all round than the nett picture size. The best veneers for this purpose are white sycamore, horse chestnut or obeche. The main requirements are that it should be light in colour and soft to cut, and should lie perfectly flat. This is called the 'waste' veneer, although it is a perfectly good veneer and usable as such. In fact, where a picture lends itself to this modification, it is possible to use the sky veneer as the waste, since it is usually a light wood and soft to cut, such as aspen, avodire, sycamore, obeche or birch. In other cases, the background veneer may be used as the waste if it fills a significant part of the picture, as in a portrait or still-life.

It is quite common practice to select the two veneers which form the major part of the background and tape them together to form the waste veneer, especially if the lower half of the picture is either walnut or harewood, both of which are easy to cut. This, of course, saves the task of cutting the woods into the picture.

The edges of the waste veneer should be bound all round with 1-in. gummed veneering tape, to protect them from tearing or splitting during the cutting process. The line drawing is then fixed to the top edges or left-hand edge of the waste veneer, with gummed paper tape, and centre lines are drawn both on the design and on the waste veneer, to ensure perfect registration as the work proceeds.

A leaf of black carbon paper is placed between the line drawing and the waste veneer. Do not use blue carbon paper, which tends to give a blurred outline. Use a hard pencil, a ball-point pen or a stencil stylus to trace the design on to the waste veneer.

To begin with, the tracing is lowered on to the waste veneer, and the centre lines checked to ensure perfect registration. The first part to be cut out will be the sky. Trace the outline of the border across the top and sides of the waste veneer where the sky veneer will fit. The sky is allowed to overlap about $\frac{1}{4}$ in. all around, into the surrounding border margin. This allows a margin for trimming the picture square and to size when the picture is completed.

Lift the tracing, and place the waste veneer on the cutting board. Using only very light pressure, cut around the line you have traced. Make only a tracing score into the veneer with the first cut, rather than trying to make a heavy cut first time, and then you will find it easier to sever the veneer with the next light stroke. Always remember to cut from the outside towards the centre of the leaf. Remove the skyline piece from the waste veneer and discard it.

A leaf of veneer is now selected which will give a suitable sky effect and this is placed in position underneath the waste veneer. Looking through this aperture or 'window' in the waste veneer (from which the method gets its name) we can then see exactly the effect of grain, figure, tone and marking, that the chosen veneer provides. The veneer can be moved around to test various sections of the leaf for better effect, watching the changing pattern through the hole in the waste veneer.

This is one of the great advantages of the window method. You can actually see the effect you will get in the finished picture and you can try all sorts of veneers under the waste veneer window, until you find one with just the right effect.

As a further example, if you are trying to capture a sky effect using aspen veneer, you can manoeuvre the veneer under the window to test the effect of the yellow sapwood towards the horizon and the pinkish heartwood towards the top of the picture. By swivelling the leaf slightly, so that the pinkish streaks appear to rise to the top right-hand corner of the opening, you might decide that this gave a more artistic effect than having the grain running parallel to the horizon.

When you are satisfied with the effect, secure both the waste veneer and the veneer to be cut to the cutting board, using hand pressure, or anchor the veneer to the waste with Sellotape in the working margin. Using the edge of the waste veneer as a template to guide the knife, follow around the contour of the window, making a light tracing cut, just sufficient to mark the veneer. Notice that it is much harder to cut a veneer across the grain than with it; it is better to make two or three light cuts than to attempt to cut through the veneer in one cut. Skill comes with a little practice, and you will soon find from experience which veneers you can get through in one or two cuts, and which require further work. Even leading marquetarians prefer to coax intricate outlines with a preliminary light tracing cut to establish the outline, following with a heavier cut which flows more smoothly along the first 'tramline' cut. After making the first tracing cut, the window veneer may be removed and the part cut out on the cutting board, without having to hold the waste veneer and design.

Having cut out the section of veneer, place it back in the window in the waste veneer, and gently smooth it into position with the finger-tips. The waste veneer is now turned over with the design underneath, and the newly cut section is taped into position along the working margin, using thin, double-gummed veneering tape. This tape will not stain delicate veneers and is specially made for easy removal later. It has sufficient strength to allow the veneers to be pulled tightly together; will stretch slightly when wet, and as it contracts will bind the picture tightly together. As you apply the tape, snip it off into half-inch lengths to avoid a build up of criss-crossing tapes. The tape has to be moistened with a warm sponge, not soaked; rubbing it with the fingertips helps to dry and stretch it.

The waste veneer is now turned again, so that the tape is underneath against the cutting board, and the join is then rubbed briskly with the rounded back of a wooden knife handle to ensure perfect adhesion. This rubbing action presses the join tightly together and smooths down any hairlike splinters which may result from a double cut.

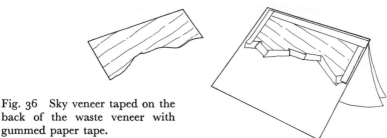

Fig. 36 Sky veneer taped on the back of the waste veneer with gummed paper tape.

The tracing is again brought over the waste veneer, the centre lines checked for perfect register and the simple process is repeated for each section of the design. The window is cut from the waste veneer; the required veneer is selected, placed under the window aperture and tested for the correct flow of grain, figure and other markings. It is then temporarily anchored on the under-side of the waste veneer with two or three small pieces of Sellotape, placed on the cutting board and, using the aperture as the template to guide the knife, the next part of the picture is lightly scored. The veneer is then released from the back of the waste veneer, and the cutting is completed on the cutting board. The piece is inserted back into the window aperture and fixed in position with small pieces of gummed tape on the under-side.

You can see the picture growing. As the picture develops, there will be a tendency to build up veneering tape which will criss-cross in every direction. This would cause some difficulty when trying to fix small details in position, and to avoid this risk, as the picture develops these small $\frac{1}{2}$-in. pieces of gummed tape may be removed and replaced with a longer strip of gummed tape along the joins.

It will soon become apparent that the less tape is used the better, since it will all have to be removed at a later stage. Expert marquetarians use an edge-to-edge butt-jointing method to assemble their veneers into the picture assembly, thereby avoiding the use of veneering tape completely. By smearing a trace of tube glue at spots around the piece to be inserted it is possible to fit it into the picture with finger pressure applied for only a few moments. Very minor detail may be fitted in by rubbing glue into the back of the picture over the joins, and sufficient will seep around the piece to secure it. It is therefore useful to have a small sheet of polythene handy to place over the back of the picture to prevent it from sticking if the work is left overnight.

There are several advantages to this method of edge-to-edge jointing. It is possible to see both sides of the picture unobstructed by tape. It enables different backgrounds to be tried and tested. For example, when making a bowl of roses, or a portrait, the assembly of individual roses, or the head of the portrait, may be removed from the waste veneer and placed on many different backgrounds for effect. Roses may be tried in the face direction or on their backs, in various positions, to effect a balanced floral arrangement, prior to letting them into the selected background.

When the design lends itself to the adoption of this refinement, the components may be made in a separate waste veneer and omitted from the first drawing. Progressive drawings would be used, the first of which would omit the detail, and the secondary drawing would contain only the detail. For example, one could position the rocks in a stream exactly where the grain and figure of the veneer used for the water might have an odd configuration around a tiny knot; in this way the natural effect of the water being disturbed by the rocks could be achieved, even though this was not envisaged when the original drawing was made.

It often works out that way. Advantage may be taken of peculiar markings in the veneers you test for special effects, and these on-the-spot alterations to the original design vastly improve the artistic result.

When the exact location of an insert is determined, secure it in position with a few drops of quick-setting cement, and use it as a template to mark the surrounding background veneer, which is then cut out and discarded and the new insert made.

Progressive tracings. As the main background parts of the picture are cut into the assembly, most of the original tracing of small detail will have been discarded with the pieces of waste veneers. The position of surrounding border lines will have been discarded too, as the picture is allowed to overlap into the border margin.

After the background parts are in, and the entire picture area is filled with the veneers which form its major components, bring the tracing down over the picture, restore the border lines, and trace in the next largest part of the picture.

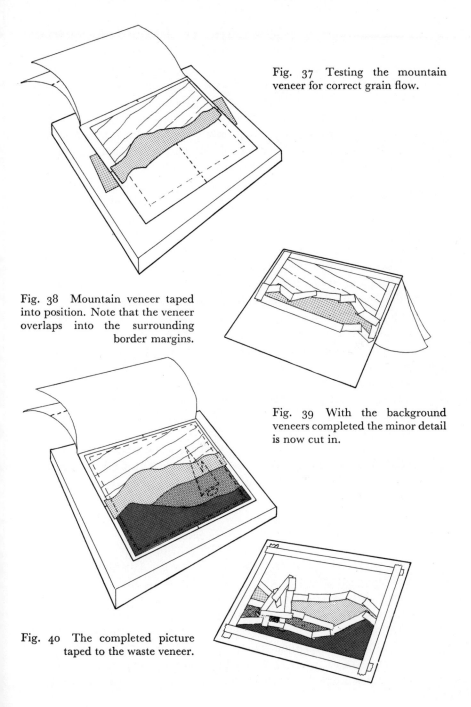

Fig. 37 Testing the mountain veneer for correct grain flow.

Fig. 38 Mountain veneer taped into position. Note that the veneer overlaps into the surrounding border margins.

Fig. 39 With the background veneers completed the minor detail is now cut in.

Fig. 40 The completed picture taped to the waste veneer.

The idea soon becomes apparent. For example, suppose there is a small wall of a house to trace on the picture, in which an even smaller door appears. There is no point in tracing the door on the picture, as the veneer waste will be discarded when you cut in the wall of the house.

By a careful study of the design, the amount of tracing is easily kept to a minimum by tracing only the peripheral outline of the next largest piece to be inserted. Hence the importance of the centre lines to ensure perfect registration of the tracing each time.

After a little experience, you will find the order of cutting a picture becomes important, to save you cutting small intricate details more than twice. To return to the example of the door in a wall, if the door was traced into the waste veneer, cut out and inserted, it would have been a wasted effort if the wall itself had not been inserted in its correct sequence, before the door.

This obvious example applies to less obvious cutting sequences, which will be demonstrated later, but to illustrate this 'order of cutting' sequence here, if you will examine the illustration of the Cornish Coast design (p. 290), it would be necessary to trace and cut the skyline first on the waste veneer and again on the No. 14 veneer. If, however, the horizon line was continued right across the design, and a complete rectangle was let into the waste veneer, *without* attempting to cut around the skyline, the outline of the hills need only be cut *once* when the window is cut in No. 14 veneer to accommodate the veneer No. 182.

With a little thought, the right order of cutting a picture will make the task much easier, especially when such details as the yacht, the rowing boat, and the church tower may be omitted completely until the whole picture background is assembled. The golden rule is to cut the part of the picture which is furthest away in perspective, before nearer objects.

Cutting hints. To maintain complete control over the knife of your choice, keep your wrist firmly on the cutting board and contrive to make the cut towards yourself, moving the work towards you with the other hand so that your hand remains in the same comfortable cutting position.

Use the tip or point of the knife, rather than the long straight part of the blade. Do not try to cut in one long continuous stroke, but make a series of short jabbing cuts or very close prickings with the knife point, then work over them, joining them together with a light score cut, tracing the outline. This prevents the knife wandering, and enables quite tricky contours to be cut with reasonable ease, and with greater accuracy of cutting.

Some professional craftsmen hold their knives – made from tempered hacksaw blades, and with smooth, rounded, wooden handles – in an almost vertical position, between thumb and index finger, with their middle finger protruding down over the back of the knife, to guide the blade and press down the veneer. This grip acts rather like a sewing-machine foot to smooth the path of the blade. The value of this style of holding the knife is felt when pivoting at sharp corners or when cutting cross-grained brittle woods.

Another refinement is that the professional cutter will sometimes cut out the waste veneer, but will not discard the cut-out. He will use it as his template to cut the required veneer, knowing that the resulting cut will be fractionally larger than the window aperture and will make a better fit.

When cutting out the waste veneer, an expert marquetarian sometimes prefers to leave the actual design line visible and will remove the waste veneer deliberately under size. When he has determined the exact flow of grain required for the picture, he cuts through both the waste veneer and the underlying veneer, exactly on the traced line. It is a simultaneous cut requiring great experience, but ensuring perfect joins. The skill lies in knowing when to use which cutting technique. Another trick of the professional is to hold the knife at a slight outward angle and to make a very slight bevel cut, fractionally wedge-shaped; when let into the picture the join is invisible. This is very useful when joins must occur between white veneers such as sycamore or horse chestnut or maple, where it is possible for dark glue lines to show if the knife is held vertically.

Another technique is to use a knife with only one bevel, to reduce the thickness of the cut by half.

Great care must be taken in making these bevel cuts, as ugly gaps will occur in the picture if the angle is made in the wrong direction. It must be kept uniformly outwards from the centre of the piece being cut.

Cleaning up. When the picture has been completely cut into the assembly, ready for trimming down to actual size, it should be laid aside for a few days. After working at the picture for some time, one's approach to the work naturally becomes subjective; one is too close to the easel and, like a true artist, needs to stand back now for an objective appraisal.

Examine the picture critically at this stage for possible flaws and weaknesses in the veneer. Errors in composition, unrealistic effects, and differences between the picture and the original drawing should be carefully noted; also bad cutting, open joins, damaged fine points and broken, cross-grained detail. In the case of pictures held together by the butt-jointing technique, tiny fragments may have fallen out in handling. These parts must be marked in pencil or chalk, removed and recut. Finally, the assembly is examined once more to ensure that the complete assembly is sound. This visual check against a strong light is applicable both to pictorial and geometric marquetry.

If any part of the picture, for any reason, does not convey the effect desired it is a simple matter to slit the veneer tape, remove the offending piece, and replace it with a veneer which will give the over-all harmony you require. Time spent on this stage of the picture will be well spent as this is the point of no return.

Many leading marquetarians have two different pictures in hand at any one time, even if one is the major work intended for an exhibition and one is just a little 'pot-boiler'. If ever one feels the frustration of not being able to get part of the major picture just right, it is advisable to leave it and turn to something else, rather than 'let it go'.

There are conflicting opinions regarding the use of wood stopping for marquetry. Those who like to exhibit their ability to cut infinitely small detail to achieve photographic realism shun the use of stopping as an excuse for poor workmanship. Artistic types, who may have searched for months to find freak veneers to provide a special effect, regard the actual cutting as merely a means to an end. They argue that an open join in such a freak wood should be filled because the freak veneer is unique and cannot be replaced. It is felt that the marquetry picture should look like a wooden picture, and poor joins underline this fact and even add their own peculiar charm to what is, after all, a hand-made work of artistry and craftsmanship.

In professional saw-cut work, where the thickness of the saw cut is visible, the joins are filled with wood stopping. This is sometimes used in the picture in a contrasting tone to emphasize fine detail, such as the veins of a leaf or a ship's rigging. This is done by making knife or saw cuts in the picture assembly and filling them with wood stopping, although whenever possible, if the detail line is not too involved, a veneer can be let in on edge. It is surprising how fine slivers of veneer can be wrapped round and twisted into curves and glued into the assembly on edge. There are many commercial wood stoppings available of the non-shrinking type, and in a wide range of intermixable tones. These are preferable to beaumontage, coloured wax or tinted shellac sticks. However, the professional method, for best work, is to rub a little transparent adhesive into the join to be filled, and to scrape dust from surrounding veneers into the join. In the case of fretsaw work with open joins, a paste is made from dust, sawn or scraped from a piece of background veneer, and glue. When this is used to fill the join it is undetectable against the background veneer from which it has been made.

Fitting the border veneers

The border surrounding a marquetry picture is fully as important as the picture itself. The wrong border can completely spoil the effect of even a well-designed and well-executed panel. Conversely, a suitable border enhances the unity and distinction of a picture. Some pictures, such as portraits, do not require a border at all – the background extends to the edge of the panel.

To decide on the best type of border for a picture, many points have to be considered. Firstly, the over-all tone is considered; whether the picture is generally light, dark or monotone. It is usually found that neutral or medium-toned woods enhance light or dark pictures, while lighter and darker borders are best with medium-toned pictures. The aim is to seek not a marked contrast but rather a blending harmony.

The subject matter of a picture is also a factor. If the picture is of a religious nature or solemn in intent, the border should also be subdued; more colourful treatment may be given to a sunny calypso scene.

As the attention of the viewer must never be diverted from the picture by the counter-attraction of the surround, a simple picture which relies on its charm may need a plain border, whereas a scene depicting plenty of life, colour and vigour can carry a border of much more character and strength of tone.

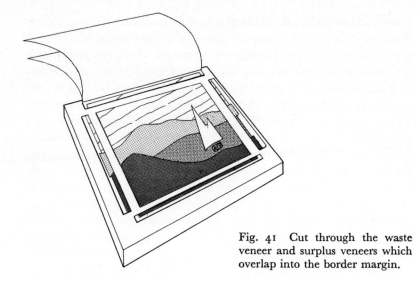

Fig. 41 Cut through the waste veneer and surplus veneers which overlap into the border margin.

The predominating wood in a picture will have a marked effect, too: in a low-horizon picture with an all-yellow sky, the choice of a yellowish veneer for the border would be wrong. This only applies where there is a predominating veneer in the picture. With a walnut foreground, for example, in an otherwise light-toned picture, there would be no objection to the choice of a walnut border, providing the grain direction of the border is in the opposite direction; or a contrasting white fillet border line could be used to make a break between the two walnut veneers.

Highly figured woods are seldom used for borders. Quarter-cut, straight-grained, ribbon-striped veneers make the best selection, such as oak, sapele, walnut, teak, afrormosia, wenge, ash, elm, rosewood, mahogany, sycamore, tola, or African walnut.

The 'temperature' of a picture can often assist the selection of a border. A winter scene with a snow-laden landscape would not require a white sycamore border, but this would greatly enhance a sunny Mediterranean scene.

The border mount may also be used to heighten the dramatic effect of a picture by allowing part of the subject to pierce or overlap the border surround – for example, a parrot's tail feathers or an eagle's wing. In one prizewinning picture, a leaping gazelle's foot is shown breaking into the fillet border, which seems to add to the desperation of the animal's leap from the attacking tiger. Another variation, used with restraint, is to permit the background or sky veneer to continue round the picture to form the fillet border.

In order to obtain perfectly mitred borders, it is essential to square the picture correctly. Place the picture assembly on the cutting board and lay the straight edge along the top border line. Cut through the waste veneer and surplus picture veneers which overlap into the border margin. When this veneer waste is discarded, use this true edge as a guide for the try-square in marking the two side edges, which are also removed with the straight edge and knife; the bottom is then trued with each side in turn to ensure perfect squareness. The overlapping of the picture veneers into the border margin prevents the chipping out of veneers when cutting across the grain.

It is permissible for the border veneers to be applied after the picture is laid, but for the purpose of this example, the borders will be laid with the picture.

The stringer, or fillet border, is a thin strip of veneer about $\frac{1}{16}$ in. wide, up to $\frac{1}{8}$ in. wide for large panoramic pictures or fire-screens. Its purpose is to stand out in contrast to the border veneers and it is fitted between the picture and borders. The usual veneers for stringers are sycamore, horse chestnut, ebony, or walnut; the main consideration is that it must contrast with the outside veneers in the picture and also with the selected border mount veneers.

The use of decorative mosaic banding, although perfect for furniture and applied marquetry, is recommended for pictorial marquetry only when of the simple 'ladder' or 'rope' type or the three-line box and black type.

Fasten the stringer fillets around the picture with pieces of gummed paper tape, overlapping at the four corners. Next, select four matching consecutive leaves of straight-grained close-striped border veneers, which must be an inch or two longer than the over-all size of the longest side of the groundwork. Look for some peculiarity of grain to ensure that the four leaves are exactly matching, and then number them with chalk A, B, C and D. Now securely bind them together at the ends with gummed paper tape, exactly one on top of the other. Place this wad on the cutting board with a straight edge on top and cut through all four leaves, one at a time, to obtain four perfectly straight, true edges; these should be marked with chalk.

Now mark, on the top veneer, the exact width of the required border veneers, to project about $\frac{1}{8}$ in. wider than the groundwork all round; this will be trimmed off later.

Cut through the four leaves again, after carefully checking the width in several places to ensure accuracy of measurement. Make several light tracing cuts to sever them, rather than one heavy cut. It is a good idea to use a new blade for this purpose.

The border veneers are now applied round the picture in sequence. Border A is taped to the top of the picture, and border B is turned over and taped to the bottom edge; piece C is taped to the left-hand side of the picture and D is turned over and taped to the right-hand side. There is now a matched, balanced border surround outside a contrasting stringer, all overlapping at the four corners.

The straight edge is placed at the intersection of the outer two border veneers at one corner, and carefully lined up, using the pointed tip of the knife, with the precise intersection of the inner stringer fillet strip at the corner of the actual picture.

Using a light score cut to establish the line, cut through both border veneers and both fillet strips from the outside of the borders towards the picture. Take care not to slip so that the knife cuts into the picture, but do not cut outwards away from the picture or the border veneers will splinter or break.

Remove the unwanted surplus pieces at the corner, and securely tape the mitred corner on the front of the picture. Repeat this at each corner.

There are objections to this form of border. A common fault is the possibility of poor mitres, especially the border and fillet border mitres failing to coincide. This type of border causes differential light reflection, the four veneers being laid in different directions, with the result that you have four different colour tones, loss of harmony, and no illusion of solidity – especially as the edges all have to be veneered long grain (fig. 52).

Where peculiar markings on a veneer are to be shown to advantage, eight-piece matches are used, the corners being mitred and the four centres butt-jointed. This type is decorative, but with no illusion of solidity (fig. 53). The cross-banded border

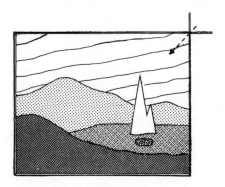

Figs. 42, 43 Fit the fillet and border veneers. Note the direction of cut, which avoids splitting the border veneers.

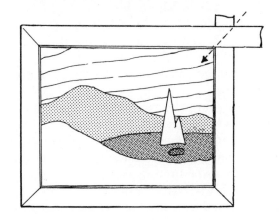

(fig. 54) serves to draw the eye towards the picture, or conversely appears to provide an 'exploded' effect, giving the picture maximum impact. One advantage of this type is that the crossbanding may be cut from veneers which do not have perfectly straight grain along their length, but which are straight in sections.

The connoisseur has a different approach to the selection of border veneers. He requires the complete panel, when laid, to resemble a solid board. This is not with any intention to deceive, but to preserve the natural appearance of a hand-made wooden picture.

The true face of the veneer is determined – the smoothest side, with the tightly closed pores. If one single leaf can be obtained, big enough to cover the picture completely, this is ideal. Where two or more leaves of narrower width are used, both are kept with the face side uppermost, never turned over, so as to provide the same tonal value by reflected light. The leaves are cut to create the effect of a picture let into a single leaf of veneer, as in fig. 57 (p. 158). The veneer on the back of the panel should also be laid as one piece. The panel's edges continue this illusion by being cross-grain veneered at the top edges and long-grain veneered to suit the face and back of the panel.

Preparation for laying

All pieces of gummed tape on the back of the picture must be removed before the picture may be laid (unless a reverse picture is required). For this purpose strips of gummed paper tape are laid right across the entire front of the picture, not overlapping each other, but butt-jointed edge to edge. These strips must be rubbed on firmly and allowed to dry thoroughly before proceeding.

Turn the picture over now, with the completely covered face side underneath, and remove the short lengths of gummed paper tape applied during the assembly. If they are moistened with warm water from a squeezed-out sponge, and the moisture is allowed time to penetrate the paper, they will peel off easily.

It is advisable to work on cleaning up the back of the picture a small area at a time, and do not allow the picture to become wet. It is better to moisten the tapes two or three times and peel them off, rather than risk introducing water to the picture.

After removing the tapes, any residue left on the back of the picture is allowed to remain and thoroughly dry out. This is easily removed with sandpaper later.

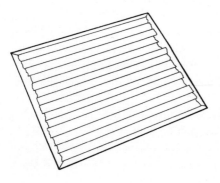

Fig. 44 To reverse the pictures tapes are laid across the face of the picture including the border veneers and the original tapes are removed from the back of the picture.

The picture is now placed in the press, or between two wooden cauls under a heavy weight until ready for laying – a process dealt with more fully later in the book (pp. 169 *ff*.).

It is now clear why many marquetarians prefer *not* to remove tapes from the back of the picture and tape the face side, only to have to remove those tapes again when the picture is laid. They prefer to work with a reverse design, leaving the original tapes on the under-side of the picture, to be cleaned off after the picture is laid.

The marquetry assembly is securely fastened to a perfectly flat surface, either by paper tape or by veneer pins through the margin. A perfectly level surface on the back of the assembly will minimize the risk of blisters, and will also reduce the amount of finishing to the face side when laid. How this is done depends on the thickness of the veneer used. European craftsmen using veneers of 0·7 mm. thickness prefer to use the scraper, very gently, or if not skilled with the scraper, a superficial coarse sanding by garnet paper grade 4/0 wrapped round a cork rubbing block. Craftsmen using $\frac{1}{28}$ in. or saw-cut veneers, which permit more robust treatment, use a toothing plane or a scraper to smooth the back.

You will need a flexible cabinet-maker's scraper, or you can make one by rubbing the back of a hacksaw blade on an oilstone and then burr over the edge by rubbing it with a chisel. In operation, hold the scraper with both hands and bend it in the middle with thumb pressure; hold it at an angle to the work surface, and use the burred edge with a scything action to prevent it digging into the veneers. This is an acquired knack, developed after a little experience, and it is surprising how much scraping even a thin veneer will stand. Scrape *with* the grain, and if this tends to roughen the grain, use the scraper diagonally. Veneers with interlocked grain need to be scraped from each end towards the middle.

Providing veneers of the same thickness have been used in the work, it is sufficient to coarse sand the back of the assembly and dispense with the scraper. This removes all glue traces, grease spots, etc., which may affect the adhesion.

If the butt-joint, edge-to-edge method of assembly has been used instead of the special veneering tape, special treatment of the back of the work is required. To prevent a possible cracked bond after laying, if the adhesive used for laying does not key with the synthetic adhesive used for edge-jointing, it is necessary to brush the back of the assembly with a bronze wire brush to remove adhesive from the back of joins which are glue-filled.

For this reason, it is best to butt-join veneers into the assembly at odd spots around the section and not all around the piece.

The working margin of waste sycamore is now trimmed off, and the picture squared with a try-square and straight edge if the fillet strip and border veneers are to be fixed (pp. 171-2); or they can be left ¼ in. over size in all directions if the border mounts are to be laid separately later.

Keep the assembly between clean sheets of paper in a folder under a board and light pressure until ready for laying.

If it is desired to lay the complete picture assembly including the border veneers, the procedure is as follows.

Trim off the surplus picture veneer and sycamore waste veneer of the working margin from the picture assembly, testing for accuracy with a try-square.

Tape the selected border and fillet border veneers into position, overlapping them at the corners. These border veneers should be larger all around than the finished panel size, to allow for trimming off after laying.

Placing the assembly on the cutting board, and using a non-slip ruler or straight edge to guide the craft tool, the mitres are cut from the outside of the panel towards the picture, using a 45° angle. Cut through both veneers, using a light tracing cut to establish the line, and then heavy pressure to sever the veneers. Then tape them together securely both at the mitres and along all joints with the picture.

When the back of the panel has been laid, the top and bottom edging strips are applied next, followed by the two side edges, and the actual picture is laid last of all, in that sequence.

By this means, the edges of the backing veneer are concealed by the edging strips; the top and bottom strips are concealed by the side strips, and all front edges are then hidden by the picture.

The problem of difficult veneers

It is ironic that the most difficult woods to cut by the knife are often the most attractive and the most interesting from a pictorial viewpoint. Ebony and rosewood are very hard, and thuya burr, ayan or pommelle and most burrs are very brittle or tend to crumble under the knife. Other woods, like wenge, will splinter or the knife will wander in the grain. Wild-grained or freak veneers often require special treatment, and some veneers which are easy to cut along the grain are most difficult to cut across the grain.

The stretching or flatting process, previously described, holds the veneer together, retaining every 'hair' in place, even if it does splinter during the cutting. If the veneer is extremely hard it may be immersed in boiling water or held with tongs in steam from a kettle, for long enough to soften it. Allow the veneer to dry off for a few minutes and then cut it to shape for the picture. Wrap this insert in paper and place it under pressure or weight until thoroughly dry. It may then be let into the softer surrounding veneers of the picture.

If this rather drastic treatment does not solve the problem, the piercing blade technique may be used; this enables veneers, no matter how hard, brittle or crumbly, to be cut in the most intricate shapes without difficulty.

Fragmentation

A technique pioneered by Mr Norman MacLeod of South London is rapidly gaining in popularity and many of the leading marquetry artists are trying their hands at 'fragmentation'.

Instead of trying to cut a very difficult burr veneer to represent a bush or tree foliage, the burr is cut into tiny fragments. In fact, several different burrs and other veneers can be cut into minute, splinter-sized pieces of various colour tones, and kept in small jars until required for use.

A 'window' or aperture is cut into the background veneer to the required outline of the bush or treetop, and a piece of gummed paper tape is fastened over the aperture on the face side.

Then the fragments of the multi-coloured veneers, mixed with a trace of transparent adhesive, are sprinkled into the aperture and pressed down with a rounded tool such as the smooth handle of a knife. They are rammed tightly into the picture background, slightly above the level surface of the back of the picture, and then left under a weight until dry. The surplus is easily sandpapered or scraped off when dry.

Surprising results are obtained by this method. The russet tones of autumn, the gold, red, brown, yellow and intermediate shades of brown-green, can transform a picture. Where a piece of dyed green might stand out incongruously in a picture made with natural woods, the tasteful use of this technique to create – for example – an ivy-covered wall, part in sunshine and part in shadow, can blend in harmoniously with the other woods, yet achieve the colourfulness desired.

Other possibilities being experimented with are the use of fragments to increase the attractiveness of seascapes. A front-lit picture which requires silver to white highlights on lapping waves, dappled with the red, orange, yellow and pink of a sunset on the water, can be created by this method. The white, silver, cream, yellow, dark blue and deep green required for moonlit subjects are also possible.

Having seen many pictures made incorporating this technique, I hasten to add that it must be used with very great restraint and taste – simply to add a finishing touch rather than to monopolize large parts of a picture.

Extending this idea, instead of cutting the veneers into fragments about $\frac{1}{16}$ in. square, another idea is to cut very fine slivers or shavings from the edges of various veneers, each shaving about two or three inches long by as fine as can be cut. (This idea originated when one enterprising customer of mine experimented with the woodwool packing which protected his veneers in the post!) The shavings are intermixed and laid into the aperture with a trace of transparent adhesive, rammed in hard, and allowed to dry before being cleaned off as before.

This produces a rather different effect from the tiny mosaic result of using fragments. It may be used for the thatched roof of a cottage, for bulrushes or reeds in streams, for weeping willow trees, for ploughed fields; and it makes superb water effects when strips of silver, grey, various blues, greens and browns for shadow are used.

Combinations of both methods are being experimented with in portraiture to depict hair, for animal subjects, for costume and many other subjects. The method enables the marquetry craftsman to tackle subjects formerly considered to be outside his scope, or for effects which could not be achieved by using natural woods in the conventional way.

British piercing blade technique

This is the most recent advance in marquetry cutting technique, pioneered by Mr Glander and Mr K. Brennand in collaboration with myself; the first demonstration of this technique was made in 1960 in my London marquetry clubroom. By this method, the most elaborate and detailed pictures may be made, involving tricky undulating contours such as tree foliage, executed in the most difficult veneers or burrs. It takes only a fraction of the time involved with knife cutting and produces excellent results without visible joins. Although leading exponents now produce complete pictures in this way, most marquetarians use the piercing blade technique in conjunction with the window method of knife cutting for the straightforward parts of the picture.

Very fine, metal-cutting piercing blades with rounded backs, specially made for jewellers, for negotiating curves and corners, are used in ordinary fretsaw frames. These blades range from grade 3, which is strong and robust, down to 2/0 – the equivalent of the special marquetry veneer sawblades previous described – and then finer still, down to 4/0 and 6/0, for extremely fine work.

To prevent these delicate blades from breaking too easily, stretch a cord across the fretsaw frame to act as a tourniquet, with a small piece of wood resting on the back of the frame. By adding turns on the tourniquet, the tension on the blade may be reduced to suit the work in hand.

These saws are used for cutting metals such as pewter, brass, and other materials for marquetry decoration, and the marquetry worker should master their use.

Use the previously described window method to cut the picture in the usual way, but this time omit all difficult or intricate, curved or serrated parts of the design requiring the use of hard, brittle or end-grain woods. Just ignore these details and complete the background assembly.

Now, for the first of these difficult parts, cut a window aperture, slightly smaller in outline than the required design line, which is left visible on the surrounding waste veneer. The veneer to be inserted is underlaid and tested for the correct flow of grain. When this has been determined, this veneer is temporarily fixed to the face side with balsa cement (rather like sticking a puncture patch to an inner tube!) and placed under a weight for a few moments for the cement to set.

A needle is then pushed through both veneers at a slight angle from the vertical, and the sawblade is entered, teeth downwards. The fretsaw frame wingnut should be securely tightened with a pair of pliers. No saw swarf is noticeable by this method, so it is unnecessary to underlay a third veneer. Keep the work as near to the edge of the saw table as possible. Hold the saw at an angle, and work it gently up and down in the same position, turning the work toward the saw. The downward drag of the teeth tends to pull the under veneer away from the picture veneer, so the two must be held down firmly. If the needle hole and saw blade are inclined in an outward direction so that the saw cuts at an angle, the bevel of the insert will fit into the bevelled aperture and the insert will fit the window perfectly with no visible sawcut. Most elaborate designs in difficult woods are cut in this way. But remember, it is possible to overdo the bevel and make the insert too big for the aperture: only a slight angle of cut is necessary, just a little off vertical.

On completion of the cut, the insert is separated from the surrounding background veneer by working a flat kitchen knife between the two veneers. The surplus veneer adhering to the background is removed with the top of the knife, used chisel fashion. This is much easier than it sounds. The whole cutting and separating operation is a matter of five minutes or so.

Several factors affect the setting time of balsa cement, such as the type of veneer, the age of the cement and the temperature of the workroom. Test the effective strength of the bond before

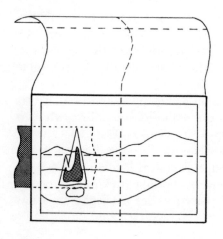

Fig. 45   Leave the required design line visible on the surrounding waste veener.

sawing – it is only necessary to form a temporary bond while sawing, sufficient to prevent the veneers from separating on the upstroke of the saw. The beginner is advised to begin by using a grade 1 blade until experience is gained.

It is only necessary to tilt the saw and cut on a bevel while you are learning this technique, using coarse blades such as grades 3 or 1. The bevel cut compensates for the thickness of the saw and of the veneer. The true value of the technique comes when experience and skill is acquired in using progressively finer blades. The angle of bevel can be reduced in proportion to the degree of fineness of the blade being used, until you can ignore the bevel cut altogether and hold the saw vertical, using the 4/0 or 6/0 blade. The cut is undetectable once the picture is laid. When this degree of proficiency is attained, the use of balsa cement is also dispensed with: the veneers are held with finger pressure only, or at most, a small piece of Sellotape is used to hold them in place.

The piercing blade technique of cutting has more recently been improved by amateurs who have tackled increasingly more ambitious projects. One marquetarian – Mr George R. Bordewick of Bellevue, Washington, USA – has adapted a fretsaw by constructing a frame made of $\frac{3}{4}$-in-square sections of maple, 48 in. long, which provided a throat of 36 in. This enabled him to cut Leonardo da Vinci's 'Last Supper' in 36 in. × 19 in. size, using the piercing-blade method.

He also constructed a working table about 30 in. square, which is set on a stand clamped to his work bench by a vice. The work table can swivel through 180° if necessary, to reverse the angle of cut or direction of cut, and although the cutting table surface is permanently fixed at 15° to compensate for the thickness of the material, he can adjust the angle of cut by adjusting the vice.

Mr Bordewick suspends his jumbo-sized fretsaw frame at the point of balance on the top bar of the frame, by a wire and chain from a ceiling joist. The cutting table has two slots sawn into it, one from each side, about $\frac{1}{8}$ in. wide and 6 in. long. The slots are not cut at right angles to the surface of the table but are vertical.

Progressive drawings
If a complete picture is planned using a combination of the knife-

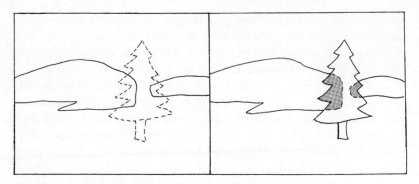

Figs. 46, 47   The line to be knife-cut is carried inside the area to be saw-cut, enabling the saw blade to remove the small surplus allowed for inside the required line.

cutting window method and the piercing-blade sawing technique, progressive drawings should be prepared, to separate the work into two phases.

The first drawing is for knife cutting, and would usually represent the simple, bold outline features of the background, straight lines and easy parts of the picture. The second drawing will show all the tricky detail, difficult contours and cuts in hard or brittle veneers, which are to be cut by saw. Both designs are reversed, and with centre lines to ensure perfect register. The object of this is to ensure that the saw cuts resulting from the second drawing do *not* coincide with the knife cuts in drawing No. 1.

To achieve this, the design lines of the background veneers to be knife-cut are carried slightly inside the area to be saw-cut, to ensure that the detail let in by the saw blade removes a small surplus, which is allowed for inside the required line.

On completion of the knife-cut background, the first-stage drawing is removed from the sycamore waste veneer, and the second-stage final drawing is fixed, checking to ensure perfect register. The new design is traced direct to the background assembly of the picture, and the approximate section is removed by the knife to make the required window. The selected veneer is underlaid in the usual way. The design line is left on the background veneer as the window is cut out deliberately under-size, as we have seen, to allow a small surplus for sawing off. The

150

required veneer is then fixed to the face side of the picture, and when the glue has set, is pierced and sawn out.

It is possible to 'let in' parts of the picture from either the face side or the back of the picture. The procedure is to locate the veneer to be inserted in the background by reference to the design. An aperture is cut in the background, slightly under-size to leave the design line visible. When the exact flow of grain has been decided, the position is marked in pencil by tracing around the window aperture. The veneer is then positioned on the back of the picture and the contour checked with the design, marking the extreme of the veneer on the background. The patch is then fixed with balsa cement or tape and the blade is entered in the usual way.

When the insert veneer is to be cut in from the back, the angle of bevel (when using fairly coarse saws) is opposite to that used when inserting from the face.

There are three advantages in letting in from the back of the picture. Firstly, the glue traces will be on the back of the picture and can be cleaned off without risk to the face of the work; secondly, the background will lie flat on the saw table and resist the downward drag of the saw teeth which tends to pull the insert veneer, when using the other method. Finally, and perhaps most

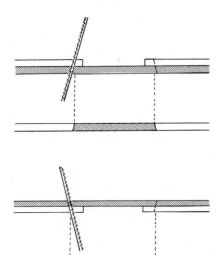

Figs. 48, 49 The angle of bevel cut is reversed when letting in from (*top*) the back of the picture or (*bottom*) the face of the picture.

important of all, motifs may be inserted into backgrounds simply by cutting them over-size, positioning them on the background, and letting them in as described, without having to go through the work of cutting a window aperture at all.

Artificial shading

In the field of pictorial marquetry there is a tremendous scope for the use of artificial shading to create the effect of depth, as in the roundness of columns, folds in costumes and drapery, and particularly in portraiture. It is possible, in fact, to introduce shading into almost every picture, with good or bad results depending on the taste and skill of the craftsman.

The marquetry artist uses artificial shading where his woods need toning to set them against one another, as for example when portraying the petals of a rose from one species of veneer.

As a successful picture depends upon the effect of freak characteristics in veneer, there is a valid argument in favour of using artificial aids to complete the picture with complementary 'supporting' woods, rather than to discard a valuable freak veneer because of some minor defect, or perhaps to search in vain for other freak natural veneers which might provide the desired effect.

When the merits of a marquetry picture are being judged, the simple use of freak veneers which succeed in achieving a true sense of depth will be of greater merit than if shading has been used for the effect – no matter how cleverly applied.

The secret of artistic shading lies in the subtle and undetectable application of the gentlest tones, which appear to merge and blend naturally into the veneer.

In short, a successfully shaded picture is one which appears *not* to have been shaded at all.

The marquetry artist has applied the methods of many other art forms to enliven and shade his work. *Pokercraft* has been used, which involves the use of heated irons and hot points for burning or branding detail into wood, and for hachuring shading in much the same way as a fine etching. From the separate art form of *pyrography*, the flame of the blow-lamp has been used to provide a large-area tonal wash to marquetry pictures.

As the wood carver has always been closely associated with marquetry, it was natural for flame-washed pictures to be engraved, to reveal the true original wood tone beneath the shading, to highlight certain features, or to create a complete wood etching in which the engraved lines were filled with black stopping, heelball or wax. Truly remarkable works have been created with this process.

However, these shading techniques were all applied *after* the picture was laid. The method of shading with hot sand is applied after the veneers are cut, but *before* assembly and laying.

Sand shading. Dipping in hot metal produced too marked a contrast between light and shade and this method gave way to the use of fine, sharp sand for shading – a method which rapidly established itself and remains until this day the best method of all for delicate, graduated shading. The skill lies in effecting only slight variations from the natural tone.

Traditionally, this job has been held to need a woman's hand, and so has been handed over to marquetry cutters' wives. In fact, even today, most marqueteurs invite their wives to carry out this part of the work, and to complete the inlaying of the assembly.

Clean, sharp-edged, fine silver sand – obtainable from pet shops – is ideal for the purpose. It is poured into a flat-bottomed metal tray or baking dish. The heat may be provided by gas ring or spirit stove, but the best results are obtained from an electric hotplate, at which one can work even in hot weather without discomfort. The heat also may be more easily regulated. After the sand has reached the desired temperature, the control should be set to maintain a constant heat. Uniform heat, not too strong, is the ideal.

Where fairly deep tones are required, the sand may be shallow and of greater heat than for the delicate and more softly gradu-

Fig. 50 Shading a leaf of veneer to various depths of tone, in hot sand.

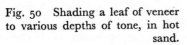

ated tones, for which the sand is heaped into mounds. The heat is lowered until the sand is merely warm and more time is allowed for the process.

The timing of the operation is quickly learned by experience after a few experiments with scraps of waste veneer. Use either the 'silent count' or a stopwatch, allowing various lengths of time at a given temperature. Most shading effects are reached in a few seconds, and you will rarely have to count more than five or six seconds.

Before deciding if the tone is correct, lightly sandpaper the veneer and then moisten it. This will remove the surface charring and roughly approximate with the tone you will obtain when the work is finally laid and polished.

The surface of the veneer tends to carbonize more quickly than the inside, which is a good fault as this is removed when the work is sanded smooth. If you stop when the outside shading is about right, the resulting effect will be just a tone more delicate. As it is a common fault with beginners to over-scorch the work, it is best to stop when you think the veneer could be given just a little bit more! It is obviously a matter of personal judgment.

When the veneer is inserted into a mound of sand, it should not be allowed to touch the metal tray as this will cause a burn and may even scorch the veneer. Hold the veneer with a pair of tweezers. It is good practice to withdraw the veneer to check the tone and to replace it for further treatment rather than risk over-shading it. Because of the greater tonal range from white to dark brown, greater subtlety of shading can be achieved with white and lighter-hued veneers than with red and brown woods, which darken very quickly.

There are four methods of working. A leaf of veneer, to suit part of a picture, is inserted in the hot sand for the required time; after a light sandpapering the leaf is then tested for effect either by using cut out 'masks' of the desired shape, or, in the window method, by placing the leaf under the aperture.

In the second method, where 'island' patches of tone are required, hot sand is poured on to the veneer, using a spoon; a grapefruit spoon is best for this. The sand is repeatedly poured and tossed back into the tray until the desired tone appears. Pour the sand on to both sides of the veneer alternately – an important point to remember when working the veneer assembly in reverse.

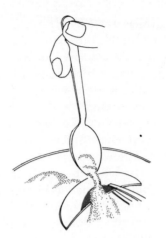

Fig. 51   Pouring sand where
'island' patches of tone are required.

The third method is to mask the veneer with a cut-out scrap, so that only the exposed area will be affected by the sand, or mask the veneer by a coat of polish where no shading is desired.

If you are cutting your work by a technique which requires that the veneers be sawn or cut to shape first, and it is not practical to shade a complete leaf of veneer to different depth of tone around its edges, as is the usual way, then the fourth method is used. The exactly shaped veneer is dipped in and out of the sand quickly (remember, the heat of the sand rapidly dries out the natural moisture content of the veneer, causing it to buckle and maybe to crack or split and curl up, if the process is prolonged) and the surface is then quickly moistened by using a damp cloth. The surface moisture applied is quickly absorbed by the heated wood and no shrinkage results. Never attempt to shade wet or moist veneers, nor try to shade too many pieces at once, in the case of a geometric shape like a Sheraton oval or fan. If the sections are placed under a light weight immediately after shading, and allowed to cool, no shrinkage will occur and the veneer will remain flat.

Many other methods of providing pictures with detail too fine to be cut in, and of shading, have been practised for centuries. The use of feathers dipped in indian ink led to the craft of quill-work. Brushes have been used to apply acids such as vitriol to shade veneers by burning. Sulphate of iron produces grey tones. One ancient method still practised today is the use of Lapis

Infernalis (silver nitrate). Diluted with distilled water to varying strengths, the chemical may be applied by brush after the picture has been assembled. At first, there is no apparent tone change, as it takes a little time for the water carrying the silver nitrate to penetrate the veneer. The effect makes its appearance slowly. The strength and the number of applications are a matter for experiment. In the main, the silver nitrate is for use as a 'touching-up' form of shading applied to the completed work.

The painting of veneers by brush is a process many true craftsmen will deplore. It is a very short step to the use of other chemicals such as hydrogen peroxide and ammonia for bleaching the veneers for cloud and water effects; or the wanton use of packets of aniline or water dyes to produce every colour of the spectrum.

A brilliantly coloured picture can best be produced by colour photography anyway; neither should a marquetry picture ever be compared with or be expected to compete with a painting.

The aim is to preserve the natural appearance of wood, to get as far away as possible from the 'painted' look. This attitude is carried to such lengths by some craftsmen that they argue that open joints, and a surface that has not been sanded perfectly level nor polished like plastic, emphasizes that the picture is made of wood. One should be able to see – and feel – that it is a wood picture. The danger in this approach is that it is also a convenient excuse for poor workmanship.

The true craftsman should apply his knowledge of artificial shading techniques with great restraint and self-discipline. The various techniques have been described, but they should not encourage the marquetarian to overstep the limits proper to the craft.

Light reflection

When a leaf of veneer is moved about and rotated before one constant source of light, the spectator receives an ever-changing tonal light reflection. The marquetarian makes use of this fact, and tests his veneers for light reflection.

This can have a great effect on a picture. An amazing likeness in a portrait, for example, when viewed from one position can vanish when the viewer moves. The moment he begins to walk around the picture the effect is lost, and where the veneer

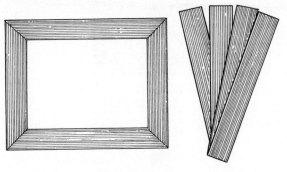

Fig. 52 The traditional border surround from four consecutive leaves of veneer.

Fig. 53, 54 *Left:* An eight-piece match with corners mitred and centres butt-jointed. *Right:* A cross-banded border which can be made from a four- or eight-piece match.

Figs. 55, 56 *Left:* Traditional cross-banding. *Right:* Unmatched borders can spoil the effect of the picture.

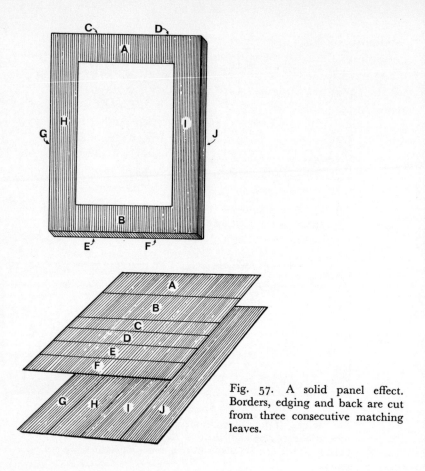

Fig. 57. A solid panel effect. Borders, edging and back are cut from three consecutive matching leaves.

sparkled before it appears dull and lifeless. A constant source of light and a single viewing position are desirable if the picture is to be seen as its creator designed it; for this purpose the angle and source of light in the viewing room and in the workroom should be similar. This is an ideal arrangement when the picture is being commissioned for a special room and this can be taken into consideration. However, for most purposes this requirement is impractical. It is useful to remember that if your work is to be viewed in a vertical position such as upon a wall, that you should test each veneer for effect by holding it in a vertical position; occasionally stand the work in progress up against a wall to get the vertical impression of the veneer.

Almost all work in veneer is carried out in the horizontal position on the work bench, and this accounts for the fact that many marquetarians, in the beginning, are surprised when they see their pictures hung at an exhibition, as they do not have the visual impact that they had created while the work was in progress. Obviously this does not apply to horizontal marquetry, which is usually viewed in the same attitude as it is made.

For this reason of light reflection, pictures which rely on the grain or figure alone can prove disappointing in certain light effects. This strengthens the argument in favour of artificial shading; for taking into consideration the source of light problem together with the changing image from various viewing positions, a picture artificially shaded will possess the desired effect, no matter how viewed and regardless of the angle and source of the lighting.

8 The groundwork

What wood to use for the groundwork upon which to lay the marquetry is not always a free choice for the marquetarian. He may, for instance, have created a piece of marquetry to be used as a decoration for a furniture panel, where other considerations have dictated the groundwork upon which the marquetry is to be laid. However, given a free choice, the following considerations should assist the craftsman designer in the planning stage. A veneered panel will only be as good as the groundwork it is laid upon and therefore it must be the correct material properly prepared.

Solid hardwoods

There may be occasions when you want to use a solid panel, especially if you already have a suitable board, but solid timber has proved to be unsuitable and inferior to man-made laminated and particle boards. As the shrinkage takes place along the growth rings, boards will tend to shrink across their width, and to warp or wind away from the heart side. (You can determine which is the heart side by looking at the end grain.) To counteract this natural tendency to warp, solid timber must always be veneered on the heart side, and in the same grain direction as the groundwork.

If there are any defects in the board, such as knots, nail holes or other blemishes, these must be chopped out, and replaced with pellets for small holes and plugs for larger ones. The grain of the pellets or plugs must run in the same direction as the grain of the board. For this reason, never use dowels to plug a board.

The best way to use a solid board as veneering groundwork is to saw it into narrow widths, and glue the strips together with the heart side alternately up and down to equalize the warping tendency. This is the principle of all core-constructed laminated boards such as laminboard, in which the core strips are only

7 mm. wide, and blockboard, in which the core strips are 1 in. wide.

If you make up your own laminated board from solid timber cut into strips, test the panel for wind. If it is not perfectly level, plane across the panel from high corner to high corner diagonally. Then tooth it with the teeth of a saw dragged across the surface in both directions, or with a toothing plane, to form a key for the adhesive and to detect any hollows missed by the plane.

The best solid timber for groundwork is Honduras mahogany, obeche, American whitewood or pine. Oak does not make suitable groundwork because flat-sawn boards are prone to warp, and quarter-sawn boards have a medullary ray figure which may show through the veneer.

Where possible, try to select a board which has been radially cut, quarter-sawn, so that the end grain shows almost vertical rings, then any future shrinkage will take place in the thickness, and this will be practically eliminated if only thoroughly well seasoned wood is used.

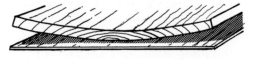

Fig. 58 Solid boards tend to shrink across their width and warp away from the heart side.

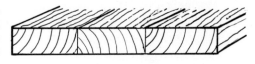

Fig. 59 Saw the board into narrow widths: the strips should be alternated with heart side up and down, so as to equalize the warping tendency.

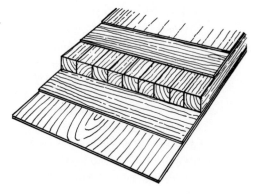

Fig. 60 Core strips, counter veneers and case veneers.

Having made the core slab from alternating strips and keyed them for veneering, you must now cross-veneer it with a cheap, soft veneer laid at right angles to the core direction. When dry, this veneer should also be keyed to receive the face veneer, which is laid in the opposite grain direction to the outer casing, i.e., in the same direction as the core strips.

The outer casing cross-veneer is applied to both sides of the core-slab and, in addition to the face veneer, a compensating backing veneer should also be applied.

Specifying groundwork

It is trade practice to state first the dimension that is 'with the grain'. A panel 18 in. × 24 in. would have its grain in the 18-in. direction, but a 24-in. × 18-in. panel would have its grain in the 24-in. direction. Therefore you should order a groundwork panel *opposite* to the predominating grain direction of your marquetry assembly, in the case of groundwork with veneered outer cases. In the case of solid groundwork specify the grain dimension in the *same* direction as the marquetry veneers.

There is little doubt that *laminboard* is the best groundwork for veneering and marquetry, but it is rather expensive. It is made as described above, but with core strips only 3 mm. to 7 mm. wide, and covered with stout outer casing veneers on both sides, laid in the opposite direction and ready to receive your face and backing veneers.

Blockboard is second only to laminboard for veneering. The core strips are up to 1 in. wide, with perhaps a fractionally greater tendency to warp in very large areas, but this can be completely ignored in the case of most marquetry panels. An 8 ft. by 4 ft. panel of blockboard veneered only on one side, on 12 mm. thickness, might have a slight tendency to warp due to the enormous pulling power of the veneer to one side; but a wardrobe door from the same material would be quite flat and trouble-free.

The same principle of construction is used in *battenboard*, except that the core strips are up to 3 in. wide and there is a greater tendency to warp in large panels.

Plywood is a much abused material and contains many pitfalls for the unwary. Most plywood is made from an odd number of laminations of constructional rotary-cut veneer, in 3-ply, 5-ply, 7-ply or 9-ply. For all practical purposes 3-ply would only be used as a core material to be built up into 5-ply for veneering. For small panels 5-ply would be excellent, but for lids, tops, doors and other hard-wearing surfaces, or large panels, the minimum recommended would be 7-ply, mahogany-faced. The act of veneering plywood unbalances it, by exerting a pull which will warp the panel unless a compensating backing veneer is laid. The golden rule is, therefore, always veneer both sides of plywood.

Where, for reasons of strength, you decide to use a panel of plywood with its outer casing veneers in the same direction as your marquetry face veneer, then an under-veneer must be laid to both sides of the panel, across the outer casing veneers, to enable your face veneer and compensating backing veneer to be laid in their correct direction, parallel with the long grain direction of the panel.

If, for reasons of economy, you have cut up a large panel of plywood, and discover that your panels have the wrong grain direction to suit your face veneers, these too must be cross-veneered to enable the face veneering to be done correctly.

The best plywood obtainable is 'marine plywood'; if 'marine ply' is not available, any exterior grade may be used with confidence.

Chipboard is universally used as a groundwork and should also be veneered two sides. If the panel has been made from two different grades of chips, lay the face veneers to the finer side, and the backing veneer to the reverse. If you have a panel of veneered chipboard, 'key' the veneer and veneer over it in the opposite

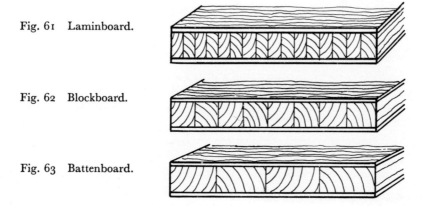

Fig. 61   Laminboard.

Fig. 62   Blockboard.

Fig. 63   Battenboard.

grain direction. Chipboard is free from all shrinkage, and most other defects.

The famous mass-produced ready-veneered panels Handiboard and Conti-board are veneered on chipboard.

For small panels, ends and plinths, and in-fillings and partition facings, *hardboard* makes satisfactory groundwork if veneered both sides; lay the face veneer on the canvas side and key the smooth side for the backing veneer. It also makes excellent core material which may be built up to form thicker panels, with veneered outer casings ready to receive the face and backing veneers.

Edges

It is not practicable to veneer the end grain of laminboard, blockboard or plywood. The usual practice is to cover the edges with a strip of solid hardwood called a lipping or facing. This may be from a strip of the same species as the veneer used for the face, but it is accepted trade practice to substitute moderately priced hardwoods for expensive ones, and those which are readily available for timbers which are difficult to obtain. African mahogany lipping is used on rosewood panels, and ramin or obeche on maple, sycamore or willow panels.

Lippings may be applied by pinning and glueing, or tonguing and grooving. However, a tongue is no longer necessary with modern adhesives. Corners should be mitred. If the edge of the panel is required to be shaped, rounded, bevelled, chamfered or fluted, the strip should be wide enough to allow for this machining.

The edges of all panels which receive hard wear, such as the front edges of lids, closing edges of doors, etc., should be lipped to protect the veneer edge, which may chip with rough handling.

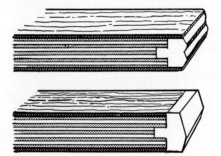

Figs. 64, 65   Edge lipping applied before and after veneering.

There are two sides to the question of whether to lip before or after veneering. The advantages of lipping before veneering are that veneers may completely cover the face of the panel, and the exact matching of one panel with another can be preserved without the edging separating them; that it is cheaper to apply the lippings before veneering; and that substitute timbers may be used instead of rare or expensive ones and the finished effect is that of a solid panel.

The advantages of lipping after the veneers have been laid are: special effects may be achieved, such as a picture frame effect (although the lipping will not match the veneer, which has been steam-treated); any chance of the lipping showing through the polished panel is eliminated (this can result if edge lipping is applied beforehand and is not rendered perfectly flush by sanding or planing the surface before veneering). The most practical advantage is that, with edge lipping, working surfaces will be able to suffer rough handling without any risk of veneer damage.

The idea is to make edge lippings which are applied after the veneers are laid part of the decorative scheme, either in contrast to or in harmony with the face veneers.

Shaped and Curved Groundwork

Here are some methods of making shaped or curved groundwork.

For slight curves, bandsaw the shape from the solid and save the waste pieces to use as cauls for laying the veneer.

For more rounded shapes, such as kidney-shaped tables, build up the groundwork from small wooden bricks, laid to a prepared template 'out of course', then bandsaw to shape.

More elaborate shapes may be built up from coopered blocks of wood.

The most common method is to laminate or bend by steaming and then clamp under pressure between curved bearers, with a greater curvature than required.

Preparation of the groundwork

For the craftsman who is determined to create a piece of work which will still be admired in a hundred years from now, who wishes to perpetuate his artistry and skill for the admiration of future generations, the preparation of groundwork cannot be stressed enough.

In a marquetry assembly, the grain direction of each component may run in a different direction. The general rule, that all face veneers must be laid opposite to the grain direction of the underlaying casing veneer of the plywood or blockboard, must be broken in *some* part of the picture. If the groundwork is for a panoramic picture 36 in. × 15 in., for example, for reasons of strength it is important to order a panel 36 in. long by 15 in. wide, with all the strength along the 36-in. direction. But for the purposes of the picture, we ought to have 15 in. × 36 in. groundwork, in order that the sea and sky veneers may run along the 36-in. direction *opposite* to the 15-in. grain direction of a cross-grained board. This is a problem which the marquetry craftsman often meets.

The answer is to lay sub-veneers, sometimes called under-veneers or counter-veneers, to *both* sides of the panel. This enables the craftsman to order a 36 in. × 15 in. panel, knowing that this will give the required strength and freedom from warp, to which he will lay cheap, soft, white veneers to both sides of the panel at 45° and parallel to each other.

There are technical reasons why sub-veneers are laid. If the grain of the groundwork runs in the same direction as the grain of a marquetry component, fine hair checks may result when the panel is laid. In the rotary cutting of veneers for the construction of plywood or the outer casing of laminboard, the action of the knife, in shearing the veneer from the log, causes fine hairchecks in the veneer, which run from the loose, open-pored under-side of the veneer, towards the closed-pore, upper side, known as the true face.

If the outer casing veneers of the plywood or blockboard are not 'true-face', the smooth side of the veneer was laid inside the glueline, leaving the coarse, open-pored surface outside; this tends to dry out and the heat applied during the original pressing of the panel dries out the moisture content of the facing veneers and may cause hairchecks.

If cheap-grade veneered plywood or outer casings are made of jointed veneers, instead of a single leaf, the joins may show through the delicate white veneers of the marquetry assembly.

Laying counter-veneers to both sides is the answer, and these should be light in colour, even grained and soft. Sycamore or obeche are ideal for this purpose. These sub-veneers should be true-faced, that is, with closed pores outwards ready to receive the marquetry assembly.

Prepare a weak glue size of ten parts of water to one part of glue. The glue may be lightened with flake white or titanium oxide, or one of the commercially available whitened glues may be used. Both surfaces of the panel are given a liberal coating and allowed to dry. The panel is then worked over in both directions with a toothing plane, with its neat vertical serrated edge finely adjusted; or the fine teeth of a hacksaw blade will do.

If edge lippings have been applied, they must be perfectly level with the surface. A superficial coarse sanding with glass-paper wrapped around a cork rubbing block, across the grain, helps to form a keyed surface, which in turn, prevents undue suction – the possible cause of blisters.

Test for a perfect level by using a straight edge in both directions.

The sub-veneers should have been given a coat of glue size and stretched as previously described (p. 57). This helps to form a glue barrier and prevents grain sinkage or the penetration of the glue to the surface during pressing.

Whether the panel has solid edge lipping applied before laying or not, it is a wise precaution to allow the panel to be very slightly over-size, in case the 'keying' tends to burr over the sharp, keen edges.

After pressing, the panel, which now has face and backing counter-veneers, is allowed to cure outside the press to restore its natural moisture content. To help this process, you should ensure a free circulation of warm, dry air to both sides of the panel.

The sub-veneered panel is then sized with glue on both sides, and allowed to dry out to prevent it from taking more than its share of glue in the final laying operation.

Keep the sized surfaces free from dust. Tooth them diagonally in both directions, or coarse-sand, and test for perfect level in both directions with a straight edge.

The panel may now be reduced to its correct size by planing the edges true and square, ready for the final pressing operation.

Continental muslin method

It might be asked, if one of the reasons for sub-veneering is the danger of the grain in a marquetry picture running in the same direction as that of the groundwork, what is the point of laying counter-veneers to both sides at 45° parallel to each other, if the picture has, for example, a mountain scene, also at 45°, in other words, parallel to the sub-veneers?

The logical answer to this – now common practice on the continent of Europe – is to lay a fine silk or muslin over the groundwork to take the marquetry assembly; this will permanently eliminate all possibility of hairline checks or splits developing. The muslin is applied on top of a coat of glue, and stretched over both sides of the groundwork to remove all wrinkles and creases. When the glue is tacky, another coat is brushed over and allowed to tack again. The groundwork is then ready for laying.

9 Laying and finishing

Before beginning the sequence of laying a picture, there are two things to be considered. Firstly, is the panel to be edge-veneered (or solid edge-lipped) before, during or after the picture is laid? Secondly, are the border veneers to be applied before or after laying the panel?

For certain artistic effects it is sometimes better to omit border veneers completely, but to use a contrasting veneer around the edges. For example, in a Chinese subject using a plain white sycamore background, a contrasting veneer in walnut would enhance the picture.

If the panel has not been fitted with solid lipped edges, it is usual to veneer the edges before the picture is laid. (Some marquetry craftsmen prefer to apply the edge veneers after the backing veneer is laid but before the picture assembly is laid.)

Strips of edge veneer are cut slightly longer and wider than the edges to be covered. The top and bottom edges are veneered first, using an impact adhesive. The veneer is pressed securely into position with a veneer hammer, seam roller or even the edge of a cork rubber block acting as a squeegee. The panel is held vertically on the cutting board, veneered edge downwards, and the surplus is trimmed off with a sharp knife. Then the two sides are applied in similar fashion.

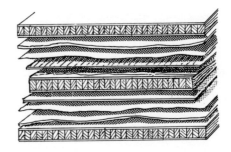

Fig. 66   The loaded press, showing upper and lower cauls, groundwork, heated linoleum sheets, polythene sheets, face and backing veneers. The glue blocks, etc., are omitted for clarity.

In this way, the edges of the backing veneer are concealed by the edge veneers; the ends of the top and bottom edges are hidden by the side veneers, and when the picture is laid, all the front edges are covered by the picture (see p. 144).

There are two basic laying methods, which allow for all the above considerations, and can be used whether the border veneers are to be laid with the picture or at a later stage.

Make sure that everything is at hand. If you are going to use heated cauls, either of wood or metal, these should be warmed but not too hot. A sheet of linoleum, plastic or rubber sheet and a wad of clean paper should be ready to be put in the press to equalize any slight unevenness of the veneers. A couple of sheets of polythene should also be handy, to prevent the glue surplus from sticking to the groundwork, the wad or the cauls.

The metal plates should be slightly larger than the groundwork. If the border veneers have been assembled to the picture, the complete assembly and the backing veneers should be oversize too, which will permit trimming them accurately to size afterwards.

It is better to lay the border veneers afterwards, by the more accurate and precise veneer hammer method (p. 175), in which case the picture veneers are allowed to overlap into the surrounding border margin of the groundwork.

The glue should be mixed in accordance with the maker's instructions, and the workroom temperature must be about 70°F.

Coating the groundwork. With the edge of a piece of veneer, coat the surface thoroughly and as thinly as possible in both directions. Bend down and look across the surface against the light to see if you have missed any single spot, and work over the surface again.

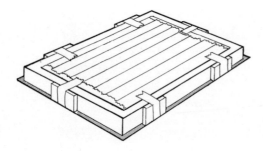

Fig. 67 The assembly ready for laying without border veneer; the glue blocks and tape are shown in position ready for simultaneous pressing.

If you are using a hot animal glue, or the traditional hot Scotch glue, the coating must be allowed to tack or chill so that the hand may be placed upon the panel surface without sticking to it. This is a safety precaution, for if the marquetry assembly is placed upon wet glue it will swell, buckle, or delaminate. Pressure alone will not cause a hot glue to run, therefore heat from cauls is essential to re-heat the glue and drive out any excess, and to evaporate the moisture from the work.

Sequence of laying a picture without border veneers (simultaneous pressing)

1 Place a warmed metal caul of aluminium or zinc, slightly larger than the groundwork, upon the bottom wooden caul of the press. Brush it with a soft brush to ensure that the surface is free from dust.

2 Lay the 'wad' in position. This may be clean paper, magazines or newspaper, or a sheet of rubber or plastic. Some people prefer to use a sheet of heated linoleum instead of metal plates and a wad of paper. The object of the 'wad' is to take up any unevenness caused by criss-crossing tapes, or slight variation in veneer thickness – a possible cause of blisters.

3 A sheet of polythene is laid in next, to prevent any glue from coming into contact with the wad or cauls. It also prevents newsprint from newspapers or magazines from off-setting on the white or pale-coloured veneers of the picture.

4 The *backing veneer* is placed on the polythene sheet, face side down. It should be $\frac{1}{4}$ in. larger all round than the groundwork.

5 The previously coated groundwork (temporarily covered with polythene to protect it from dust) should be tacky now. Remove its polythene cover and lay the groundwork directly on top of the backing veneer. Take care that it is placed centrally, with an equal $\frac{1}{4}$-in. margin of backing veneer all round. Glue blocks of $\frac{1}{4}$-in. thickness can be fixed in position, to ensure that this margin is even and accurate.

6 The groundwork should have four pencil lines diagonally drawn across from corner to corner; now place the picture assembly on the groundwork, face side (tape side, or paper side) uppermost. The picture assembly will be larger than the actual nett area it will finally occupy, and will be overlapping

into the surrounding border margin. However, it will be smaller than the groundwork and the pencilled guide lines should be rapidly aligned with the veneer surplus.

7 The gummed veneer tapes which have been fastened to the backing veneer should now be moistened, brought up and over, and fastened to the face of the picture to prevent any possible movement.

8 Spread a polythene sheet over the face of the picture.

9 A wad of linoleum, plastic or rubber, newspapers or magazines, etc.

10 The second heated metal caul.

11 The upper wooden caul.

12 Tighten down the bearers, to squeeze out all glue surplus.

13 After five minutes, tighten the press firmly down.

14 Leave the panel in the press overnight.

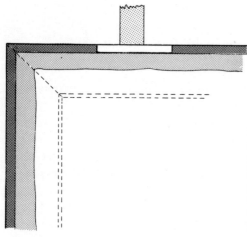

Fig. 68 Plan view of picture, without border veneers, in the press, showing veneer tape, glue block, protruding backing veneer, groundwork and surplus picture veneer. The dotted lines mark the eventual position of the fillet and border veneers.

Sequence of laying a picture with border veneers

This is a two-operation sequence in which only the bottom caul has any heat (optional) or wad. It has the advantage that, by laying the veneer on the lower caul only, the glue which is squeezed out at the edges is easily removed when the $\frac{1}{4}$-in. surplus veneer is trimmed off. Where veneers are applied to both sides of a panel simultaneously, the surplus glue squeezed from the uppermost veneer runs down the edges of the panel and requires scraping off later. This is why we only use the simultaneous pressing where the picture overlaps into the border margin but without borders being fitted. The surplus glue in that case is trimmed off with the picture veneer surplus.

1 A warmed sheet of linoleum is laid on the press on the bottom wooden caul.
2 A sheet of polythene is placed over the linoleum.
3 The backing veneer, face side downwards, is placed on the polythene sheet. The veneer should be $\frac{1}{4}$ in. larger all around than the groundwork.
4 The groundwork, already coated and tacky, is laid in position, with a sheet of polythene over it in case there are any glue traces on the upper caul.
5 The upper wooden caul is placed in position.
6 Tighten down the bearers.
7 Remove from the press after ten minutes to check that the panel has not moved. If any adjustment is required, put it on a flat surface and slide the groundwork into correct alignment. Return to the press and leave overnight.

When laid, the oversize backing veneers and the remnants of glue are trimmed off by laying the panel on a perfectly flat surface and cutting through the veneer surplus with a sharp knife. Paper the edges smooth.

At this stage, the veneer edges may be applied. The above sequence is then repeated, this time placing the picture assembly, face side (taped side) downwards.

1 The optional sheet of heated linoleum is placed on the bottom wood caul.
2 The sheet of polythene is laid in position.
3 The picture is laid, face downwards, with six small veneer tapes protruding.
4 The groundwork, tacky with glue, is carefully positioned with its corners precisely over the mitred corners of the border veneers.
5 Four $\frac{1}{4}$-in. glue blocks are placed in position to prevent the picture from moving, and the veneer tapes are moistened and brought over to adhere to the back of the picture.

6 A sheet of polythene is laid to prevent any glue traces on the upper caul from affecting the backing veneer.

7 The top caul is positioned, and the bearers tightened in sequence.

8 After ten minutes, remove from the press and check to see that the picture has not moved – any fractional adjustment can still be made by moving the groundwork.

9 Tighten down in the press and leave overnight.

The disadvantage of the double operation method is that if you veneer only one side, it is possible for the panel to warp if the second phase of the operation is postponed for some time, especially if the panel is not left under pressure. However, in practice it is usual for the backing to be laid in the morning, the edge veneering and trimming off tackled in the afternoon and the picture laid in the evening. The complete panel is then left under pressure for the ensuing 24 hours.

If a centre-screw type of book press has been used, it is advisable to work over the veneer assembly with a seam roller, or an electric iron set at 'silk', to force out all air bubbles and excess glue before placing the panel in the press because this type of press gives uniform pressure simultaneously, and may trap the surplus glue and air pockets.

Having explained at length the elaborate laying procedure necessary for the very best work, I must also stress that practically every amateur craftsman that I know ignores all the rules. He opens his book press, lays in the picture, plywood baseboard and backing veneer between the pages of a weekly magazine, and tightens the press down, without fuss or ceremony. The amateur prefers to use Croid Universal cold glue: if he manages to blister the picture, the panel can always be heated and relaid with an ordinary domestic iron. This careless attitude brings its own peril of the blistered panel; the correct sequence of operations ensures perfect results every time.

On removal of the panel from the press, the panel should be superficially cleaned of all surplus glue only, then allowed to stand on wooden blocks to permit a free circulation of warm dry air around it. The action of the glue will continue to work for several days, drawing the veneer down tightly to the groundwork and also causing grain sinkage. Allow the panel to cure for 3 to 5 days and do not attempt to level off the picture or remove tapes, etc., at this stage. What you can do is to examine the surface of it the panel for possible blisters, determined by tapping with the fingertips or a lightly held pencil. A hollow sound indicates the presence of a blister, which should be slit with a knife; fresh glue should be inserted and the panel laid back in the press.

If the border veneers have not been laid this can now be done; if the panel has not been solid-edge lipped, the edges must be veneered so that they are not visible from the front of the panel. It is preferable to veneer the edges of a panel before the face and backing veneers are laid.

The edges are veneered first, and then the oversize backing veneers are trimmed down to size by laying the panel on a perfectly flat surface, with the face of the panel uppermost, and trimming off the backing veneers with a sharp knife.

Use a cutting gauge to true the picture with the groundwork and remove the surplus veneer with a chisel. If this work is done immediately after removal from the press, the surplus veneer will peel off without difficulty. Apply the border and fillet border mounts with the help of the veneer hammer – or the rounded pene of an ordinary hammer – and an electric iron. Cut accurate mitres or joins to eliminate the danger of the panel slipping slightly out of true while in the press – the cause of many poorly bordered pictures.

The assembly is then placed in the press for a further period until dry, when the completed panel is laid face downwards on a clean board and the oversized border veneers are trimmed to fit.

Gummed paper tapes may be removed at this stage, by wiping them carefully with a sponge moistened in warm water; take care that the moisture does not penetrate the veneers, which would cause the end grain veneers such as burrs to delaminate unless a waterproof glue has been used. If you allow a few minutes for the moisture to penetrate the paper, the tapes will peel off easily. Take care *not* to use a metal scraper on damp veneers for this could result in iron mould stain on veneers with a high tannin content, such as oak, obeche, or afrormosia. If the panel is lightly brushed with a bronze wire brush, this will remove glue from the upper pores of open-grained veneers and provide a better surface for polishing. This is done while the panel is still slightly damp from the removal of tapes. Then stack the panel on its blocks, to normalize or acclimatize for a period of up to seven days, making sure that there is a free circulation of warm dry air around it. It is a good idea to weight the panel down with more blocks immediately above it.

During this period, it will fully dry out and adjust itself to workshop conditions before further processes are carried out.

By tradition, the marquetry cutter's work was completed when the motif or picture had been cut: he had no part to play in either laying or polishing his work. Even today, few professional marquetarians see their work through to its completion. The past decade, however, has brought about a break with tradition, and the complete marquetarian now needs to be the master of several skills; he also gains his reward in seeing his project right through to completion.

The polishing of wood has always been a business of rubbing by hand with beeswax, or, since the days of Louis XIV, the classic 'French polishing' techniques. Although period furniture must still be finished, in keeping with the style of the piece, with either a waxed or a shellac surface, the modern craftsman can endow his work with a protection and finish superior to anything known even a decade ago.

Until modern times, polishes have relied upon the evaporation of the solvents into the atmosphere, either by friction or by the chemical action of highly volatile solvents, as used in nitro-cellulose lacquers. The residue of polish which remained on the wood surface was not proof against heat, water or chemicals, and most finishes required careful handling. The celluloses, although they had disadvantages for the amateur woodworker, did make a hard film, and could be applied quickly with either brush or spray.

The last ten years have brought a revolution in materials and techniques for the surface treatment of wood. The plastics industry has now produced synthetic resins which rely upon chemical reaction, accomplished by the introduction of a curing agent, or catalyst, which itself remains stable, with little or no loss by evaporation into the atmosphere. As all, or most of, the body solids remain, subject to chemical reaction only, the resulting film is from five to ten times thicker than that obtainable by any other type of material. The new resins are not inflammable, are non-toxic, and they polymerize at room temperatures.

A marquetry polish must not alter materially the natural hue or colour tone of the veneers; it must provide maximum vividness, contrast and clarity of grain, texture and figure. It should have low viscosity, to allow the lacquer to penetrate into the wood pores for maximum adhesion, and to prevent dampness from getting behind the film. It should have a high solid content, forming a deep, tough film which will resist damage from abrasion, yet will remain flexible, durable and not brittle. It should retain an enduring sheen during normal usage. The polish should be resistant to heat, water, alcohol, chemicals, impurities in the air (brine near the coast, for instance). It should also contain an effective ultra-violet light absorber to filter out the detrimental photo-chemical action of the rays, which are present in both natural and artificial light and which cause some veneers to darken or fade.

To meet these requirements, it is the general practice today to finish marquetry veneering with either a nitro-cellulose lacquer or one of the new polyurethane or urea-formaldehyde resins, such as Furniglas Hardset, rather than the traditional French polish.

Preparation of the panel

The panel should have previously had all gummed paper veneering tapes removed, and been given a resting period of about one week to allow for grain sinkage and shrinkage. The surface must now be cleaned of all traces of paper, glue spots, dirty fingermarks, or any obvious unevenness of certain veneers. It is not necessary to render the surface perfectly flat and smooth at this stage.

There have been many advances in the world of abrasives. The new aluminium oxide papers are coated by an electromagnetic treatment instead of the traditional gravity-feed process. The result is that all the sharp edges and points of the abrasive particles are uppermost, giving a much better cut, with longer life and with no tendency to clog. These papers can be obtained down to the equivalent of 10/0 in polishing garnet paper and are ideal for levelling veneers.

'Lubrisil' paper contains its own lubricant, and acts like 'wet and dry' paper; it is excellent for marquetry. If it cannot be obtained locally, or from your specialist supply house, use the finest grade of garnet polishing paper, after preliminary work with the scraper.

Cleaning up

The initial cleaning up of the work is best done with a scraper – which many people find difficult to use, especially on end grain or difficult interlocking grains. These veneers require special care to prevent digging in or lifting of the grain. An excellent scraper can be made from the back of a hacksaw blade, or an old razor blade. The particles of fibre and tiny shavings made by the scraper are too big to clog the pores of open-grained woods and can be easily removed. The larger fibres of the more grainy veneers, which may have been pressed down flat during the pressing of the panel, can be cleaned off with the scraper.

The scraper can be used quite boldly on the veneers used by transatlantic craftsmen, using $\frac{1}{28}$-in. thick veneers, and on sawcut woods, which are usually from $\frac{1}{20}$ in. to $\frac{1}{16}$ in. thick. However, the craftsman using the thinner decorative veneers – which offer a far wider variety of woods to choose from – may be reluctant to use a scraper upon them and prefer to use an abrasive paper wrapped around a cork rubber.

Two very important points should be remembered if abrasion is used instead of the scraper. The pores of the veneer will tend to fill with the dust caused by rubbing, and dark dust may be transferred to the open pores of adjacent lighter veneers, which could cause discoloration when the polish is applied. Many natural woods, such as padauk, rosa peroba, rosewood etc., have a natural pigment which will stain the sycamores, chestnuts and open-grain woods like obeche. Secondly, the act of abrasion can cause a fuzziness of grain, or minute scratches on the surface of some veneers, which will blurr their vividness and be difficult to remove.

After the initial scraping or sanding, thoroughly brush the surface with a soft hairbrush to make sure that every trace of dust has been removed. Some craftsmen use a vacuum cleaner on their work after sanding, to make sure all dust is clear.

The fixative coat. Perhaps the most vital part of the whole sequence of polishing a marquetry panel, the fixative coat has two objectives. Firstly, it partially fills the open-pored woods, and completely seals the closed-pore, harder types. This is to prevent any particles of wood filler showing in the grain of the darker woods, if a filler is applied at the next stage of the polishing procedure. Secondly, it raises the grain of the veneers, to facilitate block-sanding of the surface without clogging the open-pored woods. The fixative coat is applied with much more care than one would normally use to apply a 'wash' coat of polish when polishing the surface of one type of veneer. It is not flowed on with a brush, because this may take the coloured pigment from certain woods and dye the surrounding lighter ones.

To begin, shape a cottonwool pad, soak the face of it in polish, then twist until the pad is damp dry, with only sufficient polish to cause the pad to glide effortlessly over the wood making a damp smear, rather than a flow of polish. Try to fill in the major portions of the picture carefully, and then continue with straight strokes, one below the other, until the surface has been completely covered. In practice, it is best to start on the back of the panel first, to get the hang of using the pad. Watch the pad, and if it begins to pick up any colour or stain from the wood, discard it and make a fresh one before working over the panel. Take particular care if you have used any dyed black veneer, such as black peartree, or the black sycamore often used in lines and bandings; it is usual to give all dyed woods a fixative coat of polish, even before cutting them into a picture. Allow the fixative coat to dry thoroughly and then work over the surface once again, this time with a more liberal coating, which can be brushed on, rather like paint – not flowed on.

A marquetarian of my acquaintance gives all his veneers a fixative coat of polish immediately after the stretching process, so that he can see the true colour of his woods as they will be seen in the finished panel. Polish always brings out the real wood tone – the full, rich beauty of their colours is never revealed until the polish is applied. By applying this coat to the veneers before they are cut into the picture assembly, he has the advantage that he sees the final colouring when making his selection; also, he is able to brush on his fixative coat just like an ordinary wash coat, with a brush, as he is only coating one veneer at a time.

The real value of this will be appreciated by all those marquetarians who have selected a veneer for a sky effect in a picture, and when it is eventually polished have been disappointed by its darkening or colouring in an unexpected way. Most important of all, the coat does more than prevent discoloration from other woods, it seals in any pigment in each veneer.

Grain-filling. As a general rule, it will not be necessary to use grain-filler on a marquetry picture, but there is no reason why it should not be used on other parts of the panel, such as the back or borders, or on surfaces such as table tops or furniture doors, where no marquetry decoration appears. If parts of a picture contain very open-grained woods, then they may require grain-filling. The correct type of filler to suit the polish film is usually supplied by the polish manufacturer. Heat-proof polishes require heat-proof fillers, and many 'two-pot' polishes also have catalyst-operated grain-fillers. There are also paste grain-fillers in a wide range of tones made to match the wood stopping supplied for filling open joins and gaps. Transparent paste wood-filler requires colouring with oil colour and is unsuitable for marquetry work.

The filler is rubbed into the grain with a circular motion, applied with a coarse rag across the grain and then allowed to set. When set, pack it tightly into the pores by rubbing across the grain, finishing off lightly in the grain direction. When it is thoroughly dry, paper the surface lightly with either aluminium oxide paper or polishing grade 9/0 garnet paper, then vigorously brush off the dust with a soft hairbrush or vacuum.

It must be stressed that this sequence is usually reserved for other parts of the work and not the actual picture; it is felt that if veneer is so open-grained that it requires filling it has no rightful place in a marquetry picture anyway.

Sanding sealer. The function of the sanding sealer is to prevent undue suction caused by the finishing coats of polish and to cut down on the number of coats of polish required; also, to seal the pores with a tough film which will permit the minimum of grain sinkage.

The correct sanding sealer is supplied by the polish manufacturer to suit the chosen polish. Use a camel-hair or squirrel-hair mop brush to apply the sealer; do not paint it on, but let it flow freely ahead of the brush to find its own level. Use plenty of sealer on the brush, working quickly without going back over the work while it is wet in case it pulls up.

Allow it two hours to dry, when the work may be lightly papered and the dust again removed by brushing or vacuum.

Hold the panel up to allow you to examine it against a strong light to see if the grain is now completely filled and sealed. If little patches of grain are still open, apply another coat of grain-filler. When it is dry, rub it down and apply another coat of sanding sealer.

Ideally, the work should now be left for a period of time to allow for thorough drying out, shrinkage of the marquetry joins, and grain sinkage. Both the filler and the sanding sealer will do their work and continue to harden and contract during this resting period. If it is not expedient to give the work time for this to take place, the remaining processes of polishing may proceed without delay, if the work is to be given a full grain finish.

Bodying-up. After about seven days, the surface will present a dry, patchy appearance, where certain veneers have soaked up the sealing coats, and appear not to have been sealed at all. Block-sand it with abrasive paper of the finest grade, to a perfectly level surface, and then brush off all dust as before. Now brush on a liberal flow of polish, aiming to get a level flow rather than ridges of polish.

In the polishing technique known as 'wet-backing', coats of polish are applied in comparatively quick succession, so that instead of forming separate layers, (which tends to happen with polyester and polyurethane lacquers), each coat bonds with the coat below. With this method, there is no need to wait about 24 hours for the first coat to dry completely: instead, after about two hours, when the drying coat has reached the stage at which it will no longer retain dust on its surface, you can brush on the next coat 'wet-backed'.

Allow 24 hours for the final coat to harden off, when it reaches the second stage of cure. In the case of melamine and nitro-cellulose lacquers, allow each coat to dry thoroughly, and then lightly sandpaper the surface before applying the next coat.

It doesn't really matter which type of white, clear polish you apply in two or three coats, once the marquetry has been filled and sealed – this part of the process is merely building a solid film of polish to protect the surface. The actual finish, whether matt or gloss, is decided later.

Fadding. The method used by most marquetarians, in the bodying-up stage, is to brush on two coats, and then abandon the brush for the fad.

When the first two coats are dry, allowing a 24-hour interval, lightly rub the surface down with 9/0 garnet paper, and brush it clean. Now prepare a mix of lacquer and solvent, half and half. Impregnate a small wad of cotton wool with this mix, and twist it until it no longer drips. Using the least amount on the fad which allows it to glide freely, reshape the fad and enclose it in a sound clean rag. Avoid too much polish on the fad or it will cause ridges in the film. Polish the whole surface in a continuously advancing spiral motion along parallel tracks. Work over the surface in this way half a dozen times, gradually increasing the time interval between successive coats, from a minute or two at first, after the first couple of coats, increasing to ten minutes after four coats, and half-hour intervals between coats five and six. This process is a patient one, unhurried, taking as long as is necessary to perfect a build of film.

Any slight ridges, fad marks, hairs or nibs of dust that may collect will be removed and smoothed away in the next phase. It must be stressed that fadding is only undertaken by those craftsmen who intend to create a full-grain, high-gloss surface, for the very best-quality work. The majority of marquetarians do not go to these lengths, but simply brush on two to four coats of lacquer, sanding down between each coat, and then finish off with very fine-grade 0000 wirewool, dipped in siliconized white wax polish, in straight strokes along the grain (which removes all polish brushmarks and ridges), and burnish off with a soft cloth.

However, I am describing the steps to perfection in polishing for the benefit of the serious craftsman; at any stage after the first sanding sealer coat, the man in a hurry can switch to the final wirewool and wax process.

Rubbing down. The protective film of polish is now complete – and is extremely hard. Modern methods of abrasion can now be applied to the surface, either to burnish it to reveal the true brilliance of the polish, or to achieve the beautiful satin matt finish preferred for marquetry.

Using a thick felt pad wrapped around a flat block, as a rubber for 'wet and dry' silicon carbide paper, apply a liberal amount of white spirit (turps substitute) to the surface and work in circular motion across the brushmarks – or scraper marks if the fadding process was not used – in the polish. Use firm pressure, and gradually straighten off with the grain, reducing pressure, keeping the surface wet with white spirit to prevent the paper clogging. If you can obtain it locally, ask for the new 'Lubrisil' type of electromagnetic silicon carbide paper, which contains its own lubricant, and may therefore be used dry. Wipe the surface and look for any patches or hollows in the film; these should be papered out using finger pressure only – not the block.

This felt block sanding with silicon carbide papers has now rendered the polished surface perfectly flat and level, free from all ridges, scratches and blemishes. But the minute fuzziness of the abrasive papering still mars the perfection we seek.

Flatting down. Dip a piece of soft cloth or rag in the flatting paste, and apply to the surface, using firm pressure in a circular motion. Work well into the corners, and along the edges too. As the paste begins to dry out, the cloth will start 'pulling' – but continue to rub, straightening out and reducing pressure. This smooths away all traces of abrasion.

A *satin matt finish* is much to be preferred to a high gloss. One can view the picture or work from many different viewing positions without having the beauty of the work ruined by reflected light. Others argue that a high-gloss finish is the most revealing of all finishes and only the very best craftsmanship dare carry such a gloss, as it reveals every defect. This, they say, is why nearly all amateur craftsmen – particularly beginners – apply a matt finish.

The matt finish is the easiest of all finishes to apply and is the one universally applied by most amateurs who take up marquetry for fun, rather than seriously as a craft.

Many amateurs complete the whole process of laying, sanding and polishing over a weekend, and wonder why their work does not compare with that of a craftsman who has taken the work phases in their correct sequence, patiently striving for perfection.

The easy matt finish does not provide the work with any of that faultless glass-like smooth quality, but does give some protection.

Professionals sometimes prefer the 'west-end' satin matt finish, which is gained by wetting the surface with turps substitute, and sprinkling it liberally with pumice powder, which is then brushed off vigorously in one direction, using a soft-haired shoe brush. This type of fine abrasion does remove brush or fad marks from a polish film applied quickly by either process, or by spraying.

However, there are many leading marquetry experts – the men who win exhibition prizes and trophies – who adhere to the opposite viewpoint, and we should respect their opinions because their work defies comparison. They feel that a matt finish does not bring out the true lustre and vitality of their work, the picture remains lifeless and dull. They argue that craftsmanship deserves the best finish attainable, defying the most minute and close inspection. They overcome the difficulty of light reflection by careful positioning of the finished work.

The *high-gloss finish* is arrived at, after flatting down with paste, by the application of burnishing cream, which is rubbed over the work in circular motions, lightly at first, to distribute the cream evenly to all corners and edges, then, with firm pressure as the cream dries, in straight lines across the picture, gradually reducing pressure as the gloss appears.

There are other forms of burnisher for different types of polish. French polish, cellulose and other types of lacquer can all be brought to a high gloss using brilliant gloss burnishing creams.

In this field of polishing, craftsmen learn by trial and error, and many develop their own tricks of their trade. One man applies four coats of lacquer and then uses a proprietary metal-cleaning polish, sold in pad form, such as Duraglit. This very fine abrasive polish removes the brushmarks from the polish film and provides a high-gloss finish; another excellent burnisher is fine-grade cellulose car-rubbing compound.

35 An Older
Civilization
C. R. Woodcock
Effective use of freak
sappy walnut foreground
light and shade to give
the picture depth and
realism. Note the fancy
figured pommelle
border veneer.

36 Godshill Village *Paul Jobling* First prize in the Marquetry Society National Exhibition, 1970, for the most original subject. Mr Jobling is a specialist in fine detail cutting, and has won the Rose Bowl twice. In this picture, every branch on the tree has been cut in, every brick and stone laid, and the bush to the left has been made by the 'fragmentation' process.

37 THE HAVEN *C. H. Good*   This picture won the Marquetry Society Rose Bowl. The sky and water are from freak blue mineral-stained obeche. The dappled sunlight and shadows on the far hills are achieved with sappy walnut. The selection of grain and shading of every leaf of the tree makes this a first-class marquetry picture. Note the unusual border surround.

38 LOCH HEID *N. Macleod*   This spectacular picture introduced two new techniques. Firstly the 'fragmentation' of tiny pieces for the tree foliage, fishing nets etc., secondly the long strips of varying woods used for the water effect, which enabled the boat reflections and highlights to be cut in, and the water given movement. Another feature was the clever use of mottled figure in the moirée willow used for the harbour wall.

39 INDIAN FISHER GIRL *Mrs G. M. Walker* This won the silver cup for the most artistic picture at the 1970 International Marquetry Exhibition. With the minimum of woods, mostly shades of walnut, on a sycamore background, this attractive portrait relies for its charm on simplicity and choice of woods.

40 HOMEWARD BOUND *S. H. Murrell* This Marquetry Society kit set is an excellent example of a low-horizon subject relying on the freak sky veneer to achieve its evening sunset sky appearance. This was especially attractive when 'sunray' Prima Vera with orange and red streaks was used.

41 ROYAL COAT OF ARMS BOX
A. Pollosch
Awarded the Marquetarian
of the Year Silver Cup at the
International Marquetry
Exhibition, 1970. The box
was beautifully decorated on
all shaped surfaces, and inside
the lid, with emblematic and
heraldic marquetry in rich
natural woods, expertly cut
and finished. It also won the
Marquetry Society Rose Bowl.

42 OFFCUTS *A. Gibbs-Murray* This abstract subject aroused considerable interest at the International Exhibition and went on to win first prize at the National Exhibition in the Beginners' Class. It is a perspective study using common woods and is an excellent practice picture.

43 CHAIN REACTION *A. Gibbs-Murray* The latest 'pop-art' abstract, shown at the 1970 International Exhibition.

44 THE GATES
E. Christopher
First prize at the 1969
National Exhibition. The
dramatic effect of the picture
being framed by the
silhouetted gates makes this a
most compelling subject.

45 WATER WHEEL
Miss M. Blunt
Snow scenes make good
marquetry subjects, especially
when glowing sunset sky is
used in contrast—in this case
Rosa Peroba. However,
notice how the lower border
veneer has not been applied
parallel to the groundwork.

46 Ye Olde Curiosity Shop *W. Dolley*   This is an Art Veneers Co. Ltd. marquetry art set and won first prize at the Marquetry Society National Exhibition, in the class for commercial kit sets.

47 THE KITE
N. A. Douglas
Any kind of bird picture is a popular subject for marquetry. 'The Kite' displays a careful selection of veneers, and cutting skill of the highest craftsmanship. One criticism which may be made is the use of a fiddleback figured sky veneer. The mottle which appears to run vertically destroys any sense of aerial perspective.

48 BAMBURGH CASTLE *Paul Jobling* 1969 Rose Bowl winner and first prize in Class I (Open section) of the Marquetry Society National Exhibition. This reproduction cannot do justice to the wooden picture. The freak obeche sky, tinged with natural blue mineral stains, sets the scene, and the very minute detailed cutting of every brick and line of mortar, the careful use of perspective and shadows give this picture realism. Mr Jobling makes his pictures from enlargements of his own transparencies to achieve photographic accuracy.

49 WHITBY HARBOUR *J. Dawson* Another prizewinning picture with photo-graphic realism, most unlike a wooden picture. Many marquetarians believe that this type of excellent craftsmanship does not give the raw material much freedom of artistic expression.

50 ABERSOCH HARBOUR *Mrs J. Holmes* This prize-winning picture again illustrates that harbour scenes make good marquetry subjects.

51 SEPTEMBER TRIO
John Savage
This delightful picture, typical cf
Savage's inimitable style, shows
artistic marquetry at its best.

52 CONTINENTAL SCENE
N. Macleod
Norman Macleod won first prize in
the Commercial Kit set class in 1969
with this Art Veneers Co. Ltd.
design, which he then proceeded to
elaborate upon. His now highly
developed 'fragmentation' technique
was used for the foliage, window
boxes, flowers etc., and he
pioneered the use of thin spill-like
strips for the water effect.

53 THE SHAPE OF THINGS *G. K. Thom* This abstract marquetry aroused
considerable interest at the 1970 International exhibition. Similar subjects
can be tackled by anyone who wants to try creating his own 'conversation
piece' from offcuts.

54 ELEGANCE
Miss M. Blunt
The Chinese style treatment of this subject with symbolic motifs is also an excellent marquetry exercise. Flamingos are popular subjects, but I wish the background had been one piece of plain white sycamore without the attempt to make the lower half appear as water (note the flamingos' legs) as no attempt to introduce naturalistic forms should be made when the motif is symbolic, and plain backgrounds are correct for Chinese subjects.

55 PINKIE
Mrs G. M. Walker
A low-horizon picture requiring a very strong sky interest, which is achieved by making a multi-piece background. Pinkie is a most charming subject and might have won the Rose Bowl in 1965 had 'Johnnie Walker' managed to find a one-piece freak sky. The fact that the sky is different both in tone, figure and markings at each side of the figure detracts from its value. Notice the clouds which have been cut in—this rarely achieves the desired effect. An artistic picture of great appeal.

56 NIGHT SKY *Israel* I once wrote to Alex Ephrat, that the true essence of marquetry was to let the wood do the work and tell its own story. He sent me this photograph of a night sky made from two matching leaves of Brazilian rosewood, one a tone darker than the other. On the horizon, the faint outline of a ship is silhouetted in the moonlight.

57 COCKER SPANIEL *America*
Anthony Guglielmo was introduced to marquetry after reading an article of mine in *Workbench* and he has become a gifted marquetarian, producing much fine work. This cocker spaniel's head won a certificate of merit in 1967. Note the ill-matched border veneers of white ash which do detract from the picture, and which can be rectified without difficulty.

58 BAZOUKI PLAYER *Yugoslavia* I bought this picture from a market stall outside the Palace of Diocletian at Split in Yugoslavia, from the man who made it; he followed me back to the *Dalmatian* and we asked the purser to act as interpreter. It has a Brazilian rosewood background, peartree flesh tones, padauk waistcoat and highly figured quilted moirée willow for the shirt. The freak natural markings of the willow make a most attractive shirt. It is knife-cut, using the 'window method'. The subject is Gushlor, the famous player.

59 CHINESE SCENES *America* George Kish of Illinois produces his
pictures by fretsaw, which he uses to advantage by leaving sawcuts
visible in his pictures and filling them with a contrasting wood stopping.
In many subjects this is a big advantage, particularly in snow scenes,
bird subjects, portraits etc.

60 HARBOUR SCENE *Denmark* This wall decoration by Herdis Möller-
Nielsen, a vivid and dynamic treatment with economy of woods and
cutting, is the type of modern decorative subject with great appeal
to the newly-married generation.

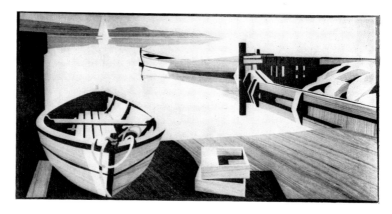

61 QUEEN NEFERTITI *Denmark*   The simple symbolic treatment of the ancient Egyptian Queen's profile typifies the modernistic style of Möller-Nielsen. This style would lend itself to creating profiles of other famous faces, especially in caricature.

62 Boy with Fish
East Germany
Made by E. Wendl, in the workshops
at Hellerau, Dresden. This modern
wall mural relies more on the
artistry and wood selection of the
marquetarian than on cutting skill,
as the individual pieces are quite
large—apart from the net which is
let in afterwards.

63 Venetian Court Scene
Italy
A masterpiece from the Trieste
artist Emanuela Marassi. The
mosaic foreground is carefully cut
in perspective and the subject
abounds in costumed figure studies
and animals. Delicate sand shading
provides the roundness vital to this
type of treatment. The lack of
shadows could be criticized.

64 THE THREE MUSES *Italy* The artistry of Emanuela Marassi, shown in this modern treatment of a musical theme, should inspire fresh thinking on the part of many traditionalists and diehards.

65 Tiger
East Germany

Gripping study of a tiger made by Max Gottschling of Leipzig. Tigers are always a popular marquetry subject using the minimum of woods, usually ebony and satinwood or ayan.

66 Dead Game
Italy

This most unusual subject is from the professional workshops of Emanuela Marassi of Trieste. Notice the crown elm background. This wall mural, 48 in. × 20 in., is fretsawn.

68 Horse's Head
East Germany

Another animal portrait by Max Gottschling of Leipzig. Notice the casual indifference to the knotty features of the background; the use of highly figured pommelle for the horse's flesh tones and the pronounced striped veneer for the neck; no attempt at the realism sought by English artists but Max is more concerned that the picture retain its wooden appearance than that it should look too much like a horse.

67 MOROCCAN JEWISH IMMIGRANT
Israel
Striking portrait by Alexander Ephrat,
who tries to achieve tonal contrasts for
successful portraits.

69 VILLAGE LANDSCAPE
France
Paul Louis Spindler is generally
considered the leading French
marquetarian and he is accepted
throughout the world as an
artist. In America the U.S.
Customs permit his pictures to
enter the country exempt from
duty as genuine works of art.
This landscape is typical of
Spindler's work, which is
fretsawn.

70 WINE HARVESTING
France
The perspective street scene is
another Spindler speciality;
notice in particular the
naturalistic people. Many of
Spindler's pictures contain people
or farm animals, and he achieves
wonderfully natural expressions
and attitudes with the minimum
of cutting, relying on artistic
flowing line.

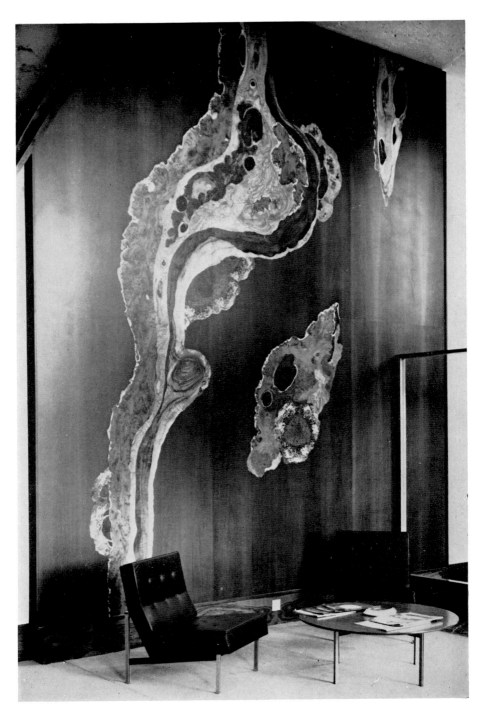

71 MODERN MOTIF *London*   In the foyer of Messrs Tersons' new building in London Robert Dunn created a massive marquetry panel, designed by George Ramon, in which the figure and peculiarities of the veneer are all important.

72, 73 WESTWARD HO! *London* Two of three large wall panels in architectural marquetry created by Robert Dunn, and designed by George Ramon,
to illustrate the early history of tobacco growing and its shipment. They are
installed in the reception hall at Granite House in Cannon Street, City of
London at the head office of Gallaher Ltd. The smaller panel portrays, in
the form of an open book, the famous passage from Charles Kingsley's story
of *Westward Ho!* In the three pictures there are more than 20,000 separate
cut pieces of veneer, cut from over 70 different woods. The book panel
measures $3\frac{1}{2}$ ft square.

74 ROBERT DUNN
One of the leading
professional
marquetarians, whose
work adorns many of
the public buildings in
all parts of the world,
at work on his 'donkey'.
Notice how the left hand
is used to turn the
veneers towards the
saw, the surprisingly
robust sawblade he uses,
and the delicate finger-
tip control on the handle
of the sawgrip. He
does not grasp this as
one would a fretsaw
frame handle, but
gently and with finesse.

75 Separating the sawn parts into a tray ready for sand shading and assembly.

10 Intarsia and decoration of furniture

The previous chapters have been concerned with the production of marquetry motifs and pictures by modern methods. The craftsman will also require to know the best methods of tackling the traditional and historic forms of decoration, in case he is asked either to restore a genuine antique or to make a reproduction piece.

A knowledge of the techniques may inspire the designer to create new forms of decorative treatment for modern furniture.

Inlay in solid wood

In the first chapter we saw that the earliest form of decoration was made by inlaying pieces in solid groundwork by chisel and shoulder knife. This is known as solid incrustation, and the finished work can be treated in many different ways: it may be carved in relief or planed, framed, etc. Multiple incrustation is possible, in which inlaid pieces can themselves be inlaid again. In addition to this, many other materials, such as mother of pearl, porcelain, metal and plastics, may be incorporated.

There are two methods of work. For old work which needs repair, the existing inlay shape is removed by chisel or router. A leaf of carbon or graphite paper is laid over a sheet of white paper, and placed over the routed section of the solid groundwork. Cover this with a second sheet of paper for protection, and tape them in position with gummed tape. Now, using a hammer, tap lightly round the contour to mark the outline on the lower paper. Alternatively, heelball can be used, as for a brass-rubbing. This imprint is then used as the design for cutting the required new section on the fretsaw.

The second method, for new work, is easier. The part to be inlaid is drawn, then cut out accurately to size on the fretsaw. The inlay part is then glued temporarily over its position on the

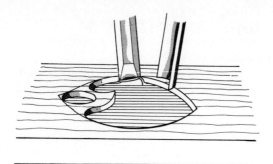

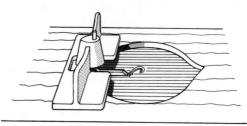

Figs. 69, 70   The groundwork is bored with expansive bits, the outline cleanly removed with chisel or gouge and levelled with router or router plane.

groundwork – taking care to cover any natural defect in the groundwork by the inlay, and also to see that the grain direction of inlay and groundwork are similar. If you find that the parts to be inlaid do not fit snugly into their allotted places traced on the design on the groundwork, they can be filed to shape with flat or key files and cleaned up with sandpaper until they all fit snugly together.

Bore out the groundwork with expansive bits, taking care not to exceed the required depth. Sharply and cleanly remove the groundwork with chisel or gouge, finishing the lowest level with router or router plane.

The parts are then brushed with glue, tapped gently into place with a mallet and pressed home with a wooden block and clamps. Take care to apply the glue sparingly, or it tends to squeeze out and may spoil the work.

The inlay can now be treated in various ways: it can be planed smooth and level; or it can be engraved, and left with the engravings open or filled with a contrasting wood stopping. The inlay may also be carved in high or low relief, or inlaid with smaller inlays of mother of pearl, ivory, metal or plastic.

Modern synthetic resin adhesives or impact adhesives should be used. Pressure should not be applied to mother of pearl, or it will break.

Solid overlays. In early fifteenth-century Germany there was a vogue of cutting out fretsawn or open-grille patterns and laying these patterns over solid groundwork, with the groundwork showing through. Sometimes the interstices would be filled with a contrasting paste called *niello*, a mixture of metallic sulphides used for decoration by the ancient Egyptians, but this filling tended to chip and drop out. Overlaying is still used today as a refinement of the solid incrustation technique just described.

There are two ways of doing this. Either the pattern is cut almost completely round, the whole overlay is bonded to the groundwork, and the cutting is completed with a chisel; or the inlaying can be done at the workbench and the complete inlaid board is then overlaid on the groundwork. This is particularly useful if it is not convenient for the work to be executed on site, or when the part to be inlaid forms part of a building on a vertical panel.

Reliefwork. The inlaid parts may be of such thickness that they can be carved in depth. If the carving is below the surface of the inlay it is known as bas-relief or deep relief. If the carved parts project above the surface this is known as haut-relief or high relief. When this work is applied to the creation of an inlaid picture it is called relief intarsia. Adam Eck of Egerland is

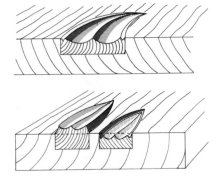

Fig. 71   The inlay may be planed smooth and level, or engraved, or carved in depth.

Fig. 72   Carved parts projecting above the surface and said to be in high relief (haut-relief), those below the surface in deep relief (bas-relief).

acknowledged to be the inventor of the technique, which was known as 'Prague work'. This type of work was also made in Paris by Fourdunois, and by Stoevesandt Karlsruhe and Heinrich Maybach, of Germany.

They enjoyed an international reputation and created works of great realism. They used the solid overlay technique, in which a solid board of about 8 mm. thickness would have other woods of different thicknesses inlaid, some 10 mm. or 12 mm. up to 18 mm. thick. The board, and the woods to be inlaid, were all cut out on the fretsaw and tailored to fit with chisel and file. Then the overlay board, with its fretsawn outlines removed, was glued to the groundwork – heart side down, to eliminate warping tendencies; any glue which seeped up into the spaces to be filled with the inlays had to be scraped clear.

The various thicknesses of shaped inlay parts were warmed up and laid in one by one and pressed until dry. Then the carver took over the work and carved the decoration in depth. This gave the opportunity to increase perspective, especially where the foreground detail was in high relief. Human figures in realistic costume were carved in crowded scenes. In some of the most spectacular and lavish work, the jewellery of women and the swords of warriors were inlaid in silver to heighten the effect.

The combination of relief inlay and marquetry offers great scope for the modern craftsman.

Layer relief inlays, also known as schraffito (hachured engraving), is used as a wall decoration, and consists of several layers of veneer in different natural colours, with the ornaments deeply chiselled in.

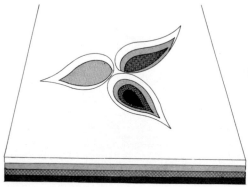

Fig. 73   Layer relief inlays.

The technique is straightforward although the drawings have to be specially designed to suit the medium. Four or five veneers of different colours are laid successively on plywood, and a corresponding thickness on the back of the panel to prevent warping. When the panel has cured, the side to be decorated is scraped – *not* sandpapered, which would dull the chisels. The design is traced on the surface and the depth of the ornament marked. Then the design is lifted by carving chisels which can remove one, two, three or four veneers to suit the design, and still reveal the lowest colour tone.

In other cases, to suit the chosen design, a repeating pattern of two woods can be laid, such as mahogany, sycamore, mahogany, sycamore, walnut (here the face veneer of the panel could be walnut), and it would only be necessary to devise an ornament in two tones, which could be shown as different depths.

Greatly enlivened surface interest is created by this method.

Engraved veneer inlays is one of the earliest known techniques, dating back to the 1500s. When the early intarsiatori made inlays with the shoulder knife, before the days of the bowsaw, they often found that the individual parts of a design were still rather large and something else was required in order to break up the detail still more and to increase the realism of their work. This led to engraving detail into the veneer with gouges and chisels, and filling the cut with a dark contrasting paste.

This led to far more elaborate work being imitated with indian ink and pen, and to a deterioration of the craft. However, it has been revived from time to time. For example, indian-inked etchings could not withstand surface treatment by sanding; but with the invention of the fretsaw it became possible to leave open sawcuts and fill them with a dark wood paste, which would still remain clearly visible when the surface veneer was sanded. Later, pictures were engraved by skilled engravers using fine chisels.

In the modern knife-cut techniques, minute details such as ships' rigging, eyelashes, etc., are often engraved with knife cuts, which are then filled with ebony dust, mixed into a paste.

Engraved tin inlays. During the rococo and baroque periods of French furniture design, there was widespread use of engraved tin inlays in a lustrous dark rosewood or ebony background veneer. These tin ornaments were then lavishly engraved and filled with a dark-coloured paste. These filled engravings helped to make a pleasant transition and soften the contrast between the black of the veneer and the silvery shine of the polished tin.

The technique is as follows. The design is traced on the solid groundwork, and the contours are marked and then chiselled with carving chisels, after being pre-cut slightly with the gouge or socket chisel to prevent breakage at the sharp edges. The chiselling is undercut, not vertical, to form a key and thus prevent the poured metal from lifting or falling out at a later date. After the contour is removed, the ground of the ornament part is routed out. The lower level is then roughened to form a key for the metal.

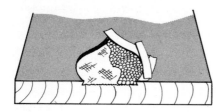

Fig. 74   Engraved tin inlays, with edges protected by asbestos strips.

Three parts of tin with one part lead are heated, and the molten metal is poured from a spoon into a bucket of cold water, while the water is beaten with a whisk or birch broom; this converts the metal into tiny kernels. These are dried, then pressed into the chiselled-out parts of the ornament. Asbestos strips are placed along the edges to protect the wood, which is also given two coats of polish, and the kernels are now worked over with a hot soldering iron, to and fro, until they melt and fuse together. More are added, until the routings are filled, and the tin is slightly heaped above the surface. The depth of this work is usually about 1 mm. and the filling is quite a rapid process. When cold, the tin is levelled with a scraper or plane, then sanded with emery or garnet paper. When it is perfectly level and smooth the tin can be worked upon by the engraver, making richly engraved patterns which are then filled in with a dark contrasting filler. The work is finally polished in the usual way.

Lacquers and plastics. The same technique can be used with any meltable material such as bronze, plastics, plaster or lacquers. Coloured polyurethane lacquer, which is a resin with a catalyst curing agent, is mixed and poured cold. It sets in two hours but while it is setting it is possible to emboss further embellishments in the lacquer, which in its turn is filled with a contrasting coloured lacquer. As polyurethane sets very hard it is possible to level and smooth it in the usual way with scraper and fine abrasives. The famous scaglio works of plaster were made in a similar way.

Boulle work

André Charles Boulle (1642–1732), architect, sculptor, cabinet-maker, engraver and marqueteur, did not invent the style of furniture decoration with which his name has become associated. Cabinets of Italian provenance which used to be imported into France up to the middle of the seventeenth century were embellished with marquetry of mosaic type in ivory, wood, tortoise-shell, silver and many other materials. But Boulle developed this technique to a high artistic level, using tortoiseshell and polished metal such as brass, copper, tin, zinc, silver or pewter. To enhance the effect he sometimes underlaid the almost transparent tortoiseshell with red or green paper or silk, and the metal parts were richly engraved and filled with a contrasting paste filler. Boulle's work, continued after his death by his four sons, has been widely copied under the name of 'boulle work' (often mis-spelt 'buhl').

Boulle work consists, for the most part, of sheet brass inlaid into a tortoiseshell background (*première-partie*, or inlay of the first part) and its reverse, tortoiseshell inlaid into brass (*contre-partie* or counter-inlay). The inlay of the first part was considered to be the more artistic and was more greatly prized. On a piece of ebony furniture, the first part and the counter-inlay were often combined, and this is generally known as counterchange marquetry. In other pieces, choice veneers were used instead of the shell, and these were also counterchanged with the metal ornament.

In order to provide a final touch of magnificence, after the metal inlays had been richly engraved and filled, Boulle ornamented the work with exquisitely modelled gilt bronze appliqué figures, masks and acanthus foliage. He also used bronze mounts at the corners of cabinets to withstand strain, and metal mouldings to prevent the marquetry from loosening. Unfortunately,

Boulle's work suffered a great deal from adhesion troubles, and one whole wall at the Palace of Fontainebleau, which was covered in this work, subsequently delaminated.

In order that both parts of the work could be counterchanged, it was necessary to cut the materials on a saw table with a perfectly vertical saw blade. This resulted in the marquetry having a noticeable join around each part of the design. Boulle accentuated this fault and converted it into a feature of the work by filling the saw cut with a dark contrasting paste.

However, for this reason, for the very best work it became fashionable for only the *première-partie* (of tortoiseshell with brass or silver inlays) to be used. The actual inlaying of the metal parts was then carried out by the bevel or conical cutting process, with the saw slightly angled to take up the thickness of the material and the saw cut. The *contre-partie* would then be unusable as a counterchange, but could be saved for another project.

The working process used to be to make a 'sandwich' of the edge-jointed tortoiseshell, metal sheet to the same thickness with the design pasted on, and a thick veneer underneath to provide some resistance to the saw and take the saw swarf. The cutting of this 'sandwich' presented a great difficulty as the saws became brittle with metal fatigue and easily snapped, and unless the pad was compressed firmly and allowed to dry very thoroughly before sawing commenced, the metal tended to buckle.

Fig. 75   Boulle (buhl) inlays. The *première-partie* on the left shows a brass ornament in a tortoiseshell background; the *contre-partie* is the reverse combination of the materials.

However, in modern times, if annealed metal sheet and plastic sheets of imitation tortoiseshell or mother of pearl are used, on power fretsaw machines with metal-piercing blades, the work is easy and very rewarding.

The metal to be used must first be annealed and roughened on the side to be glued. The roughening is done by dipping the metal in weak nitric acid for a minute, or by scraping with a rasp or toothing plane. A specially viscous glue is required. In the past it was made from strong Scotch glue with the addition of lime and glycerine, stirred in when the glue was hot. This was then liberally spread on the pre-warmed metal parts in the thickness of syrup and a few days were allowed for this to harden, before the work was removed from the press.

However, with modern synthetic adhesives, the problem of adhesion does not arise; any adhesive recommended for bonding metal to wood will serve, especially the epoxy resin types with hardener, such as Araldite.

The tortoiseshell – taken from the back of ocean turtles – is prepared into small plates, which are brittle and break easily when cold. They are heated and rendered supple in hot water.

After sawing, the parts are separated and assembled on a copy of the design, which has been glued ready to receive them. The joints are then filled with wood stopping paste and allowed to dry under light pressure. Then the inlays should be cleaned and bonded to the wooden groundwork with any of the recommended adhesives. After laying, the paper design must be cleaned off the face side of the work. The metal parts are finely sanded and burnished, and then the work can be richly engraved, and the engravings filled with a contrasting paste to enhance and enrich the whole decoration.

Metal inlays

In the Regency period, brass inlaid into rosewood enjoyed a popular vogue and this is one of the forms of inlay work most widely practised today.

Because brass sheeting is very hard, a special composition bronze is required for veneer work, in the proportion of about sixty to forty of brass and copper. Care has to be taken that the bright yellow-gold of the brass is not darkened too much by the addition of the copper, which is soft to cut, but darker in colour.

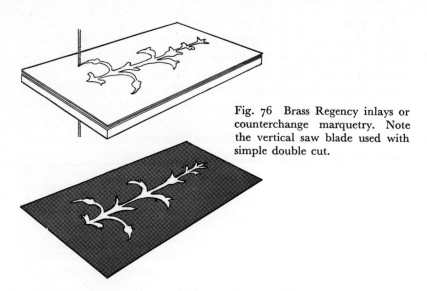

Fig. 76 Brass Regency inlays or counterchange marquetry. Note the vertical saw blade used with simple double cut.

Alternatively, use specially annealed brass or soft brass. It is possible for the layman to tell whether the brass is hard, 'half-hard' or soft by turning up one corner of the sheet to test its springiness. If the corner stays turned up without resistance, the material is soft. If it turns up but with a great effort, it is half-hard; if by finger pressure alone it is very difficult to turn it up at all, it is hard brass.

It is possible for the layman to anneal his own material. Anneal the brass by marking one surface of the sheet with ordinary household soap, and then hold it with tongs over a flame until the soap markings turn brown and either bubble or sizzle. This is a rough-and-ready indication that annealing temperature has been reached.

This is one of the tricks of the masters, to aid correct annealing. Do not plunge the metal in water, but allow it to cool off naturally. To clean the metal and dull it ready for roughening, prior to bonding it into a sawing 'sandwich', another master's device was to wipe the surface to be glued with an onion, or wash it with vinegar to degrease it.

The surface may be roughened, as in boulle work, by dipping in weak nitric acid, or with a rasp or toothing plane.

Now glue the brass and the rosewood veneer together, with the design on the rosewood, the brass underneath, and a piece of

$\frac{1}{16}$ in. plywood or stout veneer under that again, to take the swarf of the saw and to offer a resistance to the brass, which may bend or tear. Metals take much longer to bond into this sandwich than wood, because the glue cannot penetrate. Synthetic resin adhesives, such as epoxy resins with hardener, are no good for this purpose, because the sandwich has to be separated after sawing and unwanted parts discarded. Therefore an adhesive which will bond the parts strongly together during the sawing operation, yet will subsequently allow separation (when the sawn parts are warmed up on a hot plate) is best. The traditional type is Salisbury glue, which is Scotch glue mixed with plaster of Paris.

Some professionals dispense with glue for making the sawing pad, and rely on stapling or pinning the parts together. If pins are used, they nip off the points and heads, to prevent splitting the veneer, and as the pins have to be nailed in the middle of the pad too, they must be clearly marked, to avoid breaking the saw when cutting.

With modern power-saw equipment, it is possible to saw up to six inlays at one cutting from the pad, but beginners should be content with making the first experiments with a single inlay, using robust grade 3 or grade 1 metal-piercing blades.

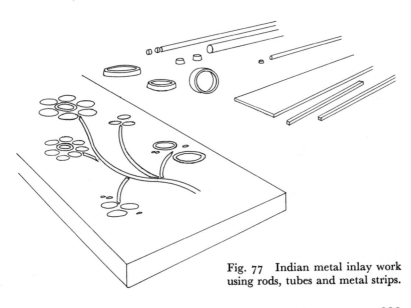

Fig. 77 Indian metal inlay work using rods, tubes and metal strips.

Indian metal inlay work. The beauty of Indian inlay work is achieved by using different metals as line ornaments. Brass, copper, tin, plated zinc and silver are commonly used, inlaid into ebony or Indian rosewood.

The design of the line ornament is traced on the groundwork, which is usually solid timber about $\frac{1}{4}$ in. thick. As the woods are dark, they are first given a brush coat of a mixture of water colour and glue, which dries quickly and is easily washed off afterwards. The design shows up well against a surface so treated. From very thin-gauge metal sheet, 0·5 mm. to about 1 mm. thick, cut narrow strips about $\frac{1}{8}$ in. wide and cut these strips into lengths about 3 to 6 inches long – the lengths will vary according to the pattern chosen. Circles can be cut from tubes of the same gauge as the metal sheets, slicing the tubes into $\frac{1}{8}$-in. sections. Wires, rods, and other extruded sections may also be cut into $\frac{1}{8}$-in. pieces, so that you can get a whole variety of shapes. All these sections are roughened with a file and given a slight bevel or mitre downwards, to form a key when laid. The groundwork is routed out or carved to a depth of $\frac{1}{8}$-in. or drilled or bored to accommodate the rods and wires. The metal parts are then glued and hammered into position, with a piece of hardwood laid over them to prevent damage. Any modern synthetic glue may be used, and this is applied, with thin veneer strips used on edge, into the grooves and chiselled dado lines. All holes, open joins, etc., are filled with a wood stopping paste made of sawdust from the groundwork and glue. The work should be left for about three days to harden off thoroughly. To clean up, the surface is filed level, then scraped, and emery cloth is used to smooth the metal parts, followed by garnet paper.

The best effects are achieved with brass, copper and tin, although silver is sometimes used.

Wirework inlays. In many respects this technique is similar to the Indian metal inlay method, except that the entire decorative treatment is executed with wires.

The initial preparation is the same, the design being chiselled or routed out to a depth of $\frac{1}{8}$-in. The width of the groove is determined by the width obtained by entwining two wires tightly together like a cord. This cord-like twist forms sufficient key to retain them in the grooves. The grooves are glued, the wires are laid in so that they come just above the surface, and

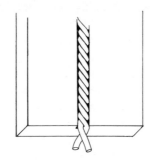

Fig. 78 Wirework inlays: two wires are entwined and the groove filled with contrasting paste.

they are hammered into the grooves. The gaps at each side of the wire are filled with wood stopping paste made from the groundwork sawdust and glue. The panel is allowed to dry, filed and emery-papered smooth, and finished with garnet paper in the usual way.

Overlaid metal inlays. The modern marquetarian who has a powered fretsaw machine can bond three veneers together, with alternating grain direction, to form a plywood with an ebony or rosewood face decoration (which may be composed of a four- or eight-piece match). The desired pattern is cut on the fretsaw machine to accommodate the metal parts, either of the Indian sheet metal types or, if a router is used, the wirework types.

The assembled inlay is then filled with the sawdust stopping and cleaned off on the back, and the whole panel is overlaid on to the eventual groundwork, where the final stages of filling the face side, levelling and polishing are completed.

Bombay mosaic

This craft, also known as Piqué, uses various woods of strong colour, even dyed woods, but with a preference for ebony and sandalwood, together with ivory, tin, mother of pearl. All these various materials are cut into sticks of triangular or rhomboidal section, glued together into a solid block under pressure and allowed to dry, before being sawn across the grain into 'veneers', each identical in pattern. This technique was revived at Shiraz in Persia, whence it travelled to Sindh and from there to Bombay, where works of this kind are a popular export item. When these veneer-thick slices are sawn, they are then arranged together and glued edge-to-edge on a paper sheet to form a pattern.

The whole assembly may then be overlaid to a groundwork in the usual way, and cleaned up, levelled and polished.

Simple mosaic-type borders and star patterns may be made this way.

Mosaic inlay bandings. The best way to describe the making of an inlay banding is to take an actual example. To begin, you have to produce the various units which form the decoration of the banding. Strips of solid wood are planed or machined into lengths of about 10 in. and of triangular, rectangular or rhomboidal section. These strips are carefully assembled, and glued together to form hexagons, octagons, stars, chessboard patterns or any of the scores of different geometric patterns used in these attractive bandings. Also machined are the pieces of wood which will appear between these geometric motifs in the finished bandings.

Having completed the first phase of the operation, you now have hundreds of glued sections about 10 in. long, with a pattern on their end grain.

Now select two or three veneers of alternating colour, such as boxwood, ebony and boxwood (which are very commonly used by banding makers) in dimensions of 1 metre ($39\frac{1}{2}$ in.) long by 10 in. wide. These three veneers are glued together in a press to form a thin three-ply. Another 'ply' of three similar veneers is also prepared.

Now the work of assembling the actual banding-block is commenced. The first 'ply' of three veneers is placed on the assembly bench, and the 10-in. solid core strips of pre-formed geometric pattern, together with the separation pieces of solid wood which have been carefully fashioned to make a complete mosaic, are glued in place side by side. Finally the second 'ply' of three veneers is placed on top of the assembly, which is then wrapped in paper, securely tied with string and held under strong pressure until dry.

Then the 'block', as it is called, is untied, the paper removed, and it is sawn on the circular saw into veneers. The saw has specially segmented teeth to provide a minimum sawcut and the sawing has to be most accurately executed to avoid wandering. The resulting veneer banding is about $\frac{1}{20}$ in., and every cut with the saw produces an identical banding. In modern mosaic banding mills multiple gangsaws are used.

It is also possible to produce mosaic bandings entirely from veneer, without using planed or machined sections for the centre. For example, one could glue together, to form a ply, nine ebony and sycamore veneers; these are sawn into veneer thickness, turned on their sides and glued together again, to form miniature chessboards when sawn through once more.

The home woodworker can produce some very attractive but simple mosaic inlay bandings in this way.

Purfling for musical instruments is of the three-line type and is made from one layer of boxwood, holly or sycamore between two layers of ebony or dyed black peartree. These three veneers are glued together, and when dry, sawn into $\frac{1}{16}$-in. strips. Purfling is used extenively for the decoration of violins, guitars, mandolins, and lutes, etc.

Inlay motifs. Ready-made decorative inlay motifs are available in all traditional styles. They have a stout paper glued to their face sides, with the back toothed flat ready for laying.

There are two ways of using these motifs. Firstly, by letting the motif into the veneer assembly before it is laid and while still in veneer form. In this way the complete assembly, including the motif, will be laid in one operation. Secondly, the traditional method is to mark the contour of the motif on the solid ground, and then rout out the base to the correct size and shape but slightly less in depth than the thickness of the inlay motif, to ensure that when pressure is applied it will bear directly on the motif; this extra thickness also allows for sanding.

After laying, the paper side is moistened and scraped off, and the motif sanded level with the surface. It is then given a coat of shellac to seal in its natural colours, or in some cases dyed black, before general polishing or staining of the surrounding veneers. This protects the inlay against discoloration, on the one hand, and the delicate white, soft, or open-grained veneers in the rest of the assembly from any possible discoloration picked up from the black parts of the inlay.

Musical instrument sound-hole inlays. Unlike the normal decorative inlay motifs which are sawn from veneers, these sound-hole inlays for guitars, mandolins, lutes, etc., are made in similar fashion to Tunbridge Ware mosaic (overleaf). However, they are also supplied in a wonderful range of decorative styles, some including mother of pearl or pearl acetate, in veneer thickness and are used in exactly the same fashion.

Tunbridge Ware (English Mosaic)

The early Victorian period saw the flowering of the unique English decorative marquetry, English Mosaic, otherwise known as Tunbridge Ware.

The craft was localized at Tunbridge Wells in Kent, and its origin can be traced to a craftsman named Jordan, about 1680–85, who practised a form of crude inlay in geometric form. The mosaic process used was exactly the same as that practised by the ancient Egyptians, and the Indian 'Bombay Mosaic' (p. 221) and the Italian 'Sorrento Ware'. The early forms produced simple geometric patterns which could be laid side by side to form continuous borders, or used as motifs on small boxes, trays, etc.

One of Jordan's apprentices went to the nearby town of Tonbridge and revealed his secrets to the old-established firm of George Wise, a family business of wood turners. The Wise family immediately produced a version of English Mosaic as stickwork turnery, turning the assembled blocks on a lathe into fruit bowls, salad bowls, etc., instead of sawing them through into identical repeating patterns.

The discovery of chalybeate springs at Tunbridge Wells made this town a fashionable spa, and this brought the English Mosaic firms to congregate at Tunbridge Wells in 1720, when inlays of shells and flowers, embellished with borders in ebony, green and white were produced for the decoration of tea caddies, workboxes and similar wares.

Long strips of carefully shaped small sticks of various coloured natural woods were assembled together and glued under pressure into a solid block. On the end grain a mosaic pattern or picture could be seen, and this was sawn transversely into veneer thickness across the grain, into a large number of exactly identical designs.

The resulting English Mosaic veneer would be laid as a marquetry assembly, exactly as any other form of marquetry. The process was inevitably a rather wasteful one, as the thickness of each sawcut resulted in valuable wastage.

The craft was raised to its zenith of artistry by about 1850 when the leading craftsmen tackled such advanced subjects as landscapes, and perspective scenes of buildings encircled with floral borders. The mosaic type of decoration was often used in conjunction with conventional marquetry, such as a central motif of birds cut in marquetry, with a border surround of roses in Tunbridge mosaic.

In 1851, Thomas Barton won the Gold Medal at the Great Exhibition, with a picture of North American bird life containing 129,500 pieces cut from 33 different natural woods.

The mosaics were used in Victorian times to decorate table tops, tea trays, firescreens, tea caddies, work boxes, snuff boxes and similar small trinkets, in the form of bandings, borders and as decorative motifs.

The vogue for Vandyke patterns became popular, featuring cubes and squares, which when viewed provided illusory perspective effects. Lozenge shapes, feather, rope, ladder, domino and many other patterns were developed for inlay mosaic borders.

Around 1840, inspired by contemporary 'Berlin-work' patterns, for embroidery in cross-stitch on squared canvas, there was a craze to reproduce these in wood, in the form of flowers, birds, butterflies and animals, which called for the use of even smaller tesserae, cut from up to 150 different woods.

The craftsman would begin with a water-colour painting of the finished picture. He would then prepare a chart on squared graph paper, with ten squares to the inch.

To make a small picture 10 in. × 8 in. for example, in the scale of 32 to the inch, this would require, on graph paper of ten squares to the inch, 320 squares horizontally by 256 squares vertically, if it was a landscape picture – total, 81,920 squares. Therefore the original water colour painting would have to be 32 in. × 25·6 in. In fact, the smaller the tesserae to be cut, the larger the original picture required for copying.

The next step was to cut strips of wood about 12 in. to 18 in. long by 1 in. wide, and the same thickness as the required tesserae, in this case 1/32 in.

The chart is carefully read, square by square, from the left-hand bottom square upwards, and strips of various woods to match the design are placed one on top of the other and glued into a solid block. When dry, this is cut into veneers $\frac{1}{32}$ in. thick; about ten cuts would be made from the assembled block, allowing for the expensive wastage due to the sawcut. Only one of these veneer cuts is required for the picture, so one block would yield sufficient veneers – all of the first column in the design – for ten 'master assemblies'.

Having now produced the first column of the graph (ten times) the second column is assembled from 1-in. wide strips again, glued, and sawn into veneer. The process is repeated until 320 such columns have been cut. These are now carefully assembled together to form a master block, 256 veneers high by 320 columns wide, and after glueing and allowing to dry, a total of ten master blocks could be prepared from the strips cut, each block being 12 in. × 18 in.

These blocks, when completely dry, are finally sawn transversely into complete Tunbridge ware pictures, each identical picture exactly corresponding with the original painting. Up to 150 pictures could be cut from one master block, and as a total of ten master blocks could be made from the original preparation, something like 1,500 identical pictures would eventually be produced.

Infinite care and patience were required of the craftsman, in carefully assembling the strips of profiled sticks to correspond exactly with a prepared graph and chart of squares. The process from beginning to end might take three months to complete.

One interesting feature of Tunbridge ware was the use of green oak, which was a freak of nature caused by an oak fungus (*Chlorosplenium aeruginosum*). This green wood was natural, and the silver harewood used by the Tunbridge Wells craftsmen was also considered to be so, as the chalybeate springs had a similar effect on sycamore, which was turned into the familiar silver-grey harewood by traces of sulphates in the water.

Sorrento Mosaic in Italy is identical in most respects, except that the Italians made use of dyed veneers, but the Tunbridge mosaics were always from natural woods.

One exception to this was the ingenious 'marblewood veneer' produced in Tunbridge Wells, made by collecting all the shavings and dust from the many natural woods used in the process, and loosely rolling them in glue. They were then compressed into solid blocks and sawn into decorative veneers, to be used for the decoration of tea caddies, work boxes and the like. After 1880 the craft rapidly deteriorated, and completely died out.

An attempt at revival in 1920 was made without repeating the success of the 1850 period, though Tunbridge ware is eagerly sought by collectors today.

'Lines' are usually the same length as bandings, i.e. 1 metre (39½ in.), and are simply strips of one wood, such as boxwood, cut to a special gauge and width. Tradition has laid down that lines are mostly cut from boxwood or dyed black in either flat or square section. Flat lines are of veneer thickness and vary in width from $\frac{1}{16}$ in. up to $\frac{1}{4}$ in. Square lines are from $\frac{1}{16}$ in. to $\frac{1}{4}$ in. both in thickness and in width. Of course, this applies to commercially available lines, but craftsmen can easily cut their own lines from a wide variety of veneers.

'Stringings' are usually very fine lines, that is veneer thickness in both width and thickness, and either boxwood or black. In application, lines and strings are used to enliven the surface of a panel without too much effort. Very often the outer edges of a door panel are crossbanded with veneers; that is, the grain of the veneer runs short-grain towards the outer edge all around, and the veneers of the main door panel are bordered by a fine line or string, to separate them from the surounding crossbanding.

A more harmonious effect can be gained by using blending tones of woods for lines rather than black and white contrasts. For example, sap walnut lines look well inlaid upon dark figured walnut panels.

It is important to examine the 'true face' of inlay lines, as they may offer a different appearance when polished, even when cut from the same leaf of veneer, if they are accidentally turned over.

There are two methods of inlaying lines, stringings and mosaic bandings. In a finished surface, the method is to use a cutting or mortice gauge and chisel, to provide a groove of the right width and depth, which should be less than the thickness of the line to be inlaid. A scratch stock may be made from two pieces of hardwood to form a handle, into which a cutter is fixed (in two notches on the inner surfaces of the wooden handle) formed by sharpening an old sawblade. This cutter, made to the exact width of the required line, is screwed into the handle, which is worked up and down over the surface until the wood is removed between the lines cut by the cutting gauge. The tool ceases to cut when the desired depth is reached.

The double knife. Professional veneer preparers make up a special knife for the inlay of curving lines. This knife may take the form of two specially prepared hacksaw blade ends, fastened into a wooden handle and bound firmly together, or two ordinary craft knives welded together. The blades can be separated by washers, as a simple means of adjusting to the required line width.

By inserting a piece of the actual line to be inlaid, between the tips of the two blades, an exact groove can be cut. This enables the craftsman to grasp the knife and to follow, free-hand, some very intricate and curving lines. I once had the task of inlaying coloured lines about $\frac{1}{16}$ in. wide, to represent garlands twining around Harlequin and Columbine figures, and attached to balloons. It was quite simple with the double knife to cut the exact outline following a curving course, which would have been impossible without templates in any other method.

The double knife also permits the actual lines themselves to be cut from any material, to any desired width.

The need for a double-knife cutting gauge will become apparent when the scratch is used across the grain; unless the fibres have been cut with the twin knives, it will be most difficult to remove. If the banding to be laid is wide enough, the unwanted wood between the twin lines may be removed by the rebate plane. Modern power-tool equipment, such as a router spindle, will make this task much easier for the craftsman new to inlaying.

When it is required to bend a line around a curved groove, for example in an oval panel, the line can be formed to the correct shape without breaking, either by steaming it or by steeping it in hot water and bending the line across a dowel or heated pipe, working it backwards and forwards and gradually increasing the curvature of the line. As it dries out, it will retain its new shape.

Providing the groove is less than the thickness of the line or banding, it needs only rubbing in with the veneer hammer. However, it is safer to apply pressure to the inlay by laying another line of equal width immediately above the actual line to be inlaid, and applying the pressure to that. Indeed, one of the tricks used by craftsmen of the past was to glue the veneer from which the line was eventually to be cut to a waste veneer before cutting the line. When the groove had been cut, the required line was laid in the groove, with the waste veneer line above it to receive the pressure. After the work was set, the surplus veneer was easily planed off to a level surface.

Attention must be paid to the type of bandings used in curved work. Traditionally, the 'herringbone' pattern is used, which may be separated by knife down its middle, when the curve is negotiated, and the pattern remains unaffected. This 'pattern-slip' is caused by the greater radius around the outside of the curve.

When inlaying square section lines at the corner of a panel, or around a curved edge, a special method is used. Battens are hand clamped near the edge to both sides of the panel, and nails are driven into them at regular intervals, around which wet string is wound, from above to below the panel, binding upon the curved line. As the string dries it presses the line tightly into position.

Insetting the line into the veneer assembly. It is, of course, more economic and simpler to assemble the lines or bandings with the other veneer faces, and lay the whole marquetry as one operation. When cutting in a pattern of lines which cross each other, always tape one line into the veneer first and then cut the next groove, rather than attempt to cut criss-crossing twin lines in the veneer. This would result in tiny cross-grained pieces breaking off. When cutting a curved line, use a pair of dividers of which one point has been flattened and sharpened into a cutter. Do not place the other point on the work, but put a scrap of veneer beneath the point, taped to the surface to stop it moving.

Lines, strings and bandings should be the same thickness as the veneers, when they are taped into marquetry assemblies. If the veneers are a shade thinner, sandpaper the bandings level with them before pressing, to avoid the risk of blisters. Use a rubber or plastic sheet in the press, as a further safeguard against blistering.

Parquetry

Parquetry is the branch of decorative veneering in which small geometric shapes are assembled to form a pattern. This is then overlaid as though it were a single veneer, in the same way as marquetry assembly. Precision and accuracy are essential in cutting parquetry, as the smallest error in cutting has an accumulative effect and multiplies with every piece of the pattern. However, special techniques have been devised to minimize the difficulties, and provided you carry out all the processes the resulting parquetry should be perfect.

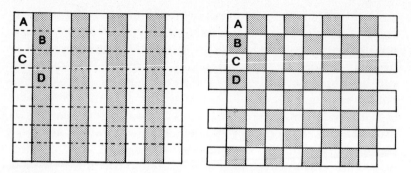

Figs. 79, 80 The chessboard. Use nine strips of two
contrasting woods; alternative rows are moved over one
square and the surplus end squares discarded.

One of the simplest forms of parquetry – and very good
practice – is the common chessboard. To make a chessboard, first
select two contrasting veneers, not black and white which would
be too tiring to the eyes in play. The brown or red tones of laurel,
rosewood, mahogany or walnut are best for the dark tones, and
antiaris, satinwood, sycamore, maple or avodire make good light
tones. Purpleheart and ayan, or rosa peroba and silver harewood, have also made up well; if a more figured appearance is
desired, walnut burr and bird's eye maple look very attractive, or
pommelle and quilted maple.

Nine 1½-in. or 1¾-in. strips are cut, 14 in. or 16 in. long. If you
have a perfectly straight edge and a very sharp knife, you can
dispense with the next phase; but craftsmen usually prefer to cut
these strips oversize, compress them between battens and shoot
the long edges with a plane, just 'kissing' the batten with the
plane. This ensures two exactly parallel, true edges.

Now edge-to-edge joint them with a fast-setting glue or impact
adhesive, or hold the strips (assembled alternately light and dark)
together with paper tape. The work is now turned and the cross-
grained edges are trued up with a try-square, straight edge and
sharp knife. Then, with a metal template to determine the exact
width which was used when cutting the original nine strips, the
assembled strips are carefully cut across the grain into eight
strips in the opposite direction. These eight strips are also cut
slightly oversize and planed to size.

Now move strips 2, 4, 6 and 8 forward by one square to bring the light and dark squares together as required for the chess-board and edge-join the complete assembly. Keep the strips pressed against a straight edge to ensure that the chessboard is perfectly rectangular. Next, trim off the unwanted 'ninth squares' which protrude at the end of each row. Now fillet border and border surrounds may be fitted, mitred towards the centre, and the surplus pieces discarded. The whole chessboard assembly is then securely taped together along the joins with gummed veneering tape, which will pull the work tightly together as it dries out. If required, inlay mosaic bandings may be fitted before assembly, between the strips, and round the outermost squares before fitting the border surround.

Diamond parquetry. There are very many geometric combina-tions possible in creating a parquetry pattern, but two of the most popular traditional types will be explained in detail to demon-strate the theory.

For best effect, quarter-cut striped woods are most effective, and great use is made of pronounced stripe, as in sapele, which has interlocked grain giving a high degree of light reflection.

The old masters used tulipwood and rosewood, but these woods relied more on a striped marking in their figure. Experience has shown that quartered woods such as sapele have the additional lustre which imparts a surface interest and increases the appeal.

There are two different types of diamond parquetry. The first type is where the grain direction is contrived to run parallel with the left-upper and right-lower sides of the vertically elongated diamond, alternating in adjacent diamonds to run in the opposite direction (right-upper, left-lower sides of the diamond). In the second type the grain direction is made to run along the axis of the diamond in one piece and at right angles to it (along the other axis) in adjacent diamonds. It is all a question of cut-ting accurately, to a fixed width and to precise angles.

For diagonal diamonds, select two matching leaves of sapele and prepare a metal template to the required width of the dia-monds, say 1 in. wide, by 18 in. long. Using the template, which must have a perfectly straight edge, cut one sheet of veneer into ten or twelve long strips 18 in. × 1 in. If you want precision, you could prepare the strips oversize, compress them between battens and shoot the long edges with a finely adjusted plane down to the exact width required. However, for this purpose we will assume that you have gained sufficient experience to cut the strips to a template, with accuracy. Put these strips on one side.

Now place a protractor on the second veneer sheet. With the base line placed along the grain, mark off an angle of 60°. Place the straight-edge template along this 60° angle and cut a number of 1-in. strips (which will appear diagonal-grained). Assemble one of the straight-grained strips with a diagonal-grain strip next to it, and repeat this pattern until all the strips are taped together.

Then place the protractor with its base line along the join, and mark off 60° angle again, right across the alternate strips. With the straight-edge template to provide the correct width again, cut the assembly into strips once more. This time, in the same way that the chessboard strips were moved along by one square, row 2, 4, 6, 8, etc., are moved along by one diamond. The whole assembly is then taped securely together with gummed veneering tape.

Trim off the parts of diamonds and odd shapes which you will find all around the edges, by placing the straight edge along the tips of the first row of diamonds. You will now have an over-all parquetry pattern of diamonds with alternating grain in diagonal directions.

The procedure for right-angled diamonds is similar. Lay the protractor with its base line along the grain on the first sheet of sapele, and mark off an angle of 30°. With the template, cut the first sheet into 1-in. strips at 30° to the grain direction. Put these strips aside, which we will call 'A' strips. Lay the protractor along the grain on the second sheet of sapele and mark off an angle of 60°, and with the template as a guide, cut this into 1-in. strips 'B'.

Assemble strips A and B alternately with gummed paper tape. Now lay the protractor base-line along the join, and mark off a 60° angle. Cut across the assembly, again using the template, into 1 in. strips 'C'. Now take each alternate row of diamonds and move them along one piece and you will see that you have now completed a parquetry pattern, where the grain of each diamond is alternately vertical to the axis and horizontal to it.

Place the straight edge along the tips of the first row of diamonds, and trim off the odd-shaped pieces at the outside edges.

Using basically the same procedure, but by varying the angles, a whole variety of different patterns can be achieved. The

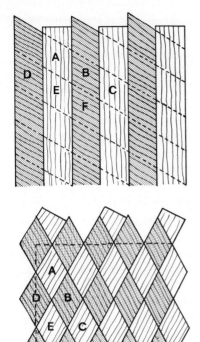

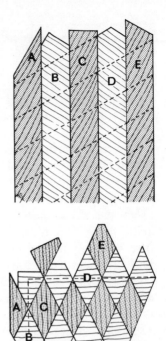

Figs. 81, 82 Diagonal diamond parquetry.

Figs. 83, 84 Right-angled diamond parquetry.

popular 'cube' type of illusion parquetry is also created from diamond shapes.

Louis parquetry. The elaborate Louis XV marquetry furniture often featured diamond or cube parquetry made from tulipwood, rosewood or amaranthe, into which exquisite floral marquetry decorations would be cut, surrounded by a boxwood scrollwork with a cross-banded border surround. The floral decoration and scrollwork would be cut into the cubes or diamonds and not on an oval panel, with the result that the cubes or diamonds were seen showing between the minute details of the petals, leafwork and ribbons.

To achieve this effect, the background parquetry is made and glued to a strong paper backing. This is then regarded as if it were a single veneer, and is used in the normal bevel cut or series-cut fretsaw techniques.

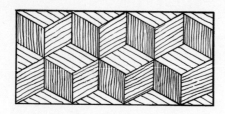

Fig. 85 Louis 'cube' parquetry, famous for its optical illusion.

For small work, it is possible to remove a section of the parquetry from the assembled leaf, and after the floral marquetry has been assembled into it, to replace it in its exact position in the larger assembly.

Line and dot parquetry makes a very attractive pattern. It is a trellis pattern of diamonds formed by diagonal crossing inlay lines, carefully mitred at the intersections. A small black dot was made at each of the four 'V' angles formed by the intersection, and sometimes a black diamond appeared in the centre of the larger parquetry diamond, with two diagonal cross saw cuts separating this into four smaller diamonds. The larger diamond was assembled with black lines as before, mitred at the inter-sections.

Trellis parquetry was the most elaborate of all forms of parquetry but did not rely on geometric precision as in the other forms. Each individual cube or diamond or oval unit was a picture in miniature, yet when the repeating unit was assembled to completely cover a surface, the over-all effect was of a trelliswork pattern entwined with flowers.

The 'units' were cut in mass production on the donkey, but can be cut on the modern power fretsaw machine. A unit would consist of a well-designed cube, oval or diamond, about 1 in. or $1\frac{1}{2}$ in. over-all, with an ornately curving or shaped scroll outline about $\frac{1}{8}$ in. wide, encompassing a small floral motif, such as a pimpernel. The trellis could be cut either from boxwood or dyed black peartree, the parquetry from basswood, magnolia or plum, and the floral motif from padauk and tulip burr.

Oyster parquetry, a peculiarly English type of parquetry, is made from saw-cut veneers cut from small stems or limbs of trees with contrasting heart and sapwood, such as walnut, laburnum, olive, lignum vitae or blackthorn. When this slice was cut at right angles to the grain, the roughly circular shape was trimmed to form an octagon, and these were assembled together to form a parquetry pattern.

234

Parquetry of this type makes a very attractive border surround, or a centrepiece ornament in an otherwise plain panel, or it can be used to cover a surface completely.

If the slice of veneer was cut at 45° tangentially, producing an oval section, with a more substantial sloping grain, which was less likely to lift when laid, these were cut into elongated octagons or irregular polygons, which were joined to form the distinctive oyster parquetry.

When the oyster veneers are first cut from the tree, they should be stacked in the same sequence as they were cut, so that they can be used to form matches. The stacking is done with small strips of wood between each veneer to allow a free circulation of air. The veneers are allowed to season in this way for a considerable period.

When they are seasoned, it is wise to glue a sheet of paper to one side, and coat the other side with glue size, before using the oysters as they are almost end-grain in texture and very brittle. They also have a tendency to cockle, and should therefore be interleaved with polythene sheets and kept under weights between boards until ready for use.

Oysters should be laid by caul pressure.

Mother of pearl inlays. Complete surfaces such as table tops have been covered in mother of pearl, although this is an exceptional use of the material. It is best used sparingly to highlight a surface.

There are four different types, the most popular being the goldfish type which possesses a wavy figure in white, yellow, blue, pink and green when viewed in changing light from different directions. Pure white mother of pearl is rare, and seldom used. Iris mother of pearl is perhaps the most colourful, being a speckled green with twisting lines of green, blue, grey and black, and marked red tinges. Black is a very rare type, which is speckled like the iris type. The most likely ones to be found today are the iris and the goldfish.

Mother of pearl will not withstand pressure at all. The usual procedure is to saw and file the ornament to shape, and locate it in position on the groundwork, marking its position with an awl. The veneer is then cut with the knife and chiselled out, and the mother of pearl inserted with hand pressure only, glued in with fish glue or leather glue to which plaster of Paris has been added.

Ivory inlays. Ivory can be sawn with the fretsaw, and perhaps finished with a file. Pure ivory has a cream to yellowish tone and also has annual rings similar to wood; it needs to be protected against humidity changes, and, when fresh, must be carefully seasoned and dried. It is used for inlay work in thin strips and plates. Because of its transparent nature, the basewood must not be dark, and the glue must also be colourless or lightened.

In ancient times, ivory was tinted green or red and used to depict foliage or parts of birds or fruit.

It must never be subjected to pressure, and is laid in the same way as mother of pearl.

Plastic veneers. Most of the traditional materials such as tortoise-shell, mother of pearl and ivory have been faithfully imitated by the plastics industry, and more recently we have seen the introduction of plastic laminates, and photographic reproductions of veneers in plastic. Most of these laminates are made of several very thin layers bonded together under heavy pressure. To the casual inspection such plastic sheets are of a uniform thickness, but in fact a microscopic examination shows them to vary quite a few thousandths of an inch. As the plastic surface cannot be scraped or planed without damage to its appearance, it should be carefully tested for accuracy of gauge before use.

As almost all materials can be cut with a power fretsaw, plastic sheet such as Formica presents no difficulty. When cutting a long joint, do so in the running direction of the board, determined by the roughened underside of the plastic sheet.

The actual cutting must be accurate, as plastics cannot be pressed together or stopped or otherwise treated like wood. Use metal-piercing blades for the actual sawing; you will find only by experiment how many layers can be cut simultaneously. When the inlay is assembled no surface treatment is possible by way of levelling – hence the importance of checking the gauge first.

Pietra Dura. This kind of inlay work was much in vogue in Renaissance Florence, about 1600, and had a revival in France under Louis XIV. Sometimes called 'hardstone work', it consists of the inlaying of cut and polished semi-precious stones in ebony or walnut, combined with ivory, mother of pearl, tortoiseshell, metals, and gilded bronze appliqués, with exotic woods also used as background decorations. The stones are cut into tesserae and assembled, in the same way as veneers, into beautiful designs featuring such subjects as birds, flowers and butterflies in vivid natural colours. The stones used were agate, amethyst, lapis lazuli, onyx, carnelian, breche d'aleps, black marble, griotte, jasper, tortosa brocatello, chalcedony, sarrancolin, yellow siena, vert des alpes, red porphyry and malachite.

Nowadays, patterns are cut on the fretsaw from marble or onyx, obtainable in sheets about $\frac{1}{4}$ in. thick and assembled into a solid groundwork, or overlaid on a plywood or laminboard groundwork. Coral, shells, pebbles and stone chips of various kinds are often used in conjunction with semi-precious stones, with highlights of mother of pearl, to form decorative works of mosaic.

Mosaic decoration. The small pieces of coloured material used in making mosaic decoration are known as tesserae. These may be simple materials such as a sorted and graded collection of beach pebbles, but generally the best mosaic materials are made of glass, ceramics or porcelain tiles. Venetian glass tesserae are available in 80 different colour tones, permitting a wonderful range of colour gradation, shadowing and other subtle effects. Venetian glass is solid, impervious and although very strong, is easily cut and shaped, and is slightly translucent. They are usually sold in $\frac{3}{4}$-in. squares with 225 tesserae of the same colour per sheet.

Italian ceramic tesserae are brightly glazed on a clay backing. These are porous, lacking the colour gradations of Venetian glass, but come in about 40 colours and in smooth, mottled or striped glaze. They are for surfaces where there is no heavy usage, being mainly decorative, and are available in the same sizes as Venetian glass.

The best and most expensive are the Byzantine tesserae, made from Venetian glass and available in small, irregular half-inch sections. They are made in thousands of shadings, but only 150 are commercially available. They are sold by weight, and about two and a half pounds are needed to cover a square foot of area.

Porcelain tiles are available in 2–in. up to 6-in. squares, and may be cut into smaller pieces to suit the work. Mosaics are cut to fit the design with tile nippers. The tesserae are assembled on a sheet of Kraft paper printed with the required design; then the spaces between them are filled with a special cement. When it is dry the whole assembly is turned over on to a glued baseboard. As soon as the glue has set, the paper can be damped and scraped off. Alternatively, the tesserae can be assembled directly to the groundwork, which will have been traced to receive them, and brushed with glue as the work proceeds. Then the gaps between the tesserae are filled with cement, which is poured over and levelled off.

Mosaic decoration in conjunction with veneers is one of the latest Italian trends.

There are two ways of doing the background: one in which the lines of tesserae are in straight rows in both directions, in which case light, plain tesserae are used so as to make the motif in the centre more prominent; in the other technique, the 'contour' background, the lines seem to have motion, and flow outwards from the motif towards the edges in swirling waves, laid to the contour of the motif.

There is also an element of symbolism in the use of the actual tesserae to represent special features: triangular shapes for grass, rectangular shapes for water, and so on.

Swirl and symbolic backgrounds are used in imaginative contemporary and abstract art forms in the mosaic field. When used in conjunction with wood, there are two methods: a solid groundwork can be routed out to take a mosaic ornament, or veneered plywood can be fretsawn to a design, then overlaid on a more substantial groundwork. The plywood thickness should equal that of the tesserae.

Wood mosaic. There have been two recent developments in wood mosaic. Imitating closely the techniques and designs used for Venetian glass and Byzantine glass mosaic, small pieces of solid wood are sawn into irregular $\frac{1}{2}$-in. squares, or odd shapes, assembled to a pattern on Kraft paper with glue, and the spaces between the tesserae filled in with plastic wood or Polyfilla coloured black or left white. The whole design can be overlaid on a plywood groundwork under pressure. When dry, the paper is sanded off. The beauty of wood mosaic is that it may be finished with ordinary wood surface treatment and polishes.

Many other materials, such as glass, can be used in conjunction with wood mosaic, if the wooden tesserae are thicker and the finished work is sanded down to the level of the other tesserae.

The other development is a form of veneer mosaic.

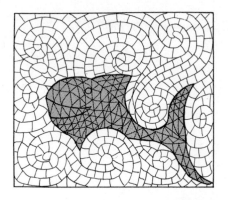

Fig. 86 Veneer mosaic
decoration.

Collect a number of different exotic veneers, cut them into strips ¼ in. to ½ in. wide, and then cut these strips into any irregular shapes or snip them with scissors into irregular rectangles, triangles or squares. These can now be assembled on Kraft paper and overlaid as before, or laid directly to the groundwork and filled in with a contrasting paste stopping. An alternative method is to use veneered hardboard, which is easier to handle in small pieces.

I introduced a form of impressionist mosaic a few years ago, using veneers of many colours, in strips like pipe-smokers' spills, about ¼ in. wide and 8 in. long. Your chosen design should have a grid of ¼-in. squares superimposed upon it, and a corresponding grid covers the groundwork, which is brushed with glue just around the section being worked. With the tip of a spill – matching the colour in the corresponding design square – placed on its square, a knife blade is held across the spill about a quarter of an inch from the tip and gentle pressure is applied. The veneer parts, leaving the tesserae in place exactly where required. By turning the grain direction in various ways, and laying the veneers either face, it is possible to create pictures of startling effectiveness. For example, the leaves in a tree can be given scores of autumnal tints; perspective is made easier because you can graduate the tonal changes with distance; and sky and water effects are given movement by using contour and swirl backgrounds. In addition, when veneer mosaic is polished the surface appeal is greatly enhanced by the light reflection of the hundreds of small irregular tesserae.

11 Repair & restoration of veneered furniture

Almost all furniture made from panels veneered over solid timber, unless correctly built and subsequently maintained, will eventually be in need of restoration or some form of surface repair. Apart from accidental damage and extremes of climate, the very dry conditions of the modern centrally heated home aggravates the damage. The treatment will be considered under three different headings.

There is the superficial damage to a polished surface caused by wear and tear, which can be repaired by polishing procedures. Then there is the damage to decorative veneers, inlays, bandings and ornaments, mostly resulting from loss of adhesion at the glueline. The commonest problem with old furniture is that of the groundwork, which may be swollen or shrunk, causing twisting, warping or splitting. We will deal with the three problems in reverse order.

The fault of most amateur restorers is that of over-restoring, of trying to improve. It should be recognized that evidence of age is something to be desired, not eliminated. The natural patina achieved by years of careful wax polishing, intermixed with layers of atmospheric grime and dust – these are welded by nature into a finish which cannot be copied easily by the tricks of the polisher, but can easily be removed or damaged by an over-enthusiastic restorer. Interference with this patina on the original veneers can quickly demote a genuine article in the antique class to a much lower-valued piece classified as 'restored'.

The amount of restoration necessary is usually found to be in proportion to the age of the item, but this is not necessarily any indication of its value, other than perhaps sentimental value. There was a large amount of junk made a hundred years ago!

Another point to consider is how far the restoration may be justified. For example, it may be possible to simply re-lay a blistered veneered surface to a table top; that will look perfectly satisfactory – for a time – whereas a permanent job may require extensive repairs to the groundwork, involving a much more lengthy process. Are you justified in making the larger restoration? Where does a restoration end and a renewal begin? A point can be reached – if the process is carried too far – where the original façade remains, but the carcass and groundwork have been virtually renewed.

It may also be discovered that previous attempts at restoration have been made or, even worse, some previous enthusiast may have added ornamentation or decoration alien to the original – a problem museum restorers are often faced with.

The general principle is: try to be faithful to the original; avoid inflicting damage to the patina; balance enthusiasm with restraint; know when to stop and never undertake work beyond your ability.

The first job of the restorer is to assess the damage – its type, extent and cause – and to consider this in relation to the nature of the old finish, the identity of the wood and whether a partial or complete repair is necessary.

Sometimes there may be more than one way of effecting the repair; the choice will depend on the equipment and ingenuity and experience of the craftsman.

Solid groundwork

The chief shrinkage of timber takes place around the annual rings as moisture dries out. Consequently, if a board is cut radially from the log, with the rings at right angles to the surface, the shrinkage takes place mainly in the board's thickness. On the other hand, if a board is cut across the crown of the log, the shrinkage will be most marked across the width, and incidentally accompanied by warping away from the heart side.

If this natural shrinkage is prevented by cross battens, screws, etc., the board will either twist or split or both.

Similarly, if solid wood has been used to make a mitred frame the joints usually open. Also, where wood of different species, with varying rates of shrinkage, has been used, or when the panel has been constructed incorrectly in a way which does not allow

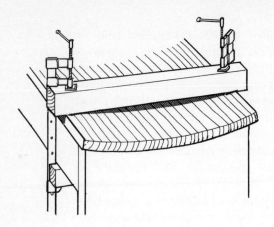

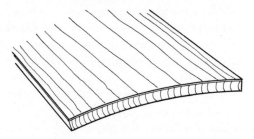

Figs. 87, 88   Treatment of warped groundwork. Veneer the heart side with the grain to counteract warping.

for this movement, the result will be a defective groundwork which must be repaired and rendered flat. Where necessary, the construction of the piece must be altered to allow for future swelling and shrinkage.

Warped groundwork. There are several methods of dealing with warped groundwork in solid wood, depending on whether you are going to try to flatten a veneered panel, or whether you propose to remove the veneer first. Boards may be flattened by mechanical pressure or by changing the humidity; but any attempt to return the board to its original shape by means of steaming or wetting the board will only be temporary remedies: it will eventually return to its warped condition when it dries out again.

A permanent cure can be made by pulling the board flat by main force if the board is neither too hard nor too thick, if there is something substantial to secure the board to, or if the additional supports you will have to fix will not spoil the appearance of the piece. Where circumstances lend themselves to this 'force and fix' technique, the back of the board is wetted either by steam or by covering with wet sawdust and leaving overnight. It is then fastened between four crossbearers which are progressively tightened. Alternatively, the back can be well sized, hand-veneered with plenty of moisture on the veneer backing, and then cramped flat under pressure and allowed to dry out for a long period.

Always veneer solid timber *with* the grain, and use a veneer of about the same thickness as the face veneer. The panel is then released from pressure and immediately fastened securely to the carcass.

In the case of a table top which has been screwed diagonally through the rail, replace this method of fastening by providing buttons fitted in grooves or mortices to allow for possible future movement. If the table top is screwed and plugged, enlarge the holes in the rail to permit shrinkage movement of the table top.

If the panel is veneered, and it is not proposed to remove the original veneer, or if the board is too thick to flatten by either of the above methods, the board should be grooved. This is done by making cuts along the length of the board on its underside to a depth of about two-thirds of its thickness. Then the board is cramped flat and strips of the same kind of wood are glued into the open grooves. Take care not to cut the grooves too deeply as this can result in showing as a series of flats on the surface. A distance of about 1 in. apart is usual, although the more grooves you make, and the closer they are together, the less obvious is

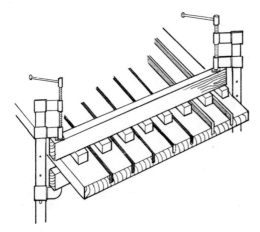

Fig. 89 Thick boards may be grooved and cramped with small blocks between the grooves under a cross bearer. The grooves should be filled with thin wooden strips planed to a finger-tight fit.

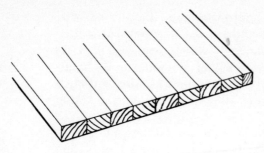

Fig. 90 The board is sawn into narrow strips and every other strip is turned over; this counteracts the tendency to warp. Note that a further strip has been added to restore the original width.

the repair when complete. Avoid grooving along the centre joint if the board has one. After grooving, place small blocks of wood between the grooves under the crossbearer, before clamping down, to enable the long strips to be glued in complete lengths. The strips should be planed to a finger-tight fit and glued in while the panel is cramped flat; the panel should be allowed to remain cramped until dry, after which the strips are planed level with the surface.

If the veneer has been carefully removed, you can saw the board into narrow strips, plane them true and edge-joint them so that each alternate strip has its heart side opposed, to even out any future warping. It is usually necessary to add a further strip to make up the original width. The board is then planed level, resulting in a thinner board than the original.

Where a board is thin, it is possible to hand veneer the back in 6-in. strips, leaving say 4 in. between the strips. This enables the amount of pull to be controlled; further strips can be added as necessary. Veneer strips laid diagonally to a corner will

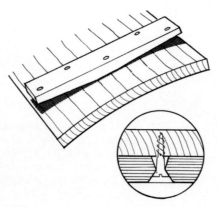

Fig. 91 Severely curved boards require battening on the underside. Elongated slots for the screws will permit future movement.

correct minor warp. When a board is wormy or defective in other ways, such as by insect attack or rot, it is sometimes practicable to cover the veneered surface with a protective layer or plywood cover, and then plane off the old board on a thicknesser, down to about $\frac{3}{16}$ in. A new board, perfectly well seasoned and of the correct type for the item concerned, can be bonded to the original, glueing the heart side of the new board to the original panel.

This 'doubling-up' technique can also be used to cure a warped panel. A combination of methods sometimes gives best results. Where the panel can be removed completely, slots are sawn in the back and the whole flattened; after strips have been glued in and planed level, a backing board is bonded to the original.

If a completely new board has to be used as a replacement, choose well seasoned, radially cut timber (Honduras mahogany is ideal). If only one veneer is to be used, lay it on the heart side, with the minimum of moisture or heat.

Wherever possible, lay an under-veneer first across the grain of the solid groundwork, and then the face veneer in the same direction as the ground and opposite to that of the under-veneer. For the best-quality work, both sides of the board should have under-veneers; the backing veneer should be of the same thickness and strength as the face veneer and laid at the same time by caul.

If the board has a severe curvature and none of the foregoing methods will work, it must be battened on the under-side. Plane the battens on the side which face the wood, to a curve in the opposite direction. Then make elongated slots for the screws to pass through, which will permit future movement.

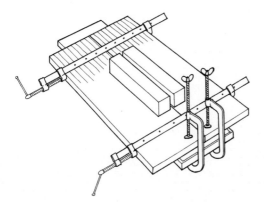

Fig. 92 Failed or broken joints are cramped with two heavy weights in position between the cramps.

245

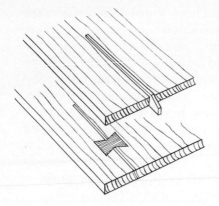

Fig. 93 Repair splits by infilling a saw cut or by inlaying a dovetailed key on the underside.

Broken joints have to be shot afresh and reglued. The two halves are rubbed together, and placed on a flat board over a sheet of clean paper. G-cramps are used at the ends and sash cramps tightened across the two boards about a third of the way from each end. If care is taken, the top need not be planed afterwards.

Splits along the grain require entirely different treatment from failed joints. The split has to be opened with the saw, especially at its narrow end, to enable a slip of wood to be inserted, which has to be tapered to follow the direction and shape of the split. It is then glued, cramped and levelled when dry.

Splits which occur at an angle to the grain require the saw cut to be made at the same angle; take care to see that the faces are in alignment when cramping as the angle may cause one piece to rise. The strip is glued in, and levelled when dry.

To make a really first-class job, let in a couple of dovetailed keys on the under-side.

Knots and plug holes should be filled with solid patches in the form of pellets, diamonds or boat shapes. The grain of these plugs must be in the same direction as the board being filled. Never use

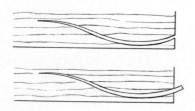

Fig. 94 Infilling splits which occur at an angle to the grain.

dowels, because the long grain will not shrink with the ground-work but will remain proud of the surface.

Plywood and laminated boards

Battenboard, blockboard and laminboard all have potential warping troubles, depending on the quality of manufacture. Laminboard is best because the smaller core strips of solid wood – no more than 7 mm. wide – are narrower and therefore mini-mize the effects of shrinkage. These boards, which are produced to an exact moisture content, are not usually troublesome but difficulty arises from the treatment they receive when being decoratively veneered.

Plywood presents the greatest difficulty. The chief problems are concerned with the outer veneers of the actual plywood, which are rotary-cut veneers, and also with the quality of the laminations. Rotary-cut veneers are produced from logs which require to be steamed. This can result in spindle-shaped or funnel-shaped holes forming on the veneer surface.

As veneers are cut on the rotary lathe, tiny knife checks run ahead of the knife towards the veneer surface on its under-side. The thicker the veneer, the more pronounced these knife checks become. If the veneer shrinks in drying, these checks can affect the surface. Very often, this open-pored, torn side is laid on the surface of the plywood. A blunt veneer knife can tear the veneer rather than cutting it smoothly. The pressure bar can cause a veneer to be ironed so smooth and be so tightly compressed, that case-hardening glue-line problems result. A chipped knife will score the face of veneers. Other common surface faults in ply-wood are caused by badly jointed core veneers in the plywood; the open join shows as stripes across the surface. Overlapped or slipped joins in the laminations also cause surface defects.

In the manufacture of plywood, the swelling and shrinking caused by humidity is usually taken up by the glue line. The thicker the glue line the greater the pressure on the veneers, and conversely the thinner the glue line, the less stress and strain on the outer casing. Hard and brittle resin adhesives, such as urea, melamine and phenolic resins, shrink considerably in hardening and are therefore more inclined to produce checks and splits which will transfer to the surface. The thicker the glue line, the more water escapes and the greater the swelling and shrinkage.

To sum up, inspection of a plywood panel can reveal any one of five defects; warping, outer casing, glue line, under-veneer, or face-veneer problems. Fortunately the restorer's job is much more straight-forward than with solid groundwork. He is not bound by respect for the age or rarity of the furniture and is free to replace any defective panel, and is reasonably certain to match the original veneer from the wide selection commercially available.

When ordering groundwork to be cut to size for veneering, bear in mind that it is trade practice to accept your first stated dimension as being *with* the grain. If you wish to renew a door panel 24 in. × 18 in., in which the decorative face veneer has its grain in the 24-in. direction, you would require your laminated groundwork to be cut 18 in. × 24 in., and would veneer across the grain of the outer casing.

However, there are exceptions to this rule. For the sake of getting the best yield from a large panel, or if you intend to underlay a counter-veneer, you could use 24 in. × 18 in. and lay the under-veneer in the 18-in. direction first, before laying the face-veneer in the 24-in. direction.

Under-veneers may be laid at right angles to the surface grain of the plywood, or at 45° to it. However, in the latter case, the under-veneer laid on the back of the panel must also be at 45°, parallel to the under-veneer on the other side and not diagonal to it. Another point to note, when laying under-veneers, is to choose light, even-textured woods such as obeche or sycamore, and lay them with their closed-pore, tight side outwards to receive the face-veneer.

Saw-cut veneer

Genuine saw-cut veneers of the thickness and type used on antique furniture are no longer available to us, and even if they were they would not match the item you want to restore, because the patina of the years, the natural ageing, cannot be faithfully reproduced by the tricks of the polisher. The would-be restorer should attend country auction sales, and haunt the second-hand furniture shops to find old pieces, no matter how badly worn – even if only the drawer fronts are in sound condition. The solid carcass top or ends will provide oddments for future restorations.

There are other advantages in acquiring an old piece of furniture of similar type to that which you have to repair. The wood will be well seasoned, and it is possible to saw-cut small-dimensioned veneers from it on a home power-saw. If the resulting veneer is thicker than required, this is a good fault and you will have the true patina of age preserved.

On the other hand, if you use a veneer which is freely obtainable from specialist supply houses in normal 0·7 mm. thickness, it is a simple matter to underlay another veneer to bring the new face veneer up to the required level of the other surface veneers. You should be careful to select a veneer lighter in tone than the original, to allow for a gradual darkening down in tone in the polishing sequence.

Veneered surfaces

The accurate identification of veneer is quite difficult, especially when one side is ingrained with stains and layers of polish and wax, and possibly the other side discoloured with glue. The patina referred to applies to waxed and oiled finishes, not to varnished and French-polished surfaces, which are easily reproduced. Identification is even more difficult with modern furniture, not only because of the far wider range of veneers in use today but because of the manufacturer's often misleading reference to 'walnut colour' or 'tola colour', which is a legal way of misrepresenting any veneer as walnut or tola after it has been through the paint shop for a colour spray.

Bruised areas. Slight knocks and minor defects can be raised by one of two methods. Fold four thicknesses of ordinary flannel; wet it, wring it dry and place it over the bruise. Work over it with an electric iron, repeating the process several times.

The other way is to prick the slight depression with a needle point in a few places, and drop a few spots of water over these minute holes. Touch each droplet, or tiny puddle, with the tip of a heated tool to turn the water droplets to steam, which will raise the depression in the veneer. This work must be done with care, to avoid delaminating the veneer.

Delaminated areas. If a patch of veneer gives a hollow sound when tapped by the fingertip or the end of a pencil, a loss of adhesion is indicated. Firstly, assume that the lifted area covers dried out glue which only requires re-heating. Place a heated wooden caul or block over a sheet of waxed paper or polythene, and apply pressure with a cramp.

Sound blisters. Where the surface contains a blister which is undamaged and therefore free from dirt, it is only necessary to slit the blister *with the grain*, gently warm the blister with an iron held over a moist paper wad, work in fresh glue and rub the blister with wet fingers to ensure glue coverage. Then rub it down with the veneer hammer and seal the slit with veneering tape. Finally, cover it with waxed paper or polythene, place a heated caul over the blister and cramp it down.

When blisters occur in the middle of a panel, it is a good tip to chalk direction marks on the panel, so that you can locate where to position the caul when fixing down the shaped crossbearer and clamps.

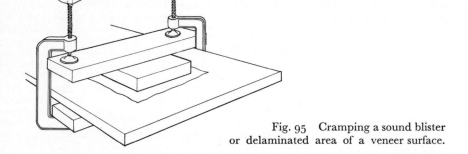

Fig. 95   Cramping a sound blister or delaminated area of a veneer surface.

Open or cracked blisters. Here it is assumed that dirt or grease has entered an open blister. First, flatten the point of a nail on an anvil to form a flat scraper. Then soften the blister by applying gentle heat, as before, with an electric iron held over a few layers of blotting paper, moistened with a sprinkling of water. Do not cut or split the blistered veneer across the grain because it is difficult to conceal a cut of this type. Try to peel the veneer gently back, sufficiently to insert the special scraper, scrape away all the old glue and dirt, and roughen the surface to form a key for the fresh glue, which is worked over the affected area. The blister is then carefully pressed down by hand and held with paper tape, covered with polythene and a heated wooden caul clamped down over it.

Broken or missing veneers. It is important to match the grain flow and figure as closely as possible, rather than be too concerned with a tone match. If you can find a veneer of the right grain and

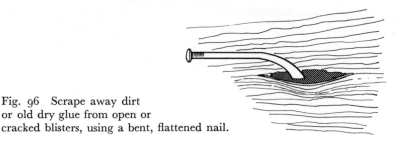

Fig. 96 Scrape away dirt
or old dry glue from open or
cracked blisters, using a bent, flattened nail.

figure which is much lighter, this can easily be darkened to match. However, the best solution is to remove a portion of veneer from an unimportant part of the cabinet in order to repair a prominent feature. This is a case of two repairs being better than one. Trim the broken edges of the part to be patched and prepare a patch slightly larger than the damaged part. Then fasten the patch in position temporarily with Sellotape while you mark round its contours with a craft knife, into the face veneer below. Remove this unwanted surplus either by applying moisture and heat, as before, or by chiselling it off. Clean off the old glue from the groundwork. Check to see that the patch is correct 'face'. If the original veneer was part of a match, in which you cannot help laying one part of the match with the closed pores inwards, then the patch must also be laid in the same way or the tone difference, when polished, will be noticeable.

These patching joins may be cut with a straight edge in certain places, but where this is undesirable, it is often possible to soften and loosen the original veneer and peel it back sufficiently to underlay the new patch. Then, using a knife, cut through both veneers freehand, allowing the point of the knife to follow the wandering grain or any prominent markings. The resulting join will be invisible.

Mitres. When the repair is to be effected at the edge of a panel, for example to a crossbanding, remove the whole veneer as far as the mitre join. When the new patch of cross-banding veneer is inserted, butted up tightly to the old join, no repair will be visible.

Irregular shapes. When patching a burr or butt or any veneer with strong markings, do *not* use the conventional straight patches, cut diamond-shaped to prevent cutting a veneer across

251

the grain. Instead, cut along a strongly marked feature of grain or figure or marking, and shape the patch accordingly. This is easiest by the underlaying method described, but if this is impossible because the original is laid with a heatproof or waterproof glue, then mark the irregular shape of the patch on tracing paper or transparent film, and then locate similar markings on the new veneer; cut it fractionally oversize, and use it as a template to cut around its contours into the original veneers. The fractional surplus of the original veneer can be chiselled off without difficulty.

Removal of old veneer. The old finish must be removed first of all. Use the appropriate solvent or de-waxing agent and glasspaper off the polish to expose the grain of the wood. Cover the surface with wet rags or wet sawdust and leave it overnight to soak. The next day, work over the surface with an electric iron pressed down over a damp cloth, and work a large flat knife between veneer and groundwork. As each piece is removed, lay it face

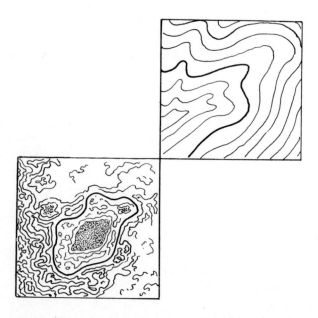

Fig. 97 Repairs to fancy veneers are made by following the contour or natural feature of the figure, grain or marking.

downwards on a flat board, and while it is still warm and moist, scrape the old glue from the back.

The removed veneers should then be laid out in the pattern they formed on the cabinet, covered with a sheet of clean paper, placed between boards and clamped down. They should be thoroughly dried out for up to two weeks.

Bad cauling. In the event of old veneers being re-cauled, and failing to go down properly, they should be gently sanded to remove any finish and damped overnight. Place a piece of hot zinc or lead on them, over a sheet of waxed paper or polythene – the metal should not be hot enough to scorch but hot enough to sizzle if wet – and clamp the whole assembly down under a wooden caul.

This treatment will soften glue which has been hardening for up to two weeks, and will relay defectively laid veneer, forcing any surplus glue out at the edges. But it will not work if resin glues have been used originally.

Curved surfaces. Repairs to curved surfaces are made by hand with the veneering hammer, or by the hot sandbag method. If cauls can be used, it is often found possible to rig up struts, to provide pressure for sustained periods, from wall to ceiling, with crossbearers and wedges to complete a makeshift press.

As alternatives to hot sand, sawdust or bran can be used; bran keeps its shape and is easily moulded.

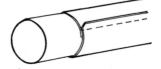

Fig. 98   Veneering a cylindrical surface.

Cylindrical surfaces. Repairs to cylindrical surfaces present no problem. Wrap the veneer round and overlap the join, securing it temporarily with veneer pins, nip the points off the pins to prevent splitting. Cut right through the overlap. Bind the assembly with webbing or canvas, which is then soaked with hot water and allowed to dry, if possible near a source of heat which will speed the contraction of the material and will exert a uniform pressure.

Mouldings. To repair a veneered moulding, first cut a caul following the contour of the moulding as closely as possible. You may have to make a plaster cast of the moulding. Now fold a few thicknesses of glasspaper to the thickness of the veneer and place this on the moulding. Rub the newly shaped caul against the glasspaper until a perfect fit results.

Broken inlays. If parts of an inlay are broken or damaged, place a piece of tracing paper over the defective inlay and rub gently with heelball or soft pencil over the outline to establish the line. The required section can then be cut and fitted into the space.

An alternative method is to place a piece of transparent plastic or perspex over the damaged inlay, preferably at a part which clearly shows a repeating pattern which can be copied. With a sharp knife, cut a guiding line into the plastic with a craft knife, carefully following the contour of the inlay below. Then this can be removed to a cutting board and cut out to form an aperture in the plastic. This, in turn, is placed over a suitable veneer and used as a template to cut the required replacement.

Modern veneer repair. Resin glue lines will not respond to either heat or water treatment. The only method is to cut a patch and place it over the defective part, securing it temporarily with a few drops of PVA adhesive. Then carefully trace the contour of the actual patch with the point of a knife into the surrounding veneer. The patch is carefully removed, and the defective section chiselled off. With practice, both the patch and surrounding veneer can be cut through simultaneously for the best fit.

Straight striped veneers. When the panel to be repaired has a quartered striped veneer in need of patching, it is often better to remove a narrow strip right across the panel, and to replace it by cutting along one of the stripes for an invisible repair, than to cut a diamond patch.

Cross-banding. If doors have been veneered over a solid frame which has shrunk and split the veneer, it pays to remove a whole strip around the door panel, and to decorate the door with a crossbanding of a new veneer – even where no crossbanding existed before – perhaps highlighted with an inlay line. In this way the mitres of the veneer and solid framework can be made to coincide.

Split and cracked veneers. Curls and burrs often show these defects, mainly caused by being laid on a groundwork with the same

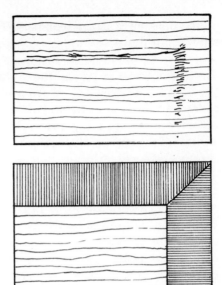

Fig. 99   In cases where doors have been veneered over a solid frame, replace with a new cross-banding.

grain direction, or by failure to flatten the veneers before laying. Veneers over elaborate joins, or on unseasoned wood, can also show these splits and cracks or minute checks. Where it is possible to repair the burrs and curls without removal, do so with wood stopping of a suitable colour. If new burrs are to be laid, be sure to coat them thoroughly with glue size, and flatten them between boards under pressure.

Inlays and burr veneers. Where the surface to be repaired is composed of a multi-joined decoration such as an inlay or marquetry, or end-grain burrs, or an eight- or sixteen-piece match with its varied grain directions, the cause of cracks and checks may be that the veneer upon which the decoration is laid has only one grain direction.

For best work, and wherever possible, the decoration must be carefully removed piece by piece and in addition to laying an under-veneer, stretch a sheet of fine Japanese silk or muslin over the under-veneer to receive the decoration.

As it is extremely difficult to match a part of a two-, four-, eight- or sixteen-piece match, it is best to remove the old parts and completely renew the match.

Repairing brass inlays. When wood is subjected to heat it tends to dry out and shrink, while a metal inlay will do the reverse and expand, forming into a loop or arched shape. It is not possible to clamp this down and apply fresh glue because the groove is now too short for the brass. The only remedy is to make a fine saw cut in the brass and re-lay it; you will find that the ends will need to be filed for a perfect fit. Place a block of heated wood over the inlay and clamp it until set, with a piece of clean paper under the block to prevent marking the surrounding veneer.

The addition of garlic to the Scotch glue, or a touch of Venice turpentine, will increase its viscosity. Salisbury glue is also a favourite with professionals, which is Scotch glue with the addition of plaster of Paris.

If new patches are to be introduced to the veneered surface, these should be cut in before the cleaning and reviving operation. It is then necessary to stain and fix them before cleaning begins.

For mahogany, use a bichromate of potash stain, made from dissolving crystals in water; make a concentration and dilute with water as required. This chemical is powerful, and if used in full strength it could turn mahogany almost black. Try the stain on a scrap of the veneer used for the patch before applying it to the repair, and wait for a period as the full effect of its darkening power only becomes apparent when the stain dries out. Then apply two rubbers of French polish to fix the stain.

In the case of oak furniture, use Vandyke crystals dissolved in water, to which a little Bismarck brown water-soluble aniline dye can be added if the colour is too cold in tone, or black to darken. These additional tones must be mixed separately into a solution and then added to the original solution.

12 Restoring the finish

The first step is to determine which of the five traditional types of finish have been used on the item to be restored – wax polish, oil polish, French polish, varnish or cellulose. Furniture made since the Second World War may have catalyst lacquer finishes or polyurethanes, but these would hardly interest the marquetry craftsman interested in restoring a valuable piece of furniture.

Test some unimportant part of the furniture to identify the finish. There are two simple ways of doing this. First, scrape the surface with a chisel: French polished surfaces will give up a thin shaving, which will crumble easily; oil varnish will yield a much tougher shaving; cellulose finishes simply come away in dust or as a white powder.

The other method is to apply different solvents by a simple process of elimination. To begin with, it is almost certain that the surface will have been wax polished, and this will need to be rubbed away with turpentine. If the surface then reacts to methylated spirits it is a shellac French-polished finish. Lacquer thinners will have no effect on a varnished surface. Acetone will soften French polish, varnish and cellulose, but have no effect on plastic finishes.

An old piece of furntiure may have been oil varnished originally, then waxed for a long period; the top may have been damaged and some restorer of bygone days may have stripped off only the damaged top, which may then have been French polished and waxed, leaving the remainder with the original finish. It is therefore useful to remember that cellulose may be applied over shellac, but never apply shellac over cellulose or crazing will result. If the surface has been cellulose sprayed, do not attempt to apply rubbers of cellulose by hand as this will soften the original finish and work it up. Oil varnish may be applied over a shellac surface but never the other way around, or again, crazing will result. Wax polish may be applied over all other finishes, and conversely nothing should ever be applied over a wax polish, as the new finish would adhere to the wax and eventually flake off.

It is well worth repeating at this stage that the sole purpose of refinishing an antique is to remove the dirt without affecting the original patina of age, to reveal the finish in its original beauty by restoring the lustre.

The minor blemishes which the surface reveals, such as digs, scratches, burns, heat or alcohol rings and ink spots, are honourable scars won in giving a lifetime of service and should be left alone. It is sobering to reflect that part of the art of the faker is to imitate these very defects, in order to pass off a reproduction piece as a genuine antique.

The techniques of refinishing are intended primarily for second-hand furniture of sentimental value rather than for genuine antiques.

Reviving and refinishing

The next step in restoring the finish on an old piece of furniture is to wash it. Practically all old furniture, of whatever type of finish, has been given a coat of wax polish at some time or other and this will have to be removed.

Wipe the surface over with turpentine, and if it is exceptionally dirty or murky-looking, use three tablespoonfuls of boiled linseed oil and an equal amount of turps. Rub the surface briskly, covering a small area at a time, until the cloth drags. Then wash with liquid soap and water for a second time, rinse with clear water, applied sparingly with a sponge, and immediately dry with a chamois leather and clean dry cloth.

Do not saturate with water, and work with some speed. This wash treatment can produce surprising results. Items which have become black with age will suddenly show the beauty of their original finish, with the fine patina of age preserved. Conversely, if the patina is artificially contrived, it may be washed away by this treatment. If the soap-and-water treatment has left the finish dull, wipe over the surface with a mixture of equal parts of boiled linseed oil, vinegar and white spirit, which will remove any trace of grease or oiliness.

Other traditional revivers are: equal parts of camphorated oil and spirits of camphor; or equal parts of vinegar and methylated spirits to make 1 pint, to which 1 oz. camphor is dissolved in the spirit, then 1 oz. linseed oil and $\frac{1}{2}$ oz. butter of antimony; or to one part of terebine, add four parts of linseed oil and twelve parts of vinegar.

Identifying the defects

Here are some of the defects often found in the film of polish.

Bleeding – where the colour of a stain or filler rises through succeeding coats. Use non-bleeding, chemically inert colours such as water or non-grain-raising stains.

Blistering, possibly caused by exposure to heat from direct sunlight or radiators, or by sealing over 'green' timber or a previously applied coat which had not dried thoroughly.

Blooming shows as a blue cast on lacquered or varnished surfaces, caused by a viscous rubbing oil, or excessive rubbing, or poor ventilation. To remove, rub with liquid soap and rotten-stone, rinse with clean water and dry with a chamois leather. Blooming is different from 'blushing', which takes place before the film is dry.

Blushing is the formation of a white film during the period of drying, and is caused by moisture, draughts, or high relative humidity. Apply thinners to the surface and increase the temperature of the workroom.

Bronzing or greening is caused by the stain being too strong, or the filler not being cleaned off thoroughly, and it causes a murky appearance.

Bubbling usually appears in varnished surfaces, caused by too thick an application of the film – the varnish being flowed-on and insufficiently brushed in – and improperly filled pores. In lacquered surfaces, it is caused by the top skin hardening before the solvents have evaporated.

Caking occurs when dirt has been allowed to settle on the film during drying out; use rottenstone and liquid soap as before.

Crazing, sometimes known as 'hair-lining' or checking, is caused by a quick-drying finish being applied over a slow-drying sealer or undercoat. It also occurs if an excessively thick coat is applied, and the top begins to dry before the bottom of the coat. Lacquer may craze or crack if applied over shellac.

Creeping of the film is caused by an oily, greasy, or wet surface, a coat being applied over a high-gloss surface, or the application of a heavy coat in a cold atmosphere.

Flaking is caused by coating varnish over too heavy a shellac coat, or applying too many shellac coats, causing the top coat to flake off. Orange peeling or pockmarking is noticed when the varnish or lacquer has been sprayed on without sufficient thinners, or with too much air pressure.

Pinholing occurs when the pores of the veneer have not been properly filled or where the varnish has been applied before the undercoat has dried.

Printing is simply an imprint of something into the varnish surface before the surface is thoroughly dry.

Runs or sags on the surface are caused by the coating being applied too thickly, or when thinned too much.

Repairing the finish

Fine surface scratches. Examine the freshly washed and dried surface in a good light, and determine whether the wash treatment alone has been sufficient, in which case the surface need only be repolished.

If the surface contains many fine scratches, which do not penetrate right through the film of polish, they may be rubbed out with flour-grade glasspaper, lubricated with boiled linseed oil and wrapped around a cork rubber. This treatment may affect the surrounding colour, if the original surface coating was coloured; this can be rectified with a rubber or two of garnet polish applied to the repaired area, toned with aniline spirit dye to match the surrounding surface. The surface may not have been previously given the wash treatment if the scratches are visible anyway, but before the above repair can be carried out, the surface should be de-waxed with detergent or white spirit. After the repair, the whole surface should be given a rubber of French polish and then re-waxed.

If the scratch – such as a dog's claw scratch – penetrates through the film into the veneer, it must be filled with coloured beeswax, or shellac applied with a pencil brush, and then scraped off level with the surface. The repair should then be lightly papered, using 6/o garnet paper lubricated with boiled linseed oil. To restore the lustre of the finish, try pumice powder and oil, and if a higher gloss is required to match the surrounding area, add more rottenstone to the compound or try all rottenstone and oil. On small surfaces, it would be easier to repolish the whole surface.

Small turnings and carvings and inaccessible parts can be refinished by sprinkling the pumice powder or rottenstone on the surface before brushing it vigorously with a short-haired stubble brush dipped in oil.

Deep jagged scratches. Where the surface has received a deep scratch through the film into the veneer below, probably caused by a sharp object accidentally striking the surface and tearing a deep scratch through the film, the scratch must first be smoothed, by cutting out all jagged edges, using a very sharp knife or razor blade. This can be done under magnification or in a very good light. The deep scratch is then filled with coloured plastic wood or stopping, scraped flat with the back of a knife, and, when dry, papered smooth with 9/0 garnet paper and boiled linseed oil. The scratch is painted over, using a pencil brush dipped in thin white shellac. The repaired scratch is then coloured in to match the surrounding surface, with a rubber of garnet polish with aniline dye added to match, and, when dry, brought up to the original lustre with pumice and rottenstone and oil.

Cracked surfaces. Mention has been made of plastic wood and wood stoppings, which are usually nitro-cellulose and sawdust mixtures, and are suitable for filling minor scratches and cracked surfaces. A more professional method of filling deep jagged scratches and cracked surfaces is by filling them with stick shellac or coloured beeswax. A range of wood-toned colours are available, and a colour should be selected one tone lighter than the surrounding surface.

Hold the blunt end of a metal file over a naked flame – a candle or small spirit lamp – and when it is hot, place the tip of the shellac stick over the file *near* the flame but not in contact with it. The melted shellac is allowed to run over the metal file tip, which is drawn along the crack to be filled. With a clean flat knife and a moistened fingertip, smooth the shellac flush with the surrounding surface. The in-filling must be done quickly to avoid damage to the old surface, and too much shellac must not be melted in as the surplus will be difficult to remove. When the repair is hard, the surface is then rubbed down with pumice powder and oil, applied with a felt pad to which a little rotten-stone is added to increase the lustre of the finish.

To complete the finish, even when the scratch or crack is across the grain, always end by polishing the entire surface with rottenstone and water, applied with the felt pad along the grain direction. The stick shellac is opaque and should therefore be used only on small defects as it shows no grain effect. If this opaque repair shows up it must be coloured out, using stain applied with a pencil brush along the grain, before the polishing process.

Plastic wood or wood stopping tends to take stain a tone darker than shellac stick, and should therefore be given a coat of shellac before the repair is coloured in and polished.

Worn edges. Lightly paper the edge with worn garnet paper, grade 9/0, taking care to remove only the film of polish. The edge may be given a rubber of garnet polish with aniline dye added to match, and the following day the surface may be re-polished with a rubber of French polish.

For small areas of edges, toned grain-filler diluted with white spirit may be sufficient, protected with a rubber of shellac, and repolished the following day.

Accidental rubbing-through. In making other repairs, sometimes the stain is accidentally rubbed through. This may be patched in with grain filler, or a rubber of garnet polish and aniline dye.

When worn edges require to be restored to their original lustre, and the felt pad is found to be inadequate in forming to the correct contour of the edge, apply a slush of pumice powder to the shaped edge and then use a stubbly bristle brush dipped in boiled linseed oil. Wipe off the oil at intervals to see the degree of shine attained, and, if necessary, finish off with a little rotten-stone applied direct to the edge. Clean the brush first, and this time apply it dipped in water.

Water stains appear as chalky-white mineral deposits on the film. Try wiping the stain with turpentine or white spirit and if the stains persist, rub them with lint-free cloth moistened with methylated spirits, taking care not to damp the surrounding surface. If the stains do not respond to this treatment, lightly rub down the stained patch with a slush of fine pumice powder and water, if on a varnished surface, or pumice and oil if on a shellacked surface. Then apply one rubber of half-and-half shellac and methylated spirits, and immediately rub off with camphorated oil. Remove all traces of the oil by wiping over the surface with a cloth dampened with vinegar.

262

Milk spots and stains. The lactic acid in milk usually forms a ring in lacquer or varnished surfaces, which is removed with the pumice powder and water treatment described above.

Ink stains. Ink stains can usually be removed with ordinary household bleach applied by brush to the stained area. When the stain is removed, wash the surface with clear water and dry with a chamois leather. Alternatives are to brush over the stain with dilute nitric acid and wipe clean with camphorated oil, followed by a wash with vinegar; or some fresh stains are removed with butter of antimony applied with a wet cloth. If the stain persists, it must be rubbed out with pumice powder and water. When the ink stain has penetrated through to the veneer below, this must be sandpapered out, and refinished as for other major damage.

Beer and spirit stains appear as white rings in the surface, made by the bottoms of glasses, and the stains may respond to rubbing out with turpentine with a sprinkle of salt added. If the stains persist they must be papered out, taking care not to rub through the stain below. The ring may then be painted out with a fine pencil brush, in light brush-strokes following the grain of the surrounding veneer, using the appropriate aniline dye in the white shellac polish. Build up the repair to the surrounding level with further brush applications of polish and allow to harden off. Then fine down the surface with flour-grade glasspaper lubricated with linseed oil, and repolish the whole surface with a rubber or two of French polish.

Damage by heat from plates or spilled hot water may be repaired by rubbing the affected area with linseed oil and turpentine applied warm with a rag. Alternatively, camphorated oil, applied vigorously, may also be tried, using several applications, removed afterwards with vinegar.

If the damage has been caused by heat from a radiator or fireplace, resulting in a blistered surface, provided that the blisters are very small or in a small cluster one can paper them out with flour-grade glasspaper lubricated with linseed oil, taking care not to rub through the stained surface, by wiping off occasionally with white spirit.

If the surface is not blistered but exposure to heat has caused a little softening and discoloration of the top film, try rubbing out with pumice powder and oil applied with the felt pad, checking the progress by wiping the patch with white spirit as before.

When the patch is rubbed out, the original lustre can be restored with the addition of rottenstone to the pumice slush.

When the light papering of the surface involves any risk of taking the film down almost to the stained surface, it is best to build up the patch with French polish.

Cigar and cigarette burns. If the burn is shallow, in the surface film only, it may be repaired with toned grain-filler and a rubber of French polish. Slightly deeper burns can be built up with coats of shellac coloured with aniline dye to match the surface.

In bad cases, the burn will have penetrated through the film to the veneer below and this, too, will have become charred. The burned or charred part must be thoroughly scraped and cleaned out with a sharp knife, taking care not to damage the surrounding polished surface.

In very deeply charred cases, where the damage penetrates the film and the veneer, either build up with plastic wood or melt in stick shellac as previously described. However, as shellac is opaque, simply fill the damaged part to the level surface, and then paint in a simulated grain with a fine pencil brush, using dyed garnet polish; when dry, protect with a rubber of French polish.

A complete refinish

If examination of the surface reveals extensive scratches, blisters, burns or stains, to attempt repairs to each imperfection would cost more than to strip off the old finish and completely repolish.

Take all reasonable precautions against splashing other parts of the item to be stripped, and surrounding floor surfaces. Do not rely on newspapers alone, but work outdoors if possible, since most paint and varnish removers are obnoxious and inflammable.

Flow on a good-quality remover with an old brush. Do not brush this on back and forth like paint, as this breaks up the film of wax that floats to the top of the remover and seals it against evaporation. Allow the remover plenty of time to work, and then scrape off the finish with a putty knife. Irregular surfaces, such as turned or carved or moulded parts, can be stripped using a coarse-grade wire wool. Apply more remover, as necessary, to remove all the old polish, and complete the task by scrubbing the surfaces with methylated spirits or white spirit, to remove all traces of the wax evaporation retardant left by the remover.

Any grease or wax remaining will be saponified, that is, changed to a soap-like substance which is easily wiped off. Allow the surface to dry overnight in a warm dry atmosphere, then lightly paper all surfaces with 9/0 garnet polishing paper.

If the surface has been stained previously, this treatment would not normally affect the stain, but careful examination is now required to make sure the stain is unaffected, and a rubber of coloured shellac should be given to any patch affected.

The furniture is now ready for normal repolishing procedure. Since most old furniture will be found to have been French polished at some stage of its life, possibly during the years on either side of the First World War, it is best to refinish the furniture with French polish, which has one or two advantages over more modern finishes. It improves upon the treacly appearance of varnished furniture, and makes an excellent base for a final siliconized wax polishing, which will prevent finger-marking. But its biggest virtue is that French polishing techniques allow new patches to be blended and harmonized into the old furniture sufficiently to escape detection.

Sources of Illustrations

The author and publisher wish to thank the following individuals, museums and other organizations for the courtesy of allowing the reproduction of pictures of objects in their collections or in their copyright:

The Department of Antiquities, Ashmolean Museum, Oxford, pl. 1; the Austrian Museum for Applied Arts, Vienna, pls. 7, 28; Messrs H. T. Biggs & Sons, Maidenhead, pl. 20; Messrs Christie, Manson and Woods Ltd, pls. 12, 26; Convento di S. Maria Novella dei Padri Domenicani, Florence, pl. 6; the Egyptian Museum, Cairo, pl. 2; the Griffith Institute, Ashmolean Museum, Oxford, pl. 3; the National Gallery of Art, Washington, D.C., pl. 24; the Pinto Collection of Wooden Bygones, pls. 17, 29; the Rijksmuseum, Amsterdam, pls. 10, 14–16; S. Domenico, Bologna, pl. 8; Messrs A. T. Silvester and Sons Ltd, Solihull, Warwickshire, pl. 23; Messrs Sotheby & Co., pl. 22; the Controller, H.M. Stationery Office, and the Director, Royal Botanic Gardens, Kew, pl. 31 (Crown copyright reserved); the Museum of Versailles, pl. 30; the Victoria and Albert Museum, London, pls. 4, 9, 11, 13, 18, 19, 21, 32, 33, 34; the Wallace Collection, pls. 25, 27.

Thanks are also due to the following marquetarians for a similar courtesy: Miss M. Blunt, pls. 45, 54; E. Christopher, pl. 44; J. Dawson, pl. 49; W. Dolley, pl. 46; N. A. Douglas, pl. 47; Robert Dunn, pls. 71, 74, 75; Alexander Ephrat, pls. 56, 67; Messrs Gallaher Ltd, pls. 72, 73; A. Gibbs-Murray, pls. 42, 43; C. H. Good, pl. 37; Max Gottschling, pls. 65, 68; Anthony Guglielmo, pl. 57; Mrs J. Holmes, pl. 50; Paul F. Jobling, pls. 36, 48 and jacket; George Kish, pl. 59; Dr Gert Kossatz, Dresden, pl. 62; N. Macleod, pls. 38, 52; Emanuela Marassi, pls. 63, 64, 66; Mr Möller-Nielsen, pls. 60, 61; S. H. Murrell, pl. 40; A. Pollosch, pl. 41; John Savage, pl. 51; Paul-Louis Spindler, pls. 69, 70; G. K. Thom, pl. 53; Mrs G. M. Walker, pls. 39, 55; E. Wendl, pl. 62; C. R. Woodcock, pl. 35; Art Veneers Co. Ltd, pl. 58.

Appendix A

VENEER AND BURR SELECTION GUIDE

The following one hundred rare and exotic marquetry veneers, with a further 18 different burr veneers, have been carefully selected for pictorial marquetry and arranged in alphabetical sequence for ease of reference.

The letter 'T' appearing in the 'treatment' column indicates that the veneer is available chemically treated in various shades of grey. All veneers can be bought in lengths of 6 ft. and up, so the width, which is the marquetry craftsman's main concern, is the only dimension shown in the table.

VENEER	origin	colour	grain	figure	texture	hard-ness
ABELE (*Populus alba*) poplar	England	white to cream	straight	plain, crown-cut heart-wood, veins	smooth	soft
ABURA (*Mitragyna ciliata*) Bahia; subaha; Nzingu	West Africa	light to medium red	interlocked	weak stripe	fine	soft
AFARA (*Terminalia superba*) limba; white afara; ofram; korina	West Africa	yellow to gold	wavy	mottled	medium	normal
AFRORMOSIA (*Afrormosia elata*) kokrodua; redbark; Devil's tree	West Africa	gold to light brown	interlocked wavy	rope stripe	coarse	hard
AFZELIA (*Afzelia spp.*) doussié	West Africa	orange-red	interlocked	weak stripe	medium	normal
AGBA (*Gossweilerodendron balsamiferum*) tolabranca; Nigerian cedar; white tola	West Africa	biscuit to light tan	straight	plain	fine	soft
ALMONDWOOD (*Chickrassia tabularis*) Copafeira	India	pink with red stripes	straight	wild markings, crown-cut heartwood	medium	hard
ANTIARIS (*Antiaris africana*) bark cloth tree	Tropical Africa	cream to yellow	interlocked	striped	medium	soft
APPLE (*Malus sylvestris*)	Europe	biscuit to light red	straight	plain	smooth	hard
ASH, EUROPEAN (*Fraxinus excelsior*)	Europe	white to cream	straight	very close stripe, crown-cut heartwood	coarse	normal
ASH, JAPANESE (*Fraxinus mandshurica*) tamo	Japan	cream to pink	wavy	wild markings, mottled	medium	hard
ASH, OLIVE (*Fraxinus excelsior*)	Europe	special figure	straight	stripy markings, streaky, wild markings	coarse	normal
ASPEN (*Populus tremula*) trembling or quaking aspen	Europe	cream to pink	straight	veins, streaky, wild markings, crown-cut heartwood	smooth	soft
AVODIRE (*Turraeanthus africanus*) apaya; lusamba; African satinwood	West Africa	yellow to gold	wavy	mottled	medium	normal
AYAN (*Distemonanthus Benthamianus*) movingui; barre; ainyeran	West Africa	yellow to gold	interlocked	mottled	coarse	hard

cutting	T	availability	width	price guide	freak types	special marquetry effects
easy	T	spasmodic	8″–12″	moderate	sky effects, water effects	'Window waster' sky effects, floral subjects, snowscenes, shades well
easy		plentiful	8″–12″	moderate		sky effects, roofs, water effects, shadows, portraiture, animal subjects
brittle		plentiful	8″–12″	moderate		cornfields, thatch, walls, doors, costume and drapery, floral subjects, shades well
normal		plentiful	8″–12″	inexpensive		borders, crossbandings, wooden subjects, cornfields, thatch, sandy beaches, walls, doors, fences, planks
brittle		plentiful	6″– 9″	moderate		wooden subjects, roofs, mid-distance fields, shadows, costume and drapery
easy		plentiful	8″–12″	inexpensive		sandy beaches, mid-distance fields, walls, doors, borders, crossbandings, fences, planks
brittle		rare	6″–9″	expensive	sky effects	sky effects, roofs, costume and drapery
easy		plentiful	8″–12″	cheap		'Window waster', sky effects, borders, crossbandings, floral subjects, shades well, walls, doors, costume and drapery
hard, brittle		scarce	6″–9″	costly		portraiture, floral subjects, shades well, costume and drapery, walls, doors
hard, brittle	T	plentiful	8″–12″	inexpensive	sky effects, water effects	sky effects, water effects, snow scenes, mountains and rocks, walls, doors, fences, planks, shades well
normal	T	spasmodic	6″–9″	moderate	water effects	floral subjects, costume and drapery, shades well, water effects
normal	T	spasmodic	6″–9″	moderate	water effects	fences, planks, roads and pathways, stonework, sky effects, water effects, shades well
easy	T	plentiful	12″ +	cheap	sky effects	'Window waster', sky effects, costume and drapery, walls, doors, shades well
easy		plentiful	6″–9″	moderate	sky effects	sky effects, mid-distance fields, walls, doors, floral subjects, shades well
brittle, crumbly, needs papering		spasmodic	8″–12″	costly		cornfields, thatch, floral subjects, portraiture, shades well, sandy beaches

VENEER	origin	colour	grain	figure	texture	hardness
BEECH (*Fagus sylvatica*)	Europe	cream to pink	straight	medullary rays	smooth	hard
BIRCH, CANADIAN (*Betula alleghaniensis*) Yellow birch; grey birch; betula	Canada and USA	cream to pink	straight	veins, mottled	smooth	hard
BIRCH, MASUR (*Betula verrucosa and pubescens*)	Finland and Norway	cream to pink	straight	wild markings	smooth	hard
BIRCH, SWEDISH (*Betula verrucosa and pubescens*) Ice birch; flame birch	Sweden	white to cream	wavy	mottled	smooth	hard
BIRD'S EYE MAPLE (*Acer saccharum*)	Canada and USA	cream to pink	straight	mottled, veins	smooth	hard
BLACKWOOD (*Acacia melanoxylon*)	Australia	light brown to mid-brown	wavy	curly, mottled	medium	soft
BUBINGA (*Guibourtia spp.*) Zebramona; Kevazinga (rotary); African rosewood	West Africa	pink with red stripes	interlocked	very close stripe, mottled	fine	hard
CANARIUM (*Canarium schweinfurthii*) aiélé	West Africa	pink to biscuit	interlocked	striped	coarse	soft
CANELLA (*Phoebe porosa*) imbuyia; Brazilian walnut	Brazil	light tan to light brown	straight	wild markings	fine	soft
CAPOMO (*Brosimum alicastrum*)	Central America	yellow to gold	straight	plain	smooth	very hard
CEDAR OF LEBANON (*Cedrus libani*) citronella	Europe	pink to biscuit	straight	striped, streaky, crown-cut heartwood	fine	soft
CEDAR, WESTERN RED (*Thuja plicata*)	Canada and USA	cream to pink	straight	very close stripe	smooth	soft
CHERRY, FRUIT (*Prunus avium*) wild cherry	Europe	pink to biscuit	interlocked	very close stripe, medullary rays	smooth	normal
CHESTNUT, HORSE (*Aesculus hippocastanum*)	Europe	white to cream	straight	plain	smooth	soft
CHESTNUT, SWEET (*Castanea sativa*) Spanish chestnut	Europe	biscuit to light tan	straight	plain	fine	soft
COURBARIL (*Hymenaea courbaril*) Surinam teak; stinking toe; locust	W. Indies, S. America	special figure	straight	streaky, wild markings	fine	very hard

cutting	T	availability	width	price guide	freak types	special marquetry effects
normal	T	plentiful	6"–9"	inexpensive		snow scenes, mountains and rocks, roads and pathways, stonework, sandy beaches, walls, doors
normal	T	plentiful	6"–9"	moderate	water effects	portraiture, floral subjects, sky effects, water effects, shades well
easy	T	rare	12"+	expensive	water effects	stonework, mountains and rocks, roads and pathways, water effects, sandy beaches
hard	T	scarce	8"–12"	costly	sky effects	floral subjects, water effects, sky effects, costume and drapery, shades well
normal	T	scarce	12"+	expensive	water effects	water effects, stonework, floral subjects, shades well, mountains and rocks, costume and drapery
easy, brittle		rare	6"–9"	costly		animal subjects, portraiture, foregrounds, wooden subjects
brittle		plentiful	8"–12"	moderate		roofs, rocks and mountains, foregrounds, floral subjects, wooden subjects, walls, doors, fences, planks
easy		spasmodic	6"–9"	moderate		floral subjects, wooden subjects, mid-distance fields, costume and drapery, walls, doors, fences, planks
easy		scarce	6"–9"	costly	water effects	foregrounds, sky effects, mid-distance fields, wooden subjects, walls, doors, fences, planks
hard		spasmodic	6"–9"	moderate		floral subjects, shades well, costume and drapery, cornfields, thatch, sandy beaches, walls, doors
easy		plentiful	8"–12"	moderate	sky effects	fences, planks, sky effects, costume and drapery, walls, doors, shades well
easy		spasmodic	8"–12"	moderate		fences, planks, walls, doors, costume and drapery, roofs
easy		plentiful	8"–12"	moderate		stonework, sky effects, roads and pathways, walls, doors, fences, planks
easy	T	in season	8"–12"	moderate	sky effects	'Window waster', snow scenes, floral subjects, sky-effects, water effects, shades well, walls, doors
easy		plentiful	6"–9"	inexpensive		walls, doors, wooden subjects, borders, crossbandings, fences, planks
hard, brittle		spasmodic	6"–9"	costly	sky effects	tree trunks, foregrounds, distant hills, wooden subjects, sky effects, reflections, roads and pathways

VENEER	origin	colour	grain	figure	texture	hard-ness
DANIELLIA (*Daniellia ogea*) ogea; faro	West Africa	light brown to mid-brown	straight	streaky	smooth	normal
DOUGLAS FIR (*Pseudotsuga taxifolia*) Oregon pine	Western USA and Canada	pink to biscuit	straight	very close stripe	medium	normal
EBONY, MACASSAR (*Diospyros celebica*) coromandel; calamander	Celebes Island	dark brown	straight	very close stripe, streaky	fine	very hard
ELM (*Ulmus procera*)	England	biscuit to light red	straight	weak stripe, crown-cut heartwood	medium	normal
EUCALYPTUS (*Eucalyptus regnans*) Tasmanian oak; mountain ash	Australia	biscuit to light tan	straight	mottled	fine	hard
GABOON (*Aucoumea Klaineana*) okoume; angouma	Gabon	biscuit to light red	wavy	mottled	fine	soft
GUAREA (*Guarea cedrata*; *G. Thompsonii*) bosse; African cedar; Nigerian pearwood	West Africa	biscuit to light red	straight	weak stripe, mottled	medium	soft
HAREWOOD (*Acer pseudoplatanus*) (chemically treated sycamore)	England	chemically treated	straight	plain	smooth	soft
HORNBEAM (*Carpinus betulus*) ironwood (USA)	Europe	biscuit to light tan	straight	striped	coarse	normal
IDIGBO (*Terminalia ivorensis*) black afara	West Africa	gold to light brown	interlocked	striped	coarse	hard
INDIAN SILVER GREYWOOD (*Terminalia bialata*) chuglam; derda; ixora	Andaman Islands	light brown to mid-brown	interlocked	very close stripe, wild markings, crown-cut heartwood	fine	normal
INDIAN WHITE MAHOGANY (*Canarium euphyllum*) safukula; Dhup. abenita	Andaman Islands	pink to biscuit	spiral, interlocked	ribbon stripe	smooth	soft
IROKO (*Chlorophora excelsa*) mvule; kambaia; African teak	West Africa	yellow to gold	wavy	mottled	coarse	normal
JARRAH (*Eucalyptus marginata*)	Australia	red to dark red	spiral, wavy	curly	coarse	very hard
KINGWOOD (*Dalbergia cearensis*) violetwood; princewood	Brazil	purple brown	straight	crown-cut heartwood	smooth	normal

cutting	T	availability	width	price guide	freak types	special marquetry effects
easy	—	spasmodic	6″–9″	moderate		mid-distance fields, tree trunks, wooden subjects, shadows, fences, planks, walls, doors
easy, brittle		plentiful	8″–12″	moderate		borders, cross bandings, costume and drapery, walls, doors, fences, planks
hard, brittle, needs papering		scarce	3″–6″	expensive		wooden subjects, shadows, tree trunks, rocks and mountains, fences, planks, reflections
easy		plentiful	6″–9″	inexpensive		mid-distance fields, roofs, foregrounds, walls, doors, fences, planks
normal		spasmodic	8″–12″	moderate		mid-distance fields, stonework, walls, doors, wooden subjects, rocks and mountains, shades well
easy		plentiful	6″–9″	inexpensive	sky effects	floral subjects, costume and drapery, walls, doors, shades well, portraiture
easy		plentiful	6″–9″	moderate	sky effects	foregrounds, portraiture, mid-distance fields, shadows, floral subjects, costume and drapery
easy	T	plentiful	8″–12″	moderate	water effects	water effects, snow scenes, stonework, rocks and mountains, costume and drapery, shades well
normal		spasmodic	6″–9″	moderate		walls, doors, fences, planks, wooden subjects
normal, brittle		plentiful	6″–9″	moderate		mid-distance fields, sandy beaches, cornfields, thatch, roads, pathways, costume and drapery
normal		scarce	8″–9″	expensive	water effects	foregrounds, mountains and rocks, distant hills, water effects, mid-distance fields
easy		spasmodic	8″–12″	moderate		floral subjects, costume and drapery, mid-distance fields, walls, doors, fences, planks
brittle, crumbly, needs papering		plentiful	8″–12″	moderate		floral subjects, cornfields, thatch, costume and drapery, walls, doors, sandy beaches
hard, brittle, needs papering		scarce	6″–9″	expensive		costume and drapery, floral subjects, foregrounds, wooden subjects, walls, doors, fences, planks
normal		rare	3″–6″	expensive		costume and drapery, rocks and crossbandings

VENEER	origin	colour	grain	figure	texture	hard-ness
LACEWOOD (*Platanus acerifolia*) planetree (sycamore in USA)	England	pink to biscuit	straight	medullary rays	medium	normal
LARCH (*Larix decidua*) golden larch	Europe	gold to light brown	straight	crown-cut heartwood, striped	medium	hard
LAUREL (*Laurel terminalia*) laurelwood; kaso kaso	India and Burma	dark brown	interlocked	curly, mottled	coarse	very hard
LIME (*Tilia vulgaris*) linden (basswood, USA)	Europe	cream to yellow	straight	plain	smooth	soft
MAHOGANY, AFRICAN (*Khaya ivorensis*) grand bassam; benin; Lagos mahogany	West Africa	red to dark red	interlocked	striped, mottled, fiddleback	fine	soft
MAHOGANY, HONDURAS (*Swietenia macrophylla*) Spanish mahogany	Central and S. America	orange-red	straight	plain, fiddleback, mottled	fine	soft
MAKORE (*Mimusops Heckelii*) African cherry; cherry mahogany	West Africa	light to medium red	straight	mottled	smooth	soft
MANSONIA (*Mansonia altissima*) aprono; ofun; African black walnut	West Africa	purple brown	straight	plain	smooth	normal
MAPLE (*Acer saccharum*) sugar maple; rock maple; sweet maple	USA and Canada	cream to pink	wavy	veins, mottled, crown-cut heartwood	smooth	hard
MAPLE, QUEENSLAND (*Flindersia Brayleyana*) maple silkwood; Australian maple	Australia	red to dark red	interlocked	very close stripe, mottled	medium	hard
MUNINGA (*Pterocarpus angolensis*) benge; kiaat; Rh. walnut	SE. Africa and Rhodesia	reddish brown	straight	very close stripe	medium	normal
SILKY OAK (*Cardwellia sublimis*) selena; lacewood (USA); gold spangled wood	Australia	reddish brown	interlocked	medullary rays	coarse	very hard
OAK (*Quercus robur* and *petraea*)	England	biscuit-light tan	straight	very close stripe, medullary rays	coarse	hard
OAK, BROWN (*Quercus robur* and *petraea*) pollard oak	England	dark brown	straight	very close stripe, medullary rays	coarse	normal

cutting	T	availability	width	price guide	freak types	special marquetry effects
normal	T	plentiful	8″–12″	inexpensive		stonework, roads and pathways, mountains and rocks, foregrounds, sandy beaches, walls, doors
brittle, crumbly		spasmodic	8″–12″	moderate		sky effects, wooden subjects, mid-distance fields, cornfields, thatch, sandy beaches
brittle, crumbly, needs papering		scarce	6″–9″	costly		mountains and rocks, wooden subjects, mid-distance fields, tree trunks, animal subjects
easy		plentiful	8″–12″	moderate		sky effects, floral subjects, shades well, walls, doors, cornfields, thatch, costume, drapery
easy		plentiful	8″–12″	cheap		borders, crossbandings, shadows, portraiture, wooden subjects, mountains and rocks, distant hills, roofs, fences, planks
easy		spasmodic	8″–12″	moderate		floral subjects, costume and drapery, wooden subjects, mid-distance fields, foregrounds, roofs, fences, planks
easy		plentiful	8″–12″	moderate		floral subjects, portraiture, roofs, wooden subjects, borders, crossbandings
easy		spasmodic	8″–12″	moderate		shadows, portraiture, wooden subjects, mountains and rocks, distant hills, foregrounds, tree trunks, fences, planks
normal	T	plentiful	8″–12″	costly	sky effects	portraiture, floral subjects, shades well, sandy beaches, stonework, water effects
hard		spasmodic	8″–12″	moderate		mid-distance fields, mountains and rocks, roofs, costume and drapery, animal subjects
normal, brittle		scarce	8″–12″	moderate		wooden subjects, borders, crossbandings, mid-distance fields, foregrounds, fences, planks, animal subjects
hard		scarce	6″–9″	costly		stonework, mountains and rocks, foregrounds, roads and pathways, wooden subjects, foliage, bushes
normal		plentiful	6″–9″	inexpensive		borders, crossbandings, fences, planks, walls, doors, wooden subjects, mid-distance fields
crumbly		spasmodic	6″–9″	moderate		portraiture, wooden subjects, tree trunks, fences, planks, mid-distance fields, mountains and rocks, roads and pathways, foregrounds, animal subjects

VENEER	origin	colour	grain	figure	texture	hardness
OBECHE (*Triplochiton scleroxylon*) African whitewood; arere; ayous; wawa; samba	West Africa	cream to yellow	straight	plain	fine	soft
OLIVILLO (*Aextoxicon punctatum*) teque; palo muerto	Chile	orange-red	straight	plain, crown-cut heartwood	smooth	normal
OLON (*Fagara macrophylla*) African satinwood	West Africa	yellow to gold	wavy	striped, mottled	medium	normal
OPEPE (*Sarcocephalus Diderrichii*) kussia; bilinga; akondoc; aloma	West Africa	gold to light brown	interlocked, wavy	rope stripe	coarse	hard
PADAUK, AFRICAN (*Pterocarpus soyauxii*) barwood; coraille; meunge	West Africa	reddish brown	straight	plain	coarse	very hard
PADAUK, ANDAMAN (*Pterocarpus dalbergiodes*)	Andaman Islands	red to dark red	interlocked	weak stripe, mottled	coarse	hard
PADAUK, BURMA (*Pterocarpus macrocarpus*) mai pi tawk; mai pradoo	Burma and Thailand	red to dark red	interlocked	very close stripe	coarse	very hard
PALDAO (*Dracontomelum dao*) dao; pacific walnut	East Indies and Philippine Islands	light brown to mid-brown	interlocked	striped, stripy markings	fine	soft
PARINARI (*Parinari spp.*) sougue; mubura; mubira (USA)	East Africa	gold to light brown	straight	plain	coarse	hard
PAU ROSA (*Swartzia fistuloides*) African tulipwood	West Africa	pink with red stripes	straight	stripy markings	coarse	hard
PEARWOOD (*Pyrus communis*) pink peartree	Europe	biscuit to light red	straight	plain	smooth	soft
PEROBA, ROSA (*Aspidosperma peroba*) palo rosa; amarillo; red peroba	Brazil	orange-red	straight	streaky, wild markings	smooth	normal
PEROBA, WHITE (*Paratecoma peroba*) golden peroba; Brazil maple	Brazil	yellow to gold	interlocked	mottled	fine	hard
PINE, SWEDISH (*Pinus sylvestris*) Scotch pine	North Europe	cream to yellow	straight	plain	coarse	soft

tting	T	avail-ability	width	price guide	freak types	special marquetry effects
asy	T	plentiful	8″–12″	cheap	sky effects	'Window waster', sky effects, water effects, shades well, walls, doors
asy		scarce	6″–9″	moderate		portraiture, floral subjects, wooden subjects, mid-distance fields, distant hills, costume and drapery, roofs, walls, doors
asy		plentiful	6″–9″	moderate		floral subjects, shades well, costume and drapery, mid-distance fields, cornfields, thatch, sandy beaches, walls, doors
ormal		spasmodic	8″–12″	costly		cornfields, thatch, portraiture, animal subjects, foregrounds, wooden subjects, fences, planks, walls, doors
ard, brittle		rare	6″–9″	expensive		borders, crossbandings, foregrounds, fences, planks, roofs, wooden subjects
ard, brittle		spasmodic	6″–9″	costly		foregrounds, floral subjects, roofs, portraiture, costume and drapery
brittle, crumbly, needs papering		scarce	6″–9″	expensive		Borders, crossbandings, wooden subjects, roofs, fences, planks, walls, doors
easy		spasmodic	8″–12″	moderate		foregrounds, tree trunks, animal subjects, mid-distance fields, mountains and rocks
brittle		spasmodic	6″–9″	moderate		shadows, animal subjects, portraiture, mid-distance fields, wooden subjects
brittle		scarce	3″–6″	expensive		roofs, costume and drapery, fences, planks, walls, doors, wooden subjects
easy		scarce	6″–9″	costly		portraiture, shadows, floral subjects, costume and drapery, shades well
easy		rare	6″–9″	expensive	sky effects	sky effects, floral subjects, walls, doors, costume and drapery, water effects, roofs, shades well
brittle		scarce	6″–9″	costly		portraiture, floral subjects, shades well, cornfields, thatch, costume and drapery
brittle, needs papering		plentiful	8″–12″	moderate		sky effects, snow scenes, shades well

VENEER	origin	colour	grain	figure	texture	hardness
POMMELLE (*Entandrophragma cylindricum*) plum pudding mahogany; snail quilt mahogany	West Africa	special figure	irregular	curly, mottled, wild markings	coarse	hard
POPLAR, YELLOW (*Liriodendron tulipifera*) magnolia; American whitewood; tuliptree	USA and Canada	greenish brown	straight	veins	smooth	soft
PRIMA VERA (*Tabebuia Donnellsmithii*) sunray; white mahogany	Central America	yellow to gold	straight	streaky, crown-cut heartwood	coarse	normal
PURPLEHEART (*Peltogyne spp.*) amaranthe; violetwood; sucupira	Central America	purple brown	interlocked	weak stripe	fine	very hard
ROSEWOOD, BRAZILIAN (*Dalbergia nigra*) palissander; jacaranda; rio rosewood	Brazil	orange-brown marbled figure	straight	wild markings, crown-cut heartwood	fine	hard
ROSEWOOD, INDIAN (*Dalbergia latifolia*) malobar; Bombay rosewood	India	purple brown	straight	very close stripe, crown-cut heartwood	fine	soft
ROSEWOOD, MADAGASCAR (*Dalbergia greveana*) French rosewood	Madagascar	pink with red stripes	wavy	very close stripe	medium	normal
ROSE ZEBRANO (*Berlinia auriculata*) zebramona; berlinia	Nigeria	pink with red stripes	irregular	stripy markings	medium	hard
SAPELE (*Entandro phragma cylindricum*) aboudikro	West Africa	light to medium red	interlocked	ribbon stripe, very close stripe, medullary rays	fine	soft
SATINWOOD (East Indian) (*Chloroxylon swietenia*) citronnier; satinato	Ceylon	yellow to gold	interlocked	very close stripe, mottled	fine	hard
SYCAMORE (*Acer pseudoplatanus*)	Great Britain	white to cream	straight	plain, fiddleback, medullary rays	smooth	soft
SYCAMORE (weathered) (*Acer pseudoplatanus*)	Great Britain	light tan to light brown	straight	plain	smooth	soft
TCHITOLA (*Pterygopodium oxyphyllum*)	West Africa	light tan to light brown	interlocked	striped, mottled, wild markings	medium	normal
TEAK (*Tectona grandis*)	Burma, Java, India, Thailand, Vietnam	gold to light brown	interlocked	very close stripe, crown-cut heartwood	coarse	normal

cutting	T	availability	width	price guide	freak types	special marquetry effects
crumbly, needs papering		scarce	6″–9″	expensive		portraiture, animal subjects, foliage, bushes, mountains and rocks, costume and drapery
easy		scarce	over 12″	costly		floral subjects, foregrounds, foliage, bushes, shades well
easy		scarce	6″–9″	costly	sky effects	floral subjects, costume and drapery, sandy beaches, sky effects, shades well
brittle		rare	8″–12″	expensive		costume and drapery, distant hills, roofs, walls, doors
hard, brittle		scarce	6″–9″	expensive		foregrounds, mountains and rocks, tree trunks, wooden subjects
easy, brittle		scarce	6″–9″	costly	water effects	borders, crossbandings, costume and drapery, wooden subjects, roofs, fences, planks
normal		spasmodic	3″–6″	expensive		borders, crossbandings, distant hills, roofs, fences, planks
brittle		scarce	8″–12″	moderate		floral subjects, costume and drapery, fences, planks
easy		plentiful	over 12″	inexpensive		borders, crossbandings, wooden subjects, costume and drapery, tree trunks, roofs, fences, planks
brittle		spasmodic	3″–6″	expensive		borders, crossbandings, cornfields, thatch, sandy beaches, floral subjects, shades well, costume and drapery
easy	T	plentiful	over 12″	inexpensive	sky effects, water effects	'Window waster', borders, crossbandings, sky effects, portraiture, snow scenes, costume and drapery, walls, doors, fences, planks, shades well
easy	T	plentiful	over 12″	inexpensive	water effects	portraiture, shadows, foregrounds, animal subjects, tree trunks, wooden subjects, fences, planks
easy		rare	6″–9″	expensive	water effects	water effects, fences, planks, mountains and rocks, foregrounds, mid-distance fields
brittle, crumbly, needs papering		plentiful	over 12″	inexpensive		borders, crossbandings, mid-distance fields, wooden subjects, tree trunks, fences, planks, roofs, mountains and rocks

VENEER	origin	colour	grain	figure	texture	hardness
TOLA (*Pterygopodium oxyphyllum*) tchitola	West Africa	light to medium red	interlocked	very close stripe, medullary rays	medium	soft
TULIPWOOD (*Dalbergia frutescens*) (pinkwood, USA)	Brazil	pink with red stripes	straight	stripy markings	fine	hard
UTILE (*Entandrophragma utile*) sipo	Africa	red to dark red	interlocked	weak stripe	fine	soft
WALNUT, AFRICAN (*Lovoa klaineana and trichiloides*) (Benin walnut, USA); tigerwood; cogowood	Africa	gold to light brown	interlocked	ribbon stripe	medium	soft
WALNUT, AMERICAN (*Juglans nigra*) claro walnut	USA	purple brown	straight	plain, crown-cut heartwood	medium	normal
WALNUT, AUSTRALIAN (*Endiandra Palmerstonii*) Queensland walnut (orientalwood, USA); Australian laurel	Australia	light brown to mid-brown	straight	streaky, wild markings	medium	hard
WALNUT, CIRCASSIAN (*Juglans regia*) Persian walnut; Caucasian walnut	East Europe	light brown to mid-brown	straight	wild markings, crown-cut heartwood	smooth	soft
WALNUT, EUROPEAN (*Juglans regia*)	Europe	light brown to mid-brown	straight	crown-cut heartwood, wild markings	smooth	soft
WALNUT, NEW GUINEA (*Dracontomelum mangiferum*) Dao; Philippine walnut	New Guinea	light tan to light brown	interlocked	ribbon stripe	fine	soft
WENGE (*Millettia Laurentii*) awong; jambiré	Central Africa	dark brown	interlocked	very close stripe	coarse	very hard
WILLOW (*Salix spp.*) moiree	Italy	white to cream	wavy	mottled, streaky, curly	smooth	soft
YEW (*Taxus baccata*) if; tasso	Great Britain, Asia Minor, North Africa, Europe	pink to biscuit		streaky, wild markings, crown-cut heartwood	smooth	hard
ZEBRANO (*Microberlinia brazzavillensis*) zebrawood; zingana (USA)	West Africa	special figure	straight	very close stripe, stripy markings	fine	hard

cutting	T	avail- ability	width	price guide	freak types	special marquetry effects
easy		plentiful	8″–12″	inexpensive		borders, crossbandings, walls, doors, roofs, shadows, wooden subjects, fences, planks
hard, brittle		scarce	3″–6″	expensive		borders, crossbandings, fences, planks,
easy		plentiful	8″–12″	cheap		borders, crossbandings, roofs, foregrounds, reflections, shadows, wooden subjects, walls, doors, fences, planks
easy		plentiful	8″–12″	inexpensive		borders, crossbandings, mid-distance fields, wooden subjects, cornfields, thatch, sandy beaches, fences, planks
easy, brittle		plentiful	8″–12″	moderate		tree trunks, mountains and rocks, distant hills, borders, crossbandings, reflections, shadows, foregrounds
hard		plentiful	6″–9″	moderate	sky effects, water effects	borders, crossbandings, tree trunks, mid-distance fields, foregrounds
easy		spasmodic	over 12″	moderate		distant hills, foregrounds, mountains and rocks, wooden subjects, tree trunks, fences, planks, animal subjects
easy		plentiful	over 12″	moderate		borders, crossbandings, foregrounds, mountains and rocks, portraiture, animal subjects, wooden subjects, tree trunks
easy		plentiful	8″–12″	moderate		portraiture, mid-distance fields, borders, crossbandings, mountains and rocks, distant hills, animal subjects
brittle, crumbly, needs papering	T	plentiful	6″–9″	moderate		borders, crossbandings, wooden subjects, tree trunks, roofs, fences, planks
easy		scarce	6″–9″	costly	sky effects	floral subjects, shades well, water effects, snow scenes, costume and drapery
hard, brittle		spasmodic	8″–12″	costly	sky effects	sky effects, wooden subjects, costume and drapery, walls, doors
brittle		plentiful	8″–12″	moderate		fences, planks, walls, doors, wooden subjects, borders, crossbandings

BURR	origin	colour	grain	figure	texture	hardness
AMBOYNA (*Pterocarpus indicus*) narra	Philippines, Borneo	gold to light brown	irregular	burr figure	coarse	hard
ASH (*Fraxinus excelsior*)	Europe	white to cream	irregular	burr figure	coarse	hard
CHERRY (*Prunus avium*)	Europe	biscuit to light red	irregular	burr figure	fine	normal
ELM (*Ulmus procera*)	England	biscuit to light red	irregular	burr figure	fine	normal
EUCALYPTUS (*Eucalyptus regnans*)	Australia	biscuit to light red	irregular	burr figure	coarse	hard
GREEN CYPRESS (*Liriodendron tulipifera*)	USA	greenish brown	irregular	wild markings	medium	hard
LACEWOOD (*Platanus acerifolia*)	England	reddish brown	irregular	burr figure	coarse	hard
MADRONA (*Arbutus menziesii*) strawberry tree	USA	light to medium red	irregular	burr figure	fine	soft
MAIDU (*Pterocarpus pedatus*)	Vietnam	light to medium red	irregular	burr figure	coarse	very hard
MAPLE (*Acer saccharum*)	USA, Canada	biscuit to light red	irregular	burr figure	smooth	soft
MYRTLE (*Umbellularia californica*) acacia burl; pepperwood; spice-tree	USA	greenish brown	irregular	burr figure	fine	soft
OAK (*Quercus robur*)	England	biscuit to light tan	irregular	burr figure	coarse	hard
OLIVE ASH (*Fraxinus excelsior*)	Europe	special figure	irregular	burr figure	coarse	hard
THUYA (*Tetraclinis articulata*)	Morocco	gold to light brown	irregular	burr figure	coarse	very hard

cutting	T	availability	width	price guide	freak types	special marquetry effects
brittle, crumbly, needs papering	–	rare	8"–12"	expensive		portraiture, foliage, bushes, animal subjects, mountains and rocks
brittle, crumbly, needs papering	T	spasmodic		moderate		foliage, bushes, snow scenes, mountains and rocks, floral subjects, stonework
easy		spasmodic		moderate		floral subjects, mountains and rocks, foregrounds, costume and drapery, foliage, bushes
easy		spasmodic		moderate		floral subjects, mountains and rocks, foregrounds, costume and drapery, foliage, bushes
brittle, crumbly, needs papering		spasmodic		moderate		mid-distance fields, mountains and rocks, roads, pathways, foregrounds, foliage, bushes, walls, doors
normal, needs papering		rare		moderate		floral subjects, foregrounds, foliage, bushes, mountains and rocks, costume and drapery
normal	T	spasmodic		moderate		mountains and rocks, roads, pathways, stonework, foregrounds, portraiture, foliage, bushes
easy		scarce	over 12"	costly		foliage, bushes, floral subjects, mountains and rocks, roofs
brittle, crumbly, needs papering		rare		expensive		portraiture, animal subjects, mountains and rocks, foliage, bushes, floral subjects
easy	T	spasmodic		inexpensive, moderate		floral subjects, costume and drapery, foliage, bushes, mountains and rocks, roads, pathways
easy, crumbly, needs papering		scarce	over 12"	expensive		foliage, bushes, water effects, floral subjects, costume and drapery
brittle, crumbly, needs papering		scarce		costly		snow scenes, mountains and rocks, roads and pathways, stonework, foliage, bushes
brittle, crumbly, needs papering	T	scarce		costly	water effects	water effects, snow scenes, mountains and rocks, roads and pathways, stonework, foregrounds
brittle, crumbly, needs papering		rare		expensive		foliage, bushes, portraiture, costume and drapery, animal subjects, mountains and rocks

BURR	origin	colour	grain	figure	texture	hardness
VAVONA (*Sequoia gigantea*) giant sequoia	USA	red to dark red	irregular	burr figure	coarse	soft
WALNUT (*Juglans regia*)	Europe	light tan to light brown	irregular	burr figure	fine	soft
WALNUT, AMERICAN (*Juglans nigra*)	USA	dark brown	irregular	burr figure	medium coarse	soft
WALNUT, CIRCASSIAN (*Juglans regia*)	East Europe	light brown to mid brown	irregular	burr figure	medium	normal

cutting	T	avail-ability	width	price guide	freak types	special marquetry effects
easy, crumbly, needs papering	—	scarce	over 12″	expensive		foliage, bushes, costume and drapery, floral subjects
easy	....	spasmodic		costly		shadows, portraiture, floral subjects, wooden subjects, mountains and rocks, distant hills, foregrounds, tree trunks, foliage, bushes, animal subjects
easy, crumbly, needs papering	....	scarce		costly		shadows, mountains and rocks, distant hills, foregrounds, foliage bushes, animal subjects, portraiture
normal	....	rare	8″–12″	expensive		foliage, bushes, tree trunks, portraiture, animal subjects, mountains and rocks, foregrounds, costume and drapery, shadows

Appendix B

VENEERS AND BURRS GROUPED BY COLOUR

GROUP 1
WHITE TO CREAM

Ash
Ash burr
Abele
Horse chestnut
Sycamore
Pine
Willow
Birch, Swedish

GROUP 2
CREAM TO PINK

Aspen
Ash, Japanese
Beech
Birch, Canadian
Bird's eye maple
Birch, masur
Cedar, western red
Maple

GROUP 3
PINK TO BISCUIT

Cedar of Lebanon
Canarium
Douglas fir
Eucalyptus burr
Yew
Elm
Lacewood
Indian white mahogany
Fruit cherry

GROUP 4
BISCUIT TO LIGHT RED

Apple
Cherry burr
Elm burr
Gaboon
Guatea
Maple burr
Pear

GROUP 5
PINK WITH RED STRIPES

Almondwood
Bubinga
Pau rosa
Rose zebrano
Rosewood, Madagascar
Tulipwood

GROUP 6
ORANGE–RED

Afzelia
Mahogany, Honduras
Rosa peroba
Olivillo

GROUP 7
CREAM TO YELLOW

Antiaris
Obeche
Pine, Swedish
Lime

GROUP 8
YELLOW TO GOLD

Afara
Avodire
Capomo
Olon
Iroko
Prima vera
Ayan
Peroba, white
Satinwood

GROUP 9
GOLD TO LIGHT BROWN

Amboyna burr
Afrormosia
Idigbo
Teak
Thuya burr
Walnut, African
Larch
Parinari
Opepe

GROUP 10
BISCUIT TO LIGHT TAN

Eucalyptus
Hornbeam
Oak
Agba
Sweet chestnut
Oak burr

GROUP 11
LIGHT TAN TO LIGHT BROWN

Canella
Courbaril
Walnut, New Guinea
Tchitola
Walnut burr, sappy
Walnut, French
Weathered sycamore
Weather maple

GROUP 12
LIGHT BROWN TO MID BROWN

Daniellia
Indian S. greywood
Walnut, English
Walnut burr, European
Walnut, Australian
Paldao
Blackwood
Circassian walnut burr

286

GROUP 13
DARK BROWN

American walnut burr
Ebony, Macassar
Laurel
Oak, brown
Wenge

GROUP 14
PURPLE BROWN

Kingwood
Mansonia
Purpleheart
Rosewood, Indian
Walnut, black American

GROUP 15
GREENISH BROWN

Green cypress burr
Myrtle burr
Yellow poplar
  (Magnolia)

GROUP 16
LIGHT TO MEDIUM RED

Makore
Madrona burr
Tola
Sapele
Maidu burr
Abura
Rault

GROUP 17
RED TO DARK RED

Jarrah
Vavona burr
Utile
Maple, Queensland
Mahogany, African
Padauk, Burma
Padauk, Andaman

GROUP 18
REDDISH BROWN

Padauk, African
Muninga
Silky oak
Pommelle
Lacewood burr

GROUP 19
SPECIAL FIGURE

Olive ash
Courbaril
Pommelle
Rio rosewood
Olive ash burr
Zebrano

GROUP 20
CHEMICALLY TREATED

Harewood (silver)
Harewood (slate)
Harewood (dark)
Lacewood (grey)
Maple (grey)
Birch (grey)
Ash (grey)

Appendix C

TRADITIONAL SAW-CUT CABINET WOODS
USED BY MARQUETRY CRAFTSMEN

Few, if any, of these woods are available today as saw-cut
veneers, but many of them are available in knife-cut
thickness. These woods were also used in TUNBRIDGE WARE.

Acacia
African cherry
African satinwood
Alder
Almond
Amaranthe
Amarillo*
Amboinawood
American poplar
Amyris
Apple
Ash
Avodire

Barberry
Baywood
Beech
Beefwood
Bermuda cedar
Birch
Bird's eye maple
Bitter orange
Blackthorn*
Bloodwood
Bog oak
Botany bay oak
Boxwood
Brazilwood
Broom
Butternut

Camphorwood
Canalette
Calamander
Canarywood
Casuarinawood
Cedar
Cedar of Lebanon
Cherry

Chestnut
Citronnier
Cocobolo
Cocuswood
Coralwood
Coromandel*
Courbaril
Cypress

Damson
Deodar
Dogwood

Eaglewood
Ebony
Elder
Elm

Furze
Fustet
Fustic

Green ash
Green ebony
Green oak
Gumwood

Hawthorn
Hazel
Hickory
Holly
Hornbeam
Horse chestnut
Hungarian ash

Ironwood

Jackwood
Japanese ash
Juniper

Kingwood*

Laburnum*
Larch
Laurel
Lignum vitae*
Lilac
Lime
Locust*
Logwood

Macassar ebony
Madeira
Magnolia
Mahogany, African
Mahogany, Honduras
Mahogany, Spanish
   (Cuban)
Manchineel
Manilawood
Mora
Mulberry

Narra

Oak
Olivewood*
Orangewood
Padauk
Palissander
Palmyra
Palmyrawood
Partridgewood*
Pear
Plane tree
Plum*
Poplar
Porcupinewood*
Princewood*
Purplewood

Red cedar
Red ebony
Red elm
Rosewood, Brazilian
Rosewood, Indian
Rosewood, Madagascar
Rowan tree
Rubywood

Sabicu
Sal
Sandalwood

Santal
Sapanwood
Satiné rouge
Satinwood, E. Indian
Satinwood, W. Indian
Savannawood
Sissoo
Snakewood*
Spanish cedar
Spindle tree
Stinkwood*
Sycamore

Teak
Thuya

Tulipwood

Violetwood

Walnut*
Whitebeam
Willow

Yew*

Zebrawood*

* These were cut into oyster veneers for parquetry.

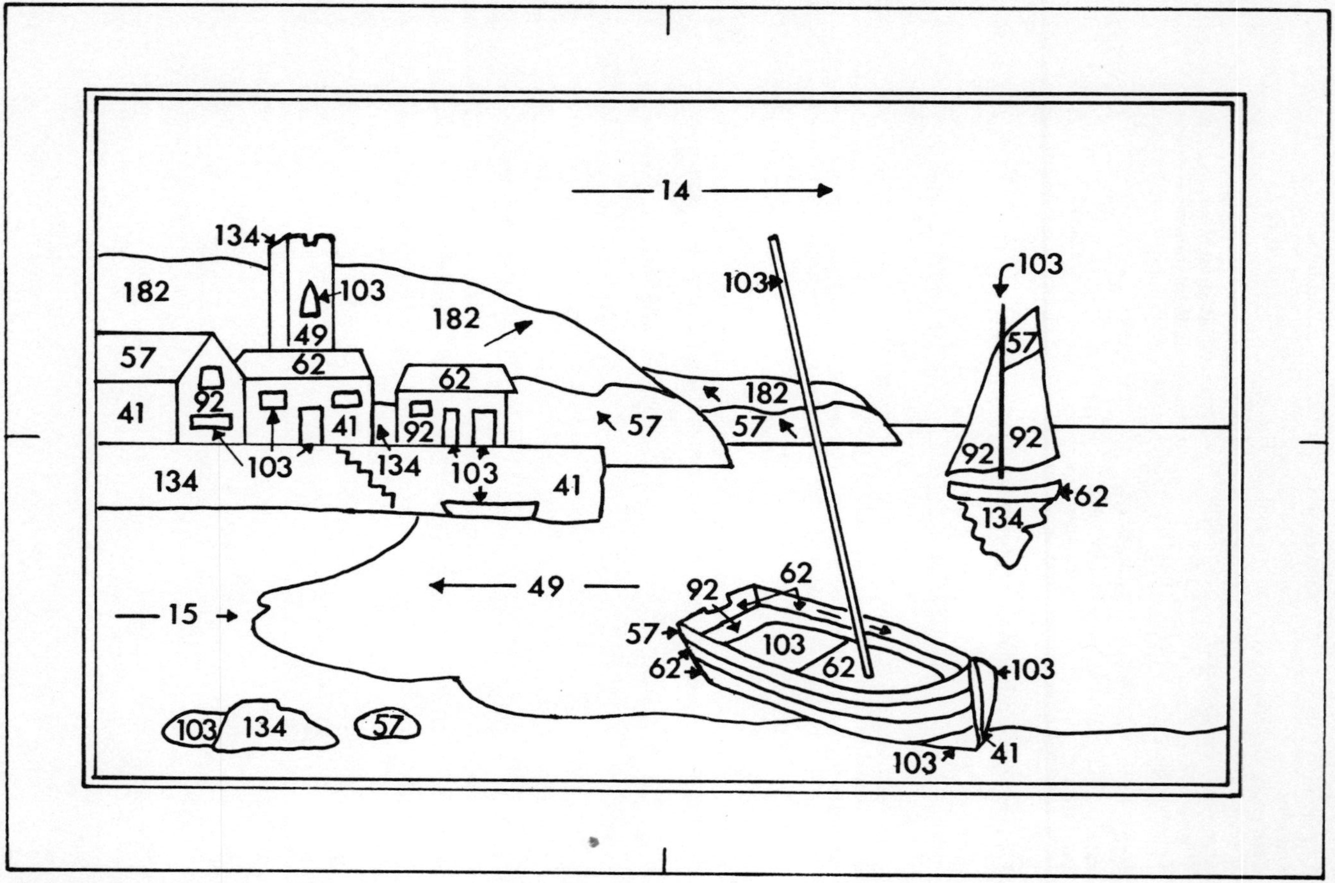
14
134
182
103
49
57
62
92
41
103
134
134
103
41
57
182
15
49
103
92
62
57
62
103
62
103
41
103
57
92
62
134
103
134
57

Appendix D

'CORNISH COAST' DESIGN

For those who would like to start the easy way there are a number of marquetry art sets available which will enable you to make a picture the first time you try. One example is the 'Cornish Coast' design opposite,* detailed instructions for which are given below.

Preparation

Trace the design on to good quality tracing paper, and fasten this along the top edge to a waste veneer $7'' \times 5''$.

Cutting sequence

1 With a hard lead pencil, trace the outline of the sky. This should be $\frac{1}{4}''$ inside the border margin at the top and sides of the picture and ignoring the yacht and hills, right across the picture from the horizon line to make a rectangle $6\frac{1}{4}'' \times 2\frac{1}{8}''$ approximately.
2 Lift the design, cut this outline from the 'waster'. Position veneer No. 14 under the window aperture, adjust it to suit the flow of grain and following the instructions previously explained cut out this veneer and tape it back into the waster with three small pieces of tape at the top and each side of the picture.
3 Next trace the outline of the sea. Its top line runs along the bottom of the skyline, and again ignoring the yacht and hills, right across the picture and down about $\frac{1}{4}''$ inside the two border margins, to the bottom of the picture. Place No. 49 veneer under the window and mark its position, remove to the cutting board, cut it out and tape the sea in position.
The picture at this stage is composed of two rectangles, butted together at the horizon position.

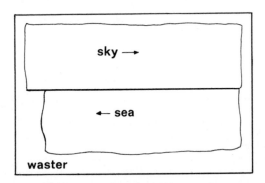

* Plywood baseboard, carbon-backed design, veneer tape, waste veneer, backing veneer, border and fillet borders, and complete set of numbered and keyed veneers to complete this picture, together with a Swann Morton craft knife and two spare blades, are obtainable direct from the manufacturers, The Art Veneers Co. Ltd, Industrial Estate, Mildenhall, Bury St Edmunds, Suffolk, price 50p post free (U.K. only).

4 Next trace veneer No. 15 on top of the sea veneer No. 49. It should also extend $\frac{1}{4}''$ into the border at each side and bottom and $\frac{1}{4}''$ *above* the line of the shore where it meets the jetty by the steps. Cut and tape this piece in position, ignoring the three little rocks.

5 Next, trace the hilltops No. 182 into the sky veneer, ignoring the church tower on the left hand hill, and the mast on the right hand hill. Cut and tape in position.

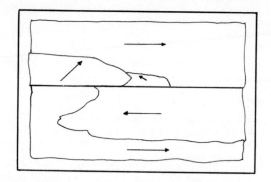

6 The left hand cliff face No. 57 should be traced and cut and taped in position; then the right hand cliff with a slightly changed appearance, by turning the veneer over, otherwise this could look like one piece when the picture is polished. Cut and tape this into position.

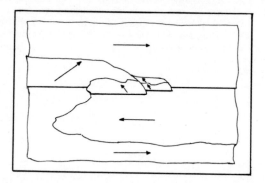

7 Now the face of the Norman tower on the church, No. 49, ignoring the window No. 103. Allow the bottom of this piece to extend beyond the rooftop No. 62.

8 The next piece is No. 134 representing the church tower in shadow, again extending down below the roof. Then these pieces are taped in position.

9 Rooftop No. 57 is now cut into the picture, extending $\frac{1}{4}''$ into the border margin.

10 Rooftop No. 62 under the church tower is next, extending to the left into the No. 92 position. Then the No. 62 roof to the right hand house.

11 The walls of the left hand house No. 41 are extended $\frac{1}{4}''$ into the border margin and to the right into the No. 92 position. The walls of the second house may extend into the same area, ignoring the tiny windows and

doors. The lower line of these houses may extend below the jetty line No. 134 and 41.

12 No. 134 piece between the two houses is next to be cut in.

13 No. 92 representing the end wall of the left hand house ignoring the windows, and the wall of the right hand house, ignoring windows and doors, and allowing the veneer to come below the jetty line.

14 No. 41 jetty is next, ignoring the boat tied up alongside, and the veneer is allowed to run to the left past the line of steps.

15 The jetty veneer No. 134 is carefully traced in, including the steps, and this veneer extends $\frac{1}{4}''$ into the border margin.

16 The beached rowboat is next, cutting in No. 103 on the foreshore, then 62 and 57 forming the front side of the boat, then No. 92 and 62 on the other side of the boat, and finally No. 103 and 62 inside the boat.

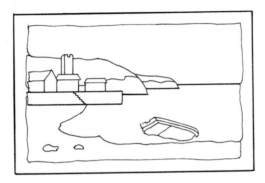

17 The mast is traced in position, and a thin sliver of No. 103 cut from the edge of a veneer is inserted. It is good practice to rub a little glue into the slot and insert a veneer on edge.

18 No. 41 veneer may also be inserted at the front of the boat.

19 The three rocks No. 103, 134 and 57 may be cut in next.

20 The yacht may be tackled now, first cutting in sail No. 57, then sails No. 92, followed by hull No. 62 and reflection No. 134.

21 Then cut a very thin line to represent the mast and insert a fine hairlike sliver off the edge of No. 103, into the groove, rub a little glue over the spot to secure it.

22 The small boat moored alongside the jetty No. 103 may be put in next, and the church window, and the windows and doors of the houses.

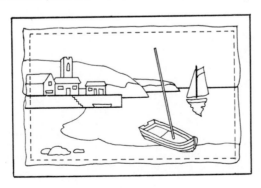

23 The design is positioned over the picture, and the centre lines checked for true register. The nett picture area line is carefully traced in, over the $\frac{1}{4}''$ surplus overlapped veneers in the border margin.

24 The surplus veneers are trimmed off, using a try square to check for perfect square, a straight edge to ensure a true, straight line.

25 The fillet strip is then cut into four equal $\frac{1}{16}''$ wide borders and fitted around the picture, overlapping at the corners, followed by the four border veneers.

26 The corners are mitred, cutting from the outside towards the picture, and the surplus end pieces discarded. Tape the face side of the borders at the mitred corners.

27 Examine the picture for flaws in cutting, small pieces which may have fallen out, or ill-chosen veneers which may not give you the effect you desire. At this stage they are simply removed and replaced.

28 Glue a sheet of paper over the face of the picture (or gummed paper tape not overlapped but edge-to-edge butt jointed).

29 Moisten and remove the tapes on the back of the picture, and allow to dry. Then fill any cracks or gaps and sandpaper smooth using a cork rubbing block and 6/0 garnet paper. The picture is now ready for laying and finishing.

Index

Italic figures refer to plate numbers

birch 50, 51, 128, 288
  Canadian 44, 270, 286
  flame 44
  grey 287
  masur 44, 270, 286
  Swedish 270, 286
blackthorn 288
blackwood 270, 286
  Australian 55
blades, double-toothed round-
  back 83, 86
  jeweller's metal-piercing 147
bleeding 259
blisters 124, 143, 167, 174, 175,
  250, 259
blockboard 161, 162, 247
bloodwood 288
blooming 259
blushing 259
bodying-up 181
Bombay mosaic 221-2
border mounts 175
border veneers *see* veneers
Bordewick, George R. 149
Boulle, André Charles 14, 78,
  215
boulle work 17, 215-17, *21*
boxwood 222, 223, 227, 288
brass 217, 220
brazilwood 288
brilliance 24
Britfix 66
British piercing blade technique
  see cutting
British piercing pad method *see*
  cutting
broken joints, repair of 246
bronzing 259
broom 288
bruises, repair and restoration of
  249
bubbling 259
bubinga 56, 270, 286
'buhl' *see* boulle work
burnishing cream 184

burns 264
burr veneers 43
  repair of 251-2, 255
butternut 24, 288
butt-jointing 131-2, 136, 143-
  144
butt veneers 43

CABINET-MAKERS, early 13
cabinet scraper 74
caking 259
camphorwood 49, 288
canalette 288
calamander 288
canarium 270, 286
canarywood 288
canella 50, 270, 286
Caniana brothers 12
capomo 270, 286
Cascamite 'One-Shot' 58, 64,
  65
casuarinawood 288
cauling, defective 253
cedar 44, 49, 50, 288
  Bermuda 288
  Lebanon 270, 286, 288
  red 289
  Spanish 289
  western red 270, 286
cement, rubber 87, 88, 95, 123,
  124, 125
  balsa 147
certomosaic 10
checking 259
cherry 282, 288
  African 288
  burr 286
  fruit 270, 286
chessboard, how to make
  230-1
chestnut 178
  horse *see* horse chestnut
  sweet 270, 286, 288
chipboard 163-4
Chlorosplenium aeruginosum 226

marquetry, history of 9–16
  definition of 16–17
  counterchange 215
'marquetry licence' 19
marquetry set method 121–4
Marquetry Society, The 52,
  125, 127
marquetry transfers 16
masking *see* shading
Maybach, Heinrich 212
mineral stains 50
mitres, repair of 251
mora 288
mosaic banding 139
  wood 238
mosaic decoration 237–9
mosaic parquetry 10
mother of pearl 211, 221
  inlays of 235
motifs, decorative, for furniture
  90
  inlay 223
moulding, repair of 254
movingui 35
mulberry 288
Multicraft tools 72
muninga 274, 287
musical instruments, decoration
  of 223
myrtle 24, 282
  burr 287

Narra 288
niello 211
nomenclature 54–6
  Anglo-American differences in
  56

Oak 47, 49, 62, 138, 161, 175,
  274, 282, 286, 288
  bog 288
  Botany Bay 288
  brown 274, 287
  burr 286
  green 226, 288
  silky 45, 274, 287

obeche 44, 48, 54, 62, 128, 161,
  164, 175, 178, 276, 286
  blue 24
odour (of veneer) 49
Oeben, Jean François 14, *24,
  30*
okpo 54
Olivetans, order of 10
olivewood 288
olivillo 276, 286
olon 276, 286
opepe 24, 276, 286
orange, bitter 288
orangewood 288
overlap technique 121
overlays, solid 211

Padauk 24, 35, 50, 178, 288
  African 276, 287
  Andaman 276, 287
  Burma 276, 287
paldeo 276, 286
palissander 288
palmyra 288
palmyrawood 288
pantograph 19
parinari 276, 286
parquetry 229*ff.*
  diamond 231–2
  illusion 233
  line and dot 234, *25*
  Louis 233–4
  oyster 234–5, *14, 15*
  trellis 234
partridgewood 288
patina 240, 241, 249, 258
pau rosa 276, 286
pear 51, 179, 286, 288
  black 223
pearwood 276
perinari 286
peroba, rosa 24, 35, 178, 276,
  286
  white 276, 286
perspective 25–6, *6–8, 70*